# Non-Alcoholic Drinks

by Ryan Foley

# Non-Alcoholic Drinks For Dummies®

Published by: **John Wiley & Sons, Inc.**, 111 River Street, Hoboken, NJ 07030-5774, www.wiley.com

Copyright © 2025 by John Wiley & Sons, Inc. All rights reserved, including rights for text and data mining and training of artificial technologies or similar technologies.

Media and software compilation copyright © 2025 by John Wiley & Sons, Inc. All rights reserved, including rights for text and data mining and training of artificial technologies or similar technologies.

Published simultaneously in Canada

No part of this publication may be reproduced, stored in a retrieval system or transmitted in any form or by any means, electronic, mechanical, photocopying, recording, scanning or otherwise, except as permitted under Sections 107 or 108 of the 1976 United States Copyright Act, without the prior written permission of the Publisher or authorization through payment of the appropriate per-copy fee to the Copyright Clearance Center, Inc., 222 Rosewood Drive, Danvers, MA 01923, (978) 750-8400, fax (978) 750-4470, or on the web at www.copyright.com. Requests to the Publisher for permission should be addressed to the Permissions Department, John Wiley & Sons, Inc., 111 River Street, Hoboken, NJ 07030, (201) 748-6011, fax (201) 748-6008, or online at http://www.wiley.com/go/permissions.

The manufacturer's authorized representative according to the EU General Product Safety Regulation is Wiley-VCH GmbH, Boschstr. 12, 69469 Weinheim, Germany, e-mail: Product_Safety@wiley.com.

**Trademarks:** Wiley, For Dummies, the Dummies Man logo, Dummies.com, Making Everything Easier, and related trade dress are trademarks or registered trademarks of John Wiley & Sons, Inc. and may not be used without written permission. All other trademarks are the property of their respective owners. John Wiley & Sons, Inc. is not associated with any product or vendor mentioned in this book.

LIMIT OF LIABILITY/DISCLAIMER OF WARRANTY: THE PUBLISHER AND THE AUTHOR MAKE NO REPRESENTATIONS OR WARRANTIES WITH RESPECT TO THE ACCURACY OR COMPLETENESS OF THE CONTENTS OF THIS WORK AND SPECIFICALLY DISCLAIM ALL WARRANTIES, INCLUDING WITHOUT LIMITATION WARRANTIES OF FITNESS FOR A PARTICULAR PURPOSE. NO WARRANTY MAY BE CREATED OR EXTENDED BY SALES OR PROMOTIONAL MATERIALS. THE ADVICE AND STRATEGIES CONTAINED HEREIN MAY NOT BE SUITABLE FOR EVERY SITUATION. THIS WORK IS SOLD WITH THE UNDERSTANDING THAT THE PUBLISHER IS NOT ENGAGED IN RENDERING LEGAL, ACCOUNTING, OR OTHER PROFESSIONAL SERVICES. IF PROFESSIONAL ASSISTANCE IS REQUIRED, THE SERVICES OF A COMPETENT PROFESSIONAL PERSON SHOULD BE SOUGHT. NEITHER THE PUBLISHER NOR THE AUTHOR SHALL BE LIABLE FOR DAMAGES ARISING HEREFROM. THE FACT THAT AN ORGANIZATION OR WEBSITE IS REFERRED TO IN THIS WORK AS A CITATION AND/OR A POTENTIAL SOURCE OF FURTHER INFORMATION DOES NOT MEAN THAT THE AUTHOR OR THE PUBLISHER ENDORSES THE INFORMATION THE ORGANIZATION OR WEBSITE MAY PROVIDE OR RECOMMENDATIONS IT MAY MAKE. FURTHER, READERS SHOULD BE AWARE THAT INTERNET WEBSITES LISTED IN THIS WORK MAY HAVE CHANGED OR DISAPPEARED BETWEEN WHEN THIS WORK WAS WRITTEN AND WHEN IT IS READ.

For general information on our other products and services, please contact our Customer Care Department within the U.S. at 877-762-2974, outside the U.S. at 317-572-3993, or fax 317-572-4002. For technical support, please visit https://hub.wiley.com/community/support/dummies.

Wiley publishes in a variety of print and electronic formats and by print-on-demand. Some material included with standard print versions of this book may not be included in e-books or in print-on-demand. If this book refers to media that is not included in the version you purchased, you may download this material at http://booksupport.wiley.com. For more information about Wiley products, visit www.wiley.com.

Library of Congress Control Number is available from the publisher.

ISBN 978-1-394-34092-7 (pbk); ISBN 978-1-394-34093-4 (ebk); ISBN 978-1-394-34094-1 (ebk)

SKY10120156_070125

# Contents at a Glance

**Introduction** ................................................................... 1

**Part 1: Kicking Things Off** ............................................. 5
- CHAPTER 1: The Rise of Non-Alcoholic Drinks ........................ 7
- CHAPTER 2: Grabbing the Right Tools and Glasses ................. 11
- CHAPTER 3: Methods to the Madness ................................... 19
- CHAPTER 4: Setting Up Your Home Bar ................................. 31

**Part 2: A World of Flavor, Without Alcohol** ................ 43
- CHAPTER 5: Non-Alcoholic Beer ........................................... 45
- CHAPTER 6: Non-Alcoholic Wine .......................................... 51
- CHAPTER 7: Non-Alcoholic Spirits ........................................ 55
- CHAPTER 8: Serving Non-Alcoholic Drinks at Home and at the Bar ........ 59

**Part 3: Sip & Savor: Non-Alcoholic Drink Recipes** ..... 65
- CHAPTER 9: Classics & Riffs on Classic Cocktails ..................... 67
- CHAPTER 10: Non-Alcoholic Drink Recipes from A to Z ............. 77
- CHAPTER 11: Drinks for Special Occasions ............................. 135
- CHAPTER 12: Non-Alcoholic Drinks from Top Bartenders ........... 149
- CHAPTER 13: Non-Alcoholic Drinks from Bars around the World ... 177

**Part 4: The Part of Tens** ............................................... 197
- CHAPTER 14: More Than Ten Tidbits of Bar Slang .................... 199
- CHAPTER 15: More Than Ten Toasts to Mark Any Occasion ........ 203

**Recipe Index** ................................................................ 205

**Topics Index** ................................................................ 227

# Table of Contents

**INTRODUCTION** ................................................................................... 1
    About This Book ............................................................................... 1
    Foolish Assumptions ........................................................................ 1
    Icons Used in This Book .................................................................. 2
    Beyond the Book ............................................................................. 2
    Where to Go from Here ................................................................... 3

**PART 1: KICKING THINGS OFF** ....................................................... 5

**CHAPTER 1: The Rise of Non-Alcoholic Drinks** ............................. 7
    Understanding the Non-Alcoholic-Drink Movement ..................... 8
    Getting a Brief History of Non-Alcoholic Drinks ............................ 9
    Meeting the New Wave of Drinkers ................................................ 9
    Having Non-Alcoholic Options at the Bar ..................................... 10
    Knowing the Difference between Low ABV and No ABV ............ 10

**CHAPTER 2: Grabbing the Right Tools and Glasses** ................. 11
    Breaking out the Basic Tools ......................................................... 11
        Wine opener ............................................................................ 12
        Cocktail shaker ........................................................................ 12
        Strainer .................................................................................... 13
        Other common tools ............................................................... 13
    Pouring into Glassware ................................................................. 16

**CHAPTER 3: Methods to the Madness** ......................................... 19
    Shaking a Drink .............................................................................. 19
    Stirring a Drink ............................................................................... 20
    Muddling ........................................................................................ 20
    Adding Flavor with Infusions ......................................................... 21
    Making Simple Syrup .................................................................... 21
    Ice, Ice, Baby .................................................................................. 22
    Stepping Up Your Garnish Game .................................................. 22
        Lemon and lime wedges ........................................................ 23
        Lemon twists ........................................................................... 23
        Lime slices ............................................................................... 24
        Lemon and orange slices/wheels .......................................... 25
        Pineapple wedges .................................................................. 26

Cucumber ribbons .................................................................................. 27
Rimming a Cocktail Glass ...................................................................... 28
Opening Wine and Champagne Bottles ............................................ 29
  Wine bottles ......................................................................................... 29
  Champagne and sparkling wine bottles ...................................... 30

**CHAPTER 4: Setting Up Your Home Bar** ................................................. 31
Getting Your Bar Ready ........................................................................ 31
  Situating the bar ................................................................................. 32
  Serving smartly .................................................................................... 32
Stocking Your Bar .................................................................................... 33
  The basic bar ....................................................................................... 34
  A more complete bar ........................................................................ 35
  The ultimate bar ................................................................................. 35
  Picking up mixers and other important supplies ..................... 36
The Party Charts: Calculating Supply Needs .................................. 38
  How much liquor should you buy? .............................................. 38
  How many supplies and mixers should you buy? .................... 40

# PART 2: A WORLD OF FLAVOR, WITHOUT ALCOHOL ........ 43

**CHAPTER 5: Non-Alcoholic Beer** ................................................................ 45
How Non-Alcoholic Beer Is Made ...................................................... 46
Exploring Types of Non-Alcoholic Beer ........................................... 47
Storing and Serving Non-Alcoholic Beer ......................................... 48
Trying a Few Non-Alcoholic Beer Brands ........................................ 49

**CHAPTER 6: Non-Alcoholic Wine** ............................................................. 51
How Non-Alcoholic Wine Is Made ..................................................... 51
Current Styles of Non-Alcoholic Wine .............................................. 52
  Red wines .............................................................................................. 52
  Rosé wines ............................................................................................ 53
  White wines ......................................................................................... 53
  Sparkling wines ................................................................................... 53
Popular Brands ........................................................................................ 54

**CHAPTER 7: Non-Alcoholic Spirits** .......................................................... 55
How Non-Alcoholic Spirits Are Made ............................................... 56
Popular Brands ........................................................................................ 56
Storing and Serving Suggestions ....................................................... 57

**CHAPTER 8: Serving Non-Alcoholic Drinks at Home and at the Bar** ................................................. 59
    Offering Options at Home ................................................................. 59
    Working Behind the Bar .................................................................... 60
        What's in a name? ...................................................................... 61
        Considering costs ....................................................................... 61
    Looking at the Future of Non-Alcoholic Drinks ..................... 62
        New products ............................................................................. 63
        Alcohol-free bars, stores, and events ..................................... 64
        Celebrity-backed brands ........................................................... 64
        Food pairings ............................................................................. 64

## PART 3: SIP & SAVOR: NON-ALCOHOLIC DRINK RECIPES .................................................................. 65

**CHAPTER 9: Classics & Riffs on Classic Cocktails** .................... 67
    Classic Non-Alcoholic Drinks ........................................................... 67
    Twists on Classic Cocktails .............................................................. 69

**CHAPTER 10: Non-Alcoholic Drink Recipes from A to Z** .......... 77

**CHAPTER 11: Drinks for Special Occasions** ............................... 135
    Party Punches ..................................................................................... 135
    Holiday Recipes .................................................................................. 143
    A Few for the Seasons ...................................................................... 145

**CHAPTER 12: Non-Alcoholic Drinks from Top Bartenders** ..... 149

**CHAPTER 13: Non-Alcoholic Drinks from Bars around the World** ........................................................................ 177

## PART 4: THE PART OF TENS .................................................. 197

**CHAPTER 14: More Than Ten Tidbits of Bar Slang** .................. 199

**CHAPTER 15: More Than Ten Toasts to Mark Any Occasion** ................................................................... 203

**RECIPE INDEX** ............................................................................. 205

**TOPICS INDEX** ............................................................................ 227

# Introduction

The non-alcoholic (NA) drinks industry has rapidly grown over the past 5-plus years. Not just pregnant people or the designated driver for the night go for non-alcoholic drinks — everyone is drinking them! No matter the reason, you can find a major place for non-alcoholic drinks in your home or on your bar's cocktail menu. This book aims to introduce you to this ever-growing industry.

When Jackie Wilson Foley and I wrote *Bartending for Dummies, 6th Edition* (Wiley) in 2023, we added two chapters about non-alcoholic drinks. And now, in *Non-Alcoholic Drinks For Dummies*, I can share over 300 recipes, as well as give you primers about the various products out there for you to enjoy.

## About This Book

I want to start by saying that this book doesn't focus on water and tea. The non-alcoholic drinks movement is on a rapid incline at the time I'm writing this, and more and more people are moving away from spirit-forward cocktails.

Whether you're an experienced bartender, home bartender, or just someone who likes making drinks, you can find something in this book for you. I really hope that you enjoy!

## Foolish Assumptions

You know what they say about assumptions: They make an . . . well, you know the saying. Even though the non-alcoholic drinks category is growing every day, people still make a lot of assumptions, such as

- » Non-alcoholic drinks are better for you than alcoholic drinks.
- » You drink non-alcoholic drinks only because you're pregnant, the designated driver, or dealing with a bad relationship with alcohol in the past.

>> Non-alcoholic drinks are just for kids.
>> Non-alcoholic drinks are just a passing trend.

All of these assumptions are false! This book can tell you a lot about the drinks industry, but I also want to continue to create a safe place for everyone ordering non-alcoholic drinks, no matter what their reason (or if they have no reason at all!). Everyone should feel safe and welcomed when they come to you for drinks, alcoholic or non-alcoholic.

## Icons Used in This Book

Icons are the images that appear in the margins of this book. Here's the guide so that you can tell what they are and what they're for:

The Tip icon calls your attention to ideas that can make your non-alcoholic drink-making job easier and help you sidestep problems. The tips often give you handy ideas on ways to create the perfect drink.

The Remember icon points out information that reinforces the concepts that I discuss. If you're in a time crunch and can't read the entire chapter, go straight to the text marked by this icon to come away with some very useful information.

The Warning icon alerts you to potential pitfalls and gives you a heads-up on mistakes to avoid. Pay attention when this icon rears its head because it points out something important.

## Beyond the Book

In addition to the material in the book that you're reading right now, I put some access-anywhere extras on the web. For some quick history, brands to stock and purchase, some quick classic recipes, and more, check out the free online Cheat Sheet (which you can find at www.dummies.com by typing "Non-Alcoholic

Drinks For Dummies Cheat Sheet" in the search bar). Also, visit www.bartender.com for more recipes, articles, and bars and bartenders to check out and get cocktails from.

## Where to Go from Here

Because this is a *For Dummies* book, you don't have to read it in order, word for word, front to back, cover to cover. If you prefer, you can go right to the recipes or start with the details on non-alcoholic spirits. You can find out what you want to know without first reading the information that precedes it. In other words, this book gives you get-in-and-get-out convenience. You can jump around and finish reading when you feel like it. If you're ready to start mixing (and drinking), check out the recipes index, which not only lists all of the recipes in the book but the ingredients as well. So grab your cocktail glass. It's time to get pouring!

# 1
# Kicking Things Off

### IN THIS PART . . .

Discover how the non-alcoholic drinks industry started and why it's growing.

Find the right tools and glassware to make you a successful bartender.

Practice essential bar techniques.

Know the right things to buy to host a successful gathering that includes non-alcoholic options.

> **IN THIS CHAPTER**
> » Discovering an industry on the rise
> » Getting some history of non-alcoholic beverages
> » Discovering the new wave of non-alcoholic drinks and drinkers

# Chapter 1
# The Rise of Non-Alcoholic Drinks

In 2023, the U.S. saw Gen-Z and millennials become more health conscious, and they started to pull back on buying alcohol. The 2020 COVID-19 pandemic also revealed a lot of negative impacts of alcohol on people who were already isolated. For social drinkers, they just wanted to enjoy a drink with friends and family, but didn't want to suffer the consequences of a hangover. Thus began the *sober-curious movement*, which continues to grow in popularity. Being *sober-curious* doesn't mean giving up alcohol entirely. It invites people to explore what life might look and feel like with less (or no) drinking, without the pressure of full sobriety or labels like "sober" or "alcohol-free." It is really about making intentional choices: skipping a drink on a night out, opting for a non-alcoholic alternative, or simply becoming more aware of when and why you drink.

Non-alcoholic (NA) or alcohol-free drinks aren't just for pregnant women or designated drivers anymore, nor should they be. For many, not drinking is simply a lifestyle choice. Everyone should be able to order whatever they want and feel comfortable when participating in a bar or party experience. At the end of the day, regardless of the reason, as a professional or home bartender, you should offer some fun and tasty non-alcoholic options (besides just soda or water) to your guests.

I'm hoping that you bought this book to find out about cocktails and drinks, not so much about The History of Water or How Tea Became Popular. In this chapter, I do cover those types of drinks briefly, but this book focuses on the rise of the non-alcoholic drinks industry, including non-alcoholic beer, wine, and spirits. And, of course, this book contains recipes for the types of amazing drinks that you can make at home or at your bar.

## Understanding the Non-Alcoholic-Drink Movement

The non-alcoholic product industry is huge, and it's just beginning to hit its stride. Various reports suggest that by 2026, the market for alcohol alternatives could reach $30 billion. Online searches for terms such as "mocktails" topped 220,000 per month as of August 2022, according to Google Trends. Although I'm not a huge fan of the term *mocktail*, clearly, people want to find complex, flavorful, non-alcoholic drinks. I prefer terms such as

- Non-alcoholic cocktails
- Zero-proof cocktails
- Non-alcoholic drinks

*Non-alcoholic drinks* is my personal favorite. After all, just look at the title of this book!

REMEMBER

I want to emphasize the importance of creating an inclusive space for everyone. I touch on this topic throughout the book because I feel strongly about it. No one should feel uncomfortable for choosing not to drink alcohol, whether they're sober, pregnant, or the designated driver — or for any other reason. Everyone deserves the chance to feel at ease and enjoy a non-alcoholic drink — not just water or soda.

And non-alcoholic drinks are so much more than simple mixed juices. A significant portion of this book presents a wide range of recipes, including Chapters 14 and 15, which feature non-alcoholic drink submissions from bars and bartenders around the globe. These drink recipes come from trial and error — as well as creativity — so I encourage you to dive into those chapters and enjoy the process. Who knows — your own recipe might just be featured in the next edition!

# Getting a Brief History of Non-Alcoholic Drinks

The first big non-alcoholic-drink movement in the U.S. happened during Prohibition, when selling any drinks that contained more than 0.5 percent alcohol by volume was illegal. So beer makers were forced to get creative. Major beer brands at the time made something they called *near beer* (around 0.4 percent) to help keep the lights on. After Prohibition, people headed back to bars and business.

Non-alcoholic beers saw a slight resurgence in the 1970s when Anheuser Busch released O'Doul's, and a German non-alcoholic beer, Clausthaler, hit the market. But the non-alcoholic movement really caught the eye of beer, liquor, and other companies that started to create these types of products around 2014.

# Meeting the New Wave of Drinkers

According to a 2024 survey by NCSolutions, 25 percent of Americans aged 21 and older reported not consuming any alcohol in the past year, and we think that even more are open to the idea of giving up drinking alcohol completely. People are exploring the idea of being *sober curious* (open to the idea of becoming sober). If I wrote this book in the early 2000's, it would have been much shorter because none of the amazing products that I talk about existed yet. While I write this book, around 60 percent of bars in the United States offer at least one non-alcoholic drink option, including a non-alcoholic cocktail or non-alcoholic beer or wine option.

TIP

I use the abbreviation NA, which stands for *non-alcoholic*. The industry uses this abbreviation a lot — we all love an acronym!

In 2000, the very small non-alcoholic beer market mostly offered options from the larger beer brands. In 2025, you can find hundreds of options from smaller producers, and our expertise expects that this market will continue to grow.

CHAPTER 1 **The Rise of Non-Alcoholic Drinks** 9

# Having Non-Alcoholic Options at the Bar

These days, bartenders spend the same amount of time creating their non-alcoholic cocktails as they do their spirit-forward cocktails, and for good reason. Non-alcoholic cocktails can make your bar great profits! I discuss margins and costing in Chapter 9, but a well-thought-out non-alcoholic drink can bring in the same amount of money as its counterparts.

You want to make a safe space for customers at your bar, and having non-alcoholic drinks on your menu allows guests to order them without feeling uncomfortable asking whether you have non-alcoholic options.

REMEMBER

At the end of the day, regardless of the reason and whether you're a professional or home bartender, offer at least one non-alcoholic drink option to your guests.

# Knowing the Difference between Low ABV and No ABV

Alcohol by volume (ABV) appears on all products that contain alcohol. Here's what the terms Low ABV and No ABV mean:

- **Low ABV:** Cocktails that usually contain less than 15 percent ABV.
- **No ABV:** These cocktails contain 0 percent ABV.

Low ABV drinks are popular in bars and restaurants, as well as with drinkers who don't want to completely remove alcohol but want a lower-proof option. Proof is a measurement of the alcohol content in a beverage. It is calculated as twice the percentage of alcohol by volume (ABV). For example, a drink with 40-percent ABV would be 80 proof.

I like to refer to these drinks as more *sessionable,* meaning you can have a few more drinks and still not fully feel the effects of alcohol, so you can extend your drinking session.

In Part 3 of this book, I share a variety of non-alcoholic recipes options for you to consider and make at your home or bar.

**IN THIS CHAPTER**

» Understanding the tools of the trade

» Getting to know glassware

# Chapter 2
# Grabbing the Right Tools and Glasses

To bartend, at home or at the bar, you need a few essentials: good people skills, general knowledge about the products that you're pouring, a collection of cocktail recipes, and the proper equipment. This chapter covers the equipment part of the equation. In Part 2, you can get the product knowledge, and Part 3 provides you with recipes. As for people skills, you're on your own, friend.

## Breaking out the Basic Tools

The most important assets for any profession are the right tools. You need basic bar tools to mix, serve, and store your drinks. Whether you're stocking a home bar or working as a professional, your basic tools are a bar spoon, cocktail shaker, strainer, and wine opener. If you want to get more tools, I suggest grabbing a mixing glass and a jigger (which I talk about in the section "Other common tools" later in this chapter).

## Wine opener

The most common wine opener is a waiter's wine opener (shown in Figure 2-1). It has a sharp blade, a corkscrew (also known as a *worm*), and a bottle opener. You can find this opener in most liquor stores and bar supply houses.

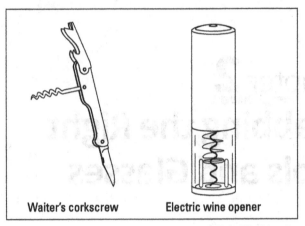

Waiter's corkscrew      Electric wine opener

© John Wiley & Sons, Inc.

**FIGURE 2-1:** A waiter's corkscrew and an electric wine opener.

Another nifty option is an electric wine opener. It's also shown in Figure 2-1. It's easy to use and a great tool to have at home if you do a lot of entertaining.

## Cocktail shaker

Figure 2-2 shows two types of shakers:

- **Boston shaker:** The one used by most professional bartenders. It commonly consists of a mixing/pint glass and a stainless steel core that overlaps the glass.

- **Cobbler shaker:** Usually consists of two or more stainless steel parts. You can find these shakers in most department stores or online shops, and they come in different shapes and designs.

© *John Wiley & Sons, Inc.*

**FIGURE 2-2:** A Boston shaker and a Cobbler shaker.

## Strainer

A couple of different types of strainers are available, and both are shown in Figure 2-3:

- » **Hawthorn:** The most popular strainer, this flat, spoon-shaped utensil has a spring coil around its head. You can use it on top of a steel shaker or a bar glass to strain cocktails.

- » **Julep:** This utensil was originally designed to help you drink a cocktail by holding back ice so that you can easily sip. It's now more commonly used to strain cocktails out of a mixing glass.

## Other common tools

The tools below are most of the tools that you will see in a bar or restaurant. Many of the following tools are shown in Figure 2-4:

- » **Bar towels:** Always smart to have so that you can wipe up spills, overpours, or sweat from glasses.

- » **Bar spoon:** A long spoon that you use to stir cocktails.

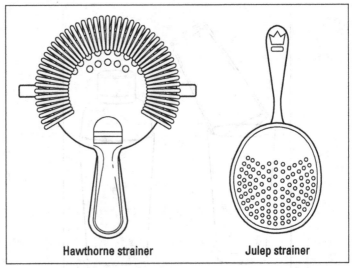

**Hawthorne strainer**  **Julep strainer**

© John Wiley & Sons, Inc.

**FIGURE 2-3:** The Hawthorn strainer and Julep strainer.

- **Blender:** You can find many types of commercial or home blenders that have various speeds. When you make a drink, always put liquid in the blender before switching the blender on; doing so helps save the blender blade and prevent spills. You can use some blenders (but not all) to make crushed ice. Check with the manufacturer before trying to crush ice in your blender — or buy yourself a dedicated ice crusher.

- **Bottle opener or church key:** Used to open bottles or cans.

- **Coasters or bar napkins:** Coasters prevent rings from developing on your bar and tables. Napkins also help your guests hold their drinks.

- **Grater:** Use to dust drinks with grated nutmeg, chocolate, and so on.

- **Ice bucket:** Pick one that can hold at least three trays' worth of ice.

- **Ice scoop or tongs:** A must for every bar. Never use your hands or glassware to scoop ice as it may break the glass into the ice, requiring you to replace all the ice in the bucket/bar well.

- **Jigger or measuring glass:** A *jigger* is a small glass or metal measuring container that usually has a ½-ounce measurer on one side and a 2-ounce measurer on the other.
- **Juicer:** To juice various fruits for cocktails.
- **Knife and cutting board:** You need a small, sharp paring knife to cut fruit.
- **Large cups or bowls:** You need something to hold garnishes such as lemons, limes, oranges, and cherries. These containers often come in a set called a *condiment caddy*.
- **Lewis ice bag:** Made of heavy-grade natural canvas, so you can smash the ice with your muddler to make crushed ice.
- **Mixing glass:** You place the ingredients for the drink that you're making into this glass to mix them.

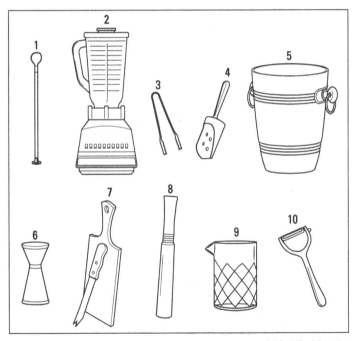

© John Wiley & Sons, Inc.

**FIGURE 2-4:** A collection of bar tools: (1) bar spoon, (2) blender, (3) tongs, (4) ice scoop, (5) ice bucket, (6) jigger or measuring glass, (7) knife and cutting board, (8) muddler, (9) pourer, and (10) peeler.

CHAPTER 2 Grabbing the Right Tools and Glasses **15**

- **Muddler:** A small wooden bat or pestle that you can use to crush fruit or herbs (or ice).
- **Peeler:** Used to peel fruits for garnishes.
- **Pourer:** This device gives greater control to your pouring. You can find many different types available, including some that have a lidded spout that prevents insects and undesirables from entering the pourer.
- **Stirrers and straws:** Used for stirring and sipping drinks.

## Pouring into Glassware

When serving and creating cocktails, you need to match your glassware to the experience of the drink so that xxx. You can find a ton of styles of glasses out there — more bar glasses than most people (and many bars) care to purchase. Figure 2-5 shows most of the kinds of glasses that you would serve a non-alcoholic drink in:

- **Champagne flute:** The bowl is tapered to prevent bubbles from escaping.
- **Martini glass:** Perfect for martinis, Manhattans, and many other classic drinks, this glass is available in 3- to 6-ounce sizes.
- **Coupe:** A stemmed glass that typically serves *up cocktails*, meaning drinks either shaken or stirred, and then strained into a glass without ice.
- **Highball and Collins glasses:** These glasses are the most versatile because of their size. Sizes range from 8 to 12 ounces.
- **Mason jar:** Originally designed for canning and preserving food, these jars have become a unique and fun way to serve drinks like an Arnold Palmer or frozen drink.
- **Red wine glass:** This glass is available in 5- to 10-ounce sizes. The bowl of a red wine glass is wider than the bowl of a white wine glass, which allows the wine to *breathe* (meaning giving it time to mix with the air and open up its aromas).

» **White wine glass:** This glass is available in 5- to 10-ounce sizes.

» **Rocks glass:** Also known as an *old-fashioned glass*. Sizes of this glass vary from 5 to 10 ounces.

» **Shot glass:** This small glass used to serve spirits in, typically 1, 1.5, or 2 ounces. You can also use the shot glass as a measuring tool. Every bar needs one (or more).

» **Stemless glasses:** These glasses have become popular in recent years, probably because they look elegant and do not break as easily due to not having a stem!

TIP

If you plan to create a bar at home or serve cocktails at a party, keep your glass selection small to save space. You can simplify by using just a few types of glasses: a stemless glass to use for most drinks, and a pint or highball glass to use for more juice or tea/lemonade-based drinks. Figure 2-5 shows a selection of glasses. Also, if you use just two glass shapes, you can make the process of cleaning and storing your glasses less complicated. Overall, the most common glasses for non-alcoholic drinks are stemless, highball/Collins, rocks, red, and white wine.

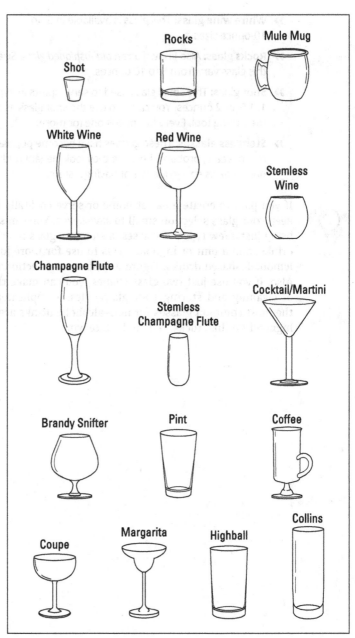

**FIGURE 2-5:** Glasses, glasses, glasses.

**IN THIS CHAPTER**

» Shaking, stirring, and muddling drinks with style

» Making infusions and syrups

» Coolin' down with ice

» Prepping some great garnishes

» Popping the champagne

# Chapter 3
# Methods to the Madness

Making good cocktails takes more effort than just pouring ingredients into a glass. This chapter shows you the techniques for how to make drinks and pull off some of the little touches that make your drinks look and taste better, with the ultimate result of happier guests.

## Shaking a Drink

You shake drinks mainly to chill a cocktail, to mix ingredients, or to put a *head* (froth) on the cocktail.

TIP

As a general rule, shake all cloudy drinks (cocktails that include citrus, milk, or cream) and stir all clear drinks. Never shake a cocktail that contains carbonated water or soda — that creates quite the mess!

To shake a cocktail in a Boston shaker (described in Chapter 2), follow these steps:

1. **Following the drink recipe, put some ice cubes in the glass container.**

   Use ice cubes only if the recipe calls for them.

2. **Add the cocktail ingredients.**

3. Place the metal container over the glass container.
4. Hold the metal and glass containers together with both hands and shake with an up-and-down motion.

Always point the shaker away from your guests to avoid spilling anything on them if you don't have the shaker sealed.

**WARNING**

The two pieces of the shaker may stick together after you shake a drink. Never bang the shaker against the bar, kitchen counter, or any other surface or object; instead, gently tap it a few times with your palm at the point where the glass and metal containers come in contact to separate them. With the containers separated, now you can pour your cocktail.

**TIP**

When pouring or straining the cocktail, always pour from the glass container because it allows for better control and ensures a clean, professional presentation.

## Stirring a Drink

The main reason for stirring cocktails is to mix, chill, and dilute.

As a general rule, stir drinks that contain only clear ingredients since the goal is to combine and chill the ingredients. To stir cocktails, follow these steps:

1. Add the cocktail ingredients and ice into the mixing glass.
2. Take your bar spoon and insert it into the mixing glass.
3. Stir in a circular motion for around 30 to 45 seconds.
4. Use your julep strainer to strain the cocktail into a glass.

You can read about the julep strainer in Chapter 2.

## Muddling

*Muddling*, which involves gently pressing ingredients like herbs, fruits, or sugar, helps release the flavors of fresh ingredients such as fruits and herbs. You often use this technique in making drinks such as a Caipirinha, Mint Julep, Mojito, or Smash.

**TIP**

To muddle a drink, follow these simple steps:

1. **Add the fresh ingredients into a glass or cocktail shaker.**
2. **Press firmly into the ingredient by using your muddler, and then twist.**
3. **Repeat Step 2 a few times till you can smell the essences from the herbs or see the juices from the fruit being released.**

   Do your best to not over muddle, which could crush certain herbs that can release bitter and unpleasant flavors, throwing off the balance of your cocktail.

4. **Follow the post-muddling part of the recipe that you're using.**

## Adding Flavor with Infusions

You can create *infusions* by soaking something in liquid to extract its flavor. For the liquid, you can use water or non-alcoholic spirits. Simple infusions involve adding in dried herbs or leaves in hot water to make teas or even adding lemon slices to water to make lemon water. Of course, you can do more complex infusions, such as adding in jalapenos to a bottle of non-alcoholic tequila to help create a spicy margarita.

When you create an infusion, allow the mixture to sit for a few hours — or, in some cases, overnight — to help extract the full flavor of whatever you want to infuse.

## Making Simple Syrup

Several cocktail recipes call for *simple syrup*, a liquid sweetener made of sugar and water. To make simple syrup, follow these steps:

1. **Boil water on a stove.**

   How much you boil depends on how much simple syrup you want to make. Use a one-to-one ratio of sugar to boiling water.

CHAPTER 3 Methods to the Madness    21

2. **Add the sugar to your boiling water and stir until it dissolves.**

3. **Turn the stove to low heat, stirring your sugar-water frequently, until it thickens.**

   You probably don't have to stir more than a couple of minutes.

You can make a variety of flavored syrups by using the same one-to-one measurements. Add in fresh fruits or herbs to make unique syrups and test them in different cocktails to make your own twist. You can also use a variety of sugar sources, such as agave, demerara sugar, or maple syrup.

## Ice, Ice, Baby

Ice is very important in cocktails because it makes the drinks cold and helps to dilute the drinks. Most bars and bartenders use a few types of ice; I explain the most common ones here:

» **Standard (1 in. by 1 in.):** The most common type of ice; used for almost everything in bartending, such as shaking, stirring, and adding to cocktails.

» **Rocks Ice:** When you hear someone say "on the rocks" or "on one rock" they most likely mean this type of ice. This ice usually comes as a larger square, but it can be a circle as well.

» **Crushed Ice:** Smaller ice pieces that are ideal for frozen drinks. Pebble and julep ice fall into this category. Bartenders often use this ice in tiki, frozen, and julep cocktails.

REMEMBER

You can find all types of ice, in addition to those in the preceding list, such as Collins spears and dry ice. Be very careful when using dry ice in cocktails because coming into direct contact with it can seriously harm a guest, employee, or yourself! Use dry ice only if you have the training on how to use it.

## Stepping Up Your Garnish Game

Many drinks require fruit garnishes. Your guests expect the garnish, so you can't forgo it — and you have to do it well. Presentation counts, big time. You may mix the best drinks on the planet, but if they don't look good when you serve them, no one wants to drink them. Garnishes also help make the cocktail(s) stand out and look good on social media.

The following sections show you how to cut the most common garnishes.

## Lemon and lime wedges

Figure 3-1 illustrates the following steps for cutting wedges:

1. **Slice the lemon or lime in half the long way.**
   Cut from end to end.
2. **Lay the cut halves flat on a cutting board and halve them again in the same direction.**
3. **Cut wedges from the lemon or lime quarters that you create in Step 2 by cutting perpendicular to your previous cuts, aiming for about ½-inch wide pieces.**

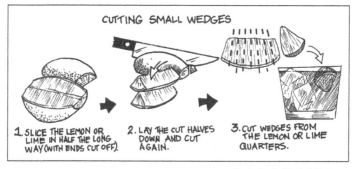

*Illustration by Elizabeth Kurtzman*

**FIGURE 3-1:** Cutting lemon or lime wedges.

## Lemon twists

Figure 3-2 illustrates the procedure for cutting lemon twists. Just follow these steps:

1. **Cut off both ends of the lemon.**
2. **Insert a sharp knife or spoon between the rind and meat of the lemon and carefully separate them.**

CHAPTER 3 Methods to the Madness    23

3. **Slice the rind into strips about ¼-inch wide — narrow enough to curl easily, but wide enough to hold their shape.**

4. **Twist the strip around your finger or a bar spoon to make a spiral.**

**TIP**

The flavor of a lemon really lies on the outside. When adding a lemon twist to a drink, slowly *rim* the glass — meaning gently run the outer peel along the edge — with the outside of the twist to release its aromatic oils. (I talk about this process in the section "Rimming a Cocktail Glass" later in this chapter.)

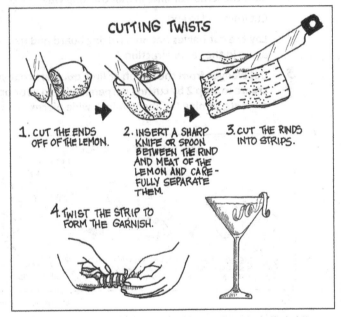

*Illustration by Elizabeth Kurtzman*

**FIGURE 3-2:** Cutting lemon twists.

## Lime slices

Figure 3-3 shows you how to cut lime slices by following these steps:

1. **Cut off both ends of the lime.**
2. **Slice the lime in half from end to end.**

3. **Lay each half flat on the cutting board and cut it into half-moon slices.**

    These slice cuts are perpendicular to the cut you make in Step 2.

4. **Lay each half-moon slice down and cut into the flesh at the fruit's middle point, being careful to slice only halfway into the wedge.**

    This small slit holds the garnish in place on the rim of your glass.

**FIGURE 3-3:** Cutting lime slices.

## Lemon and orange slices/wheels

Follow these steps to cut lemon and orange slices (as shown in Figure 3-4):

1. **Cut off both ends by slicing off a small piece from both the top (stem) and bottom of the fruit to create flat surfaces.**

2. **Place the fruit on one of the flat ends and cut it in half horizontally.**

3. Lay one half cut-side down on the cutting board. Cut across the fruit to create thin round slices, about ¼-inch thick.

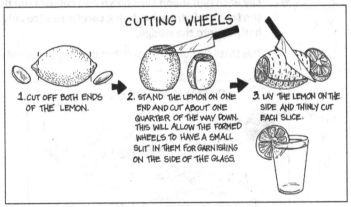

FIGURE 3-4: Cutting lemon or orange slices.

## Pineapple wedges

Figure 3-5 and the following steps show you how to cut pineapple wedges:

1. Cut off the top and bottom of the pineapple. Remove the tough outer skin by slicing downward along the sides, following the curve of the fruit.

2. From top to bottom, cut the pineapple in half.

3. Lay one half flat on the cutting board and cut it in half again lengthwise to create quarters.

4. Cut out the hard core from each pineapple quarter by slicing it out at an angle.

5. Cut wedges by slicing across the quarters — perpendicular to the lengthwise cuts — into pieces about ½- to ¾-inch thick.

6. Cut a small notch in the center of each wedge to easily rest it on the rim of a glass.

*Illustration by Elizabeth Kurtzman*

**FIGURE 3-5:** Cutting pineapple wedges.

## Cucumber ribbons

Long cucumber ribbons make great garnishes for sodas and for cocktails such as a non-alcoholic Collins and Gimlets. Follow these steps to slice them (and check out Figure 3-6):

1. **Cut off both ends to create a clean starting surface.**
2. **Hold the cucumber firmly on a cutting board. Using a vegetable peeler, drag it lengthwise down the cucumber to create long, thin ribbons. A mandoline on the thinnest setting also works great to create more slices.**
3. **Keep peeling from the same side until you reach the seeds, then rotate the cucumber and repeat.**
4. **Use ribbons right away or store them in ice water for a few minutes to keep them crisp and curly until ready to garnish.**

    If you want to make cucumber slices or wheels, follow the same steps as you would the orange slices/wheels.

TIP

You can roll a cucumber ribbon into a spiral and skewer it, or drape it along the inside of the glass, creating a cool and elevated look for your non-alcoholic cocktails.

CHAPTER 3 **Methods to the Madness** 27

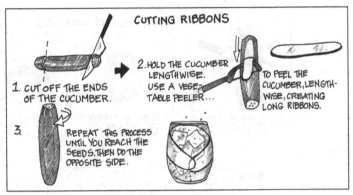

*Illustration by Elizabeth Kurtzman*

**FIGURE 3-6:** Cutting cucumber ribbons.

## Rimming a Cocktail Glass

To help balance flavors and add a bit of flare to your cocktails, you can rim the glass with salt, sugar, or a spice mixture; for example, you can rim the glass with salt when making a margarita. To rim a glass, follow these steps:

1. **Prep your rim mixture in a dish or bowl.**

   Add in your sugar, salt, or spice mixture into your bowl

2. **Cut a citrus wedge (lime or lemon) in half.**

   You can also use water or simple syrup in a dish or bowl (similar to the one you use for the rim mixture).

3. **Rub the citrus flesh up against the outside rim of the glass.**

   Or if you're using water or simple syrup, place the rim of the glass into the liquid, coating the entire rim.

4. **Place the glass into the mixture bowl, coating the outside rim in the mix.**

5. **Set the rimmed glass to the side while you prepare your cocktail.**

6. **Pour your cocktail into the glass and serve!**

> **DON'T FORGET THE MARASCHINO CHERRIES**
>
> All kinds of drinks are garnished with Maraschino cherries, including the Shirley Temple and the non-alcoholic Manhattan. You can find Maraschino cherries in small jars at any food store. And the best thing about them: You don't have to cut them before serving.

TIP

If you plan to serve a lot of rimmed non-alcoholic cocktails, you can prep the rims in advance. This prepping gives the rims time to dry and stick to the glass better; and it also saves you time so that you can make more drinks and serve your guests more quickly. In addition, some modern techniques have bartenders rimming only half the glass, which gives the guest the option to taste the rim or not.

## Opening Wine and Champagne Bottles

Opening bottles doesn't take much skill and just a little practice. The more you practice, the easier opening wines and champagnes becomes.

### Wine bottles

To open a wine bottle, get yourself a waiter's opener, which I show you in Chapter 2. Then follow these steps:

1. **Using the blade on the opener, cut the lead foil or capsule at the middle of the bulge near the bottle neck.**
2. **Remove the foil and wipe the bottle top with a cloth to remove any foreign particles.**
3. **Line up the opener's screw or worm directly over the bottle, and with gentle downward pressure, screw the worm clockwise into the cork.**

WARNING

Don't break the end of the cork (which can happen if you screw too far or use too much force), and screw in just enough to extract the cork.

CHAPTER 3 Methods to the Madness    29

4. **Attach the lever of the opener to the lip on top of the bottle, and while holding the bottle firmly, slowly lift the cork straight up.**
5. **After you remove the cork, wipe the neck of the bottle.**
6. **Present the cork to your guest and pour a small amount of wine into their glass.**

If the wine is to your guest's satisfaction, pour more. Keep your towel handy to wipe the neck of the bottle while you pour the wine for other guests.

## Champagne and sparkling wine bottles

You don't use a corkscrew or any other wine-opening tool when opening sparkling wine bottles; you simply use your hands.

1. **Remove the wine hood** (protective covering over the cork) **and foil capsule.**
2. **Hold the bottle at an angle and point it away from you and anyone else (and anything valuable).**
3. **While holding the cork in one hand, twist the bottle with the other hand and gently remove the cork.**

REMEMBER

Twist the bottle, not the cork, because it gives you better control and reduces the chance of the cork breaking or flying out unexpectedly.

4. **Just before the cork is about to pop, place a bar towel over the cork and bottle, and loosen the cork the rest of the way.**

The towel can catch the cork when it pops and prevent it from becoming a UFO.

TIP

Keep another towel handy in case the bottle bubbles over after you remove the cork. To avoid the overflow, don't shake the bottle before you open it.

> **IN THIS CHAPTER**
> » Purchasing the right products
> » Figuring out how much to buy

# Chapter 4
# Setting Up Your Home Bar

When you're doing any sort of entertaining, one of the biggest mysteries is figuring out how to set up your bar and how much you need to buy.

If you're like me and enjoy throwing parties, or you're just looking to start a nice home bar, this chapter can help.

You can easily make a punch or a drink ahead of time and not add in any alcohol. You can later add in alcohol if one of your guests wants, or they can add in a non-alcoholic spirit option. These little changes can make guests who aren't interested in alcohol feel included, not having to worry about whether they can get a non-alcoholic drink.

## Getting Your Bar Ready

The following sections give you some pointers on how to set up a bar for a party.

## Situating the bar

When setting up a home bar, find an area that fits the flow of the room, whether you want your home bar in your living or dining room. When setting up a bar for a party, put the bar as close to running water or a sink as you can to help with rinsing glassware and tools — and, of course, cleaning up any spills. Here are a few things to consider:

- » Keep the bar as far as possible from your food and snacks to prevent large groups of people from staying in one area. You want folks to mingle and not crowd certain areas.

- » If possible, have a self-serve wine and beer bar in one area and a cocktail bar in another.

- » You can clean up spills much more easily if you put the cocktail bar in your kitchen. What's more, you do less running around when you're close to the sink and refrigerator.

- » If you have to set up your bar in a location other than your kitchen, put a small rug or mat under and behind the bar to protect the floor or carpet. You can find a lot of affordable machine-washable rugs that you can use both for your bar and around your kitchen.

- » No matter where your bar is, use a strong, steady table so that you don't have to worry about it tipping or collapsing.

## Serving smartly

When hosting a party, especially when you're expecting 20-plus guests, your best bet is to hire a professional bartender.

TIP

Although this book's focus is on non-alcoholic drinks, I also make some suggestions for cocktails that contain alcohol.

Take the following suggestions to heart to make your party run smoothly and to keep your guests happy:

- » Be sure to have at least one non-alcoholic beer, wine, and spirit option available for your guests. You can find non-alcoholic sparkling wines at many grocery and liquor stores, and they make a nice addition to any party.

- » Make a non-alcoholic punch for all guests to enjoy, and have both non-alcoholic spirits and alcoholic spirits near the punch so that guests can add what they want to their punch.
- » When serving cocktails that contain alcohol, don't add more than 2 ounces of liquor to a drink to avoid overserving any of your guests.
- » Use only fresh ice and fresh fruit.
- » If possible, chill glasses and don't put them out until five minutes before the party begins as it not only keeps them cold but ensures they're fresh and clean when guests arrive.
- » When serving hot drinks, make sure that the cups or glasses have handles. Have tea and coffee at the ready to save yourself a lot of time while you're busy slinging drinks.
- » Use a scoop, tongs, or a large spoon to serve ice. Never use your hands.
- » If you don't have bottle pourers, rub waxed paper over the tip of liquor bottles to prevent dripping.
- » Use a champagne bucket or any type of small bucket to dump out any extra liquid or ice from your shakers if you don't have a sink nearby.
- » Close the bar an hour to an hour and a half before the end of the party. You can then continue to offer your guests tea and coffee.

## Stocking Your Bar

When setting up your home bar, always use popular name brands, even when it comes to non-alcoholic drinks. These brands aren't always the most expensive, but they're the most recognizable and relatable for your guests.

The following sections present three different levels of bar stocking: basic, more complete, and the ultimate bar.

TIP

I recommend that you use mostly premium brands. You don't want your guests to think that you'd serve them anything but the best. Work with someone at the liquor store to help guide you on what's best for the type of bar that you want to build. Also, if

CHAPTER 4 Setting Up Your Home Bar    33

you have an affinity for one brand or type of spirit over another, purchase that!

## The basic bar

A basic bar setup for your home and for spur-of-the-moment entertaining should consist of the following. Have one 750 ml bottle of each of the following:

- A non-alcoholic spirit
- Vodka
- Gin
- Rum (light or dark)
- Blended scotch
- Bourbon
- Blanco tequila
- Dry or sweet vermouth (you use dry in Martinis and sweet in Manhattans)
- Brandy or cognac
- Non-alcoholic wine (white, red, or sparkling)
- Sparkling wine or champagne
- White wine (I suggest a Pinot Grigio because it is a light, crisp white wine)
- Red wine (A Cabernet Sauvignon is a full-bodied red wine that would work well for many palates)

Also have these drinks available:

- Six 12-ounce bottles or cans of non-alcoholic beer
- Twelve 12-ounce bottles of beer (domestic or imported)
- One bottle of Angostura bitters

The estimated cost to set up this bar falls somewhere between $500 and $600 if you're using domestic and local brands. If you use premium brands, add 20 to 30 percent.

## A more complete bar

If you plan to serve more than the basics at your bar, add the following items to the ones outlined in the preceding section. Get one 750 ml bottle of

- » An additional non-alcoholic spirit (such as non-alcoholic whiskey, tequila, gin, or rum)
- » Flavored vodka (such as lemon or orange)
- » Single malt scotch
- » Rye whiskey
- » Irish whiskey
- » Reposado or añejo tequila
- » VS (Very Special) or VSOP (Very Superior Old Pale) cognac
- » Irish cream liqueur
- » Italian liqueur

Also, get two 750 ml bottles of

- » Non-alcoholic wine (one white or red, and one sparkling)
- » Red wine (such as Pinot Noir and Merlot because it is nice to have additional versatility in your offerings)
- » White wine (go for Chardonnay and Sauvignon Blanc as they are also crowd favorites)

And finally, add six 12-ounce bottles or cans of non-alcoholic seltzers.

The estimated cost of these items adds an additional $600 to $700 to the basic bar setup in the preceding section.

## The ultimate bar

If money is no object and you want the most complete home bar, or if you have the basics covered and want to expand, then add the following items to those in the preceding two sections. Get yourself one 750 ml bottle of

- » Each non-alcoholic spirit that you don't yet have (non-alcoholic whiskey, tequila, gin, and rum)

- A non-alcoholic aperitif
- Super-premium gin
- Dark rum or light/flavored rum (whichever kind you didn't get in your basic bar)
- Japanese whiskey
- Canadian or Tennessee whiskey
- Reposado tequila or añejo tequila (whichever tequila you didn't select in your more complete bar)
- Mezcal
- Triple sec/orange liqueur
- Sherry
- Non-alcoholic white wine, red wine, and sparkling wine

Also get two 750 ml bottles of super-premium vodka.

The estimated cost of the ultimate bar is roughly $650 to $750, in addition to the basic and complete bar setup prices.

## Picking up mixers and other important supplies

Here are the typical mixers and supplies to have on hand in your bar:

- Cola or diet cola
- Cranberry juice
- Energy drinks (Red Bull and Monster in original and sugar-free varieties)
- Ginger ale
- Ginger beer
- Grapefruit juice
- Lemon juice or lemon juice
- Lemon-lime soda
- Lime juice
- Orange juice
- Pineapple juice

- Pomegranate juice
- Seltzer water or club soda
- Tomato juice
- Tonic water

You also need the following fruits and garnishes (see Chapter 3 for cutting instructions):

- Lemon and orange twists
- Lime and lemon wedges
- Maraschino cherries
- Olives
- Orange slices

Don't forget these items:

- Simple syrup (Chapter 2 provides a simple recipe)
- Grenadine
- Salt and pepper
- Superfine sugar
- Tabasco sauce
- Worcestershire sauce

Finally, bar tools: Here's a list of the must-haves (refer to Chapter 2 for full descriptions):

- Cocktail shaker
- Strainer
- Bar spoon
- Mixing glass
- Jigger
- Wine opener/corkscrew
- Peeler
- Muddler

**TIP** You can get a full cocktail set for a reasonable price from online vendors such as Bull in China PDX (https://bullinchinapdx.com).

## The Party Charts: Calculating Supply Needs

If you're throwing a party and don't know how much is enough for the number of guests you've invited, the tables in the following sections have all the answers when it comes to stocking up on liquor and supplies for any size get-together.

### How much liquor should you buy?

Table 4-1 shows the amount of liquor you should buy for the number of guests at your party. The left column lists the products, and the remaining columns list the number of bottles of that product you should purchase, depending on how many guests you're having. The first row of the table lists the total estimated cost.

**TABLE 4-1 How Much Liquor to Purchase for a Party**

| Product (750 ml Bottles) | 10–30 Guests | 30–40 Guests | 40–60 Guests | 60–100 Guests |
|---|---|---|---|---|
| Estimated total cost | $500–$600 | $600–$650 | $650–$725 | $725–$800 |
| Non-alcoholic (NA) spirits | 1 | 2 | 4 | 6 |
| NA wine (red/white/sparkling) | 1 | 2 | 4 | 6 |
| White wine, domestic | 5 | 5 | 6 | 8 |
| White wine, imported | 2 | 2 | 2 | 3 |
| Red wine, domestic | 1 | 2 | 3 | 3 |
| Red wine, imported | 1 | 1 | 2 | 2 |
| Blush wine | 1 | 2 | 2 | 2 |
| Sparkling wine | 2 | 3 | 4 | 4 |
| Champagne, imported | 2 | 2 | 2 | 2 |

| Product (750 ml Bottles) | 10–30 Guests | 30–40 Guests | 40–60 Guests | 60–100 Guests |
|---|---|---|---|---|
| Vermouth, extra dry | 1 | 1 | 2 | 2 |
| Vermouth, red | 1 | 1 | 1 | 1 |
| Vodka | 3 | 3 | 3 | 4 |
| Rum | 2 | 2 | 2 | 2 |
| Gin | 1 | 2 | 2 | 3 |
| Scotch | 1 | 2 | 2 | 3 |
| Whiskey, American or Canadian | 1 | 1 | 2 | 2 |
| Bourbon | 1 | 1 | 1 | 1 |
| Irish whiskey | 1 | 1 | 1 | 2 |
| Tequila | 2 | 2 | 2 | 3 |
| Brandy/cognac | 1 | 2 | 2 | 3 |
| Aperitifs (your choice) | 1 | 1 | 2 | 2 |
| Cordials (your choice) | 3 | 3 | 3 | 3 |
| Hard seltzers (12 oz. cans) | 24 | 48 | 72 | 96 |
| NA beer (12 oz. cans/bottles) | 48 | 72 | 72 | 96 |
| Beer (12 oz. cans/bottles) | 48 | 72 | 72 | 96 |

With the exception of beer and wine, I based the costs in Table 4-1 on pouring 1¾ ounces of liquor per drink. Cost totals are in U.S. dollars.

REMEMBER

The size of a crowd isn't the only factor to consider when buying liquor:

» **Age:** The number of products that you purchase varies depending on the age of the crowd. If people between the ages of 21 and 35 dominate a crowd, increase the amount of vodka, whiskey, tequila, and beer by one-half.

CHAPTER 4 **Setting Up Your Home Bar** 39

- » **Season:** Think about the time of year. In the fall and winter, consider serving less gin and more beer or whiskey because people tend to crave warmer, fuller flavors that feel cozy and comforting. Darker spirits like whiskey or spiced rum complement the season's mood and pair well with heartier foods. In the spring and summer, I suggest leaning into hard seltzers, vodka, gin, and tequila because they're lighter, more refreshing, and often mix well with citrus, herbs, and fresh seasonal fruits, which are perfect for warm weather and outdoor gatherings.

- » **Geographical location:** Consult a local bartender or liquor clerk to find out what the most popular products are in your area. For example, if you live in an area that has a lot of wineries, consider carrying those products. If you're in Kentucky, have more bourbons (both alcoholic and non-alcoholic) because both locals and tourists want to have those kinds of products when they're in that part of the country.

## How many supplies and mixers should you buy?

Your bar needs more than just liquor. Table 4-2 lists the other supplies that you want to purchase. The total costs (in U.S. dollars) are listed in the first row.

**TABLE 4-2 Mixers and Other Bar Supplies**

| Product | 10–30 Guests | 30–40 Guests | 40–60 Guests | 60–100 Guests |
|---|---|---|---|---|
| Estimated Total cost | $100–$125 | $125–$150 | $150–$175 | $200–$225 |
| Soda (2-liter bottles) | | | | |
| Club soda/seltzer water | 3 | 3 | 4 | 5 |
| Ginger ale | 2 | 2 | 2 | 3 |
| Cola | 3 | 3 | 3 | 4 |
| Diet cola | 3 | 3 | 3 | 4 |
| Lemon-lime soda | 2 | 3 | 3 | 4 |

| Product | 10–30 Guests | 30–40 Guests | 40–60 Guests | 60–100 Guests |
|---|---|---|---|---|
| Tonic water | 2 | 2 | 3 | 3 |
| Juices (quarts) | | | | |
| Tomato | 2 | 2 | 3 | 3 |
| Grapefruit | 2 | 2 | 3 | 3 |
| Orange | 2 | 2 | 3 | 3 |
| Cranberry | 2 | 2 | 3 | 3 |
| Miscellaneous Items | | | | |
| Ice (bags) | 10 | 15 | 20 | 30 |
| Napkins (dozen) | 4 | 4 | 6 | 8 |
| Stirrers (1,000/box) | 1 | 1 | 1 | 1 |
| Angostura bitters (4 oz. bottles) | 1 | 1 | 1 | 2 |
| Cream of coconut (cans) | 1 | 2 | 2 | 2 |
| Grenadine (12 oz. bottles) | 1 | 1 | 1 | 2 |
| Energy drink | 6 | 6 | 12 | 12 |
| Horseradish (small jars) | 1 | 1 | 1 | 2 |
| Lime juice (12 oz. bottles) | 1 | 1 | 1 | 2 |
| Lemons | 3 | 4 | 5 | 6 |
| Limes | 2 | 3 | 3 | 4 |
| Maraschino cherries (jars) | 1 | 1 | 1 | 1 |
| Olives (jars) | 1 | 1 | 1 | 1 |
| Oranges | 1 | 2 | 2 | 3 |
| Milk (quarts) | 1 | 1 | 1 | 2 |

*(continued)*

**TABLE 4-2** *(continued)*

| Product | 10–30 Guests | 30–40 Guests | 40–60 Guests | 60–100 Guests |
|---|---|---|---|---|
| Mineral water (1L bottles) | 2 | 3 | 4 | 5 |
| Superfine sugar (boxes) | 1 | 1 | 1 | 1 |
| Tabasco sauce (bottles) | 1 | 1 | 1 | 1 |
| Worcestershire sauce (bottles) | 1 | 1 | 1 | 1 |

# 2
# A World of Flavor, Without Alcohol

**IN THIS PART . . .**

Discover the growing market of non-alcoholic beer, wine, and spirits.

Prep your home bar for non-alcoholic drink-making magic.

Get to know the dollars and cents of non-alcoholic drinks at your bar or restaurant.

IN THIS CHAPTER

» Discovering how non-alcoholic beer is made

» Exploring different varieties to try

# Chapter 5
# Non-Alcoholic Beer

People have brewed beer for thousands of years, and today, drinkers all over the world enjoy thousands of different varieties of beer, including non-alcoholic beer. The Business Research Company put out a report in 2025 that the global non-alcoholic beer market would grow from $21.94 billion in 2024 to $35.35 billion in 2029. With this trend, we imagine that more non-alcoholic beer offerings will continue to be added to the market.

Legally, non-alcoholic beer in the U.S. must contain 0.5 percent alcohol by volume (ABV) or less. If you see a beer labeled as "0.0," that means that specific beer has a zero percent ABV. And 0.5 percent ABV is a small amount of alcohol; it typically doesn't cause intoxication, but helps keep the beer tasting like beer.

With more than 8,000 craft breweries in the United States and more opening up each year, the number of breweries that offer non-alcoholic beer will continue to increase.

# How Non-Alcoholic Beer Is Made

*Beer* is an alcoholic beverage that's fermented and brewed from barley, hops, water, and yeast (along with corn and rice in some recipes). The process for making non-alcoholic beer is the same as making alcoholic beer, and then the brewer reduces or removes the alcohol after brewing.

To make non-alcoholic beer, you mash malted barley, and then boil the wort, at which point you add the hops. After you boil for about 60 minutes, you move on to the fermentation process — just like regular beer — but later remove or limit the alcohol.

After fermentation, the process for non-alcoholic beer becomes different than your typical beer. The brewers now have to remove or reduce the alcohol, depending on what ABV they want to create, and they have a few ways that they can do it.

Brewers most often use either vacuum distillation or reverse osmosis because those two methods preserve the most flavor:

- **Vacuum distillation:** Lowers the boiling point of alcohol by using a vacuum. In a vacuum, the alcohol evaporates at a much lower temperature, but the beer's flavor profile remains.
- **Reverse osmosis:** Filters out alcohol through a membrane filter while retaining the flavors and characteristics of the beer, ensuring minimal loss of flavor.

Both of the processes in the preceding list require special equipment, so brewers have to make an investment to create non-alcoholic beers.

Overall, the total process takes about four to six weeks.

TIP

This chapter gives you just a generic overview of beer production; for much more information on beer, check out *Beer For Dummies* by Marty Nachel and Steve Ettlinger (Wiley). If you're interested in actually making your own beer, grab Marty Nachel's *Homebrewing For Dummies* (Wiley).

## A QUICK HISTORY OF BEER

Beer enjoys the distinction of coming to the Americas on the *Mayflower* and, in fact, seems to have played a part in the Pilgrims' decision to land at Plymouth Rock, rather than farther south as intended. A journal (now in the U.S. Library of Congress) written by one of the passengers states in an entry from 1620 that the *Mayflower* landed at Plymouth because "we could not now take time for further search or consideration, our victuals being much spent, especially our beer."

The first commercial brewery in America was founded in New Amsterdam (New York City) in 1613. Many patriots owned their own breweries, among them General Israel Putnam and William Penn. Thomas Jefferson was also interested in brewing and made beer at Monticello. George Washington even had his own brewhouse on the grounds of Mount Vernon, and his handwritten recipe for beer — dated 1757 and taken from his diary — is still preserved.

Non-alcoholic beer first made its appearance around the time of Prohibition in the 1920s and was known as *near beer*. Although near beer did contain alcohol (around the legal limit of 0.5 percent), it helped kickstart the development of non-alcoholic beers. The German brand Clausthaler is credited with creating the first genuine non-alcoholic beer around 1979, using methods like vacuum distillation. Later, in 1994, the international brewing company Heineken introduced Heineken 0.0, and Budweiser, another major international brewer, followed suit shortly after.

## Exploring Types of Non-Alcoholic Beer

You've probably seen some of the following terms on beer labels, or maybe you've heard them in beer commercials. You can find all of these types of beers in non-alcoholic versions:

- **Amber or red ale:** Caramel and toasted flavors.
- **Cider:** Apple flavors; usually either dry or sweet.
- **India pale ale (IPA):** A style within the pale ale category that's typically made with more hops than other pale ales.

CHAPTER 5 **Non-Alcoholic Beer** 47

- **Lager:** Usually a lighter style of beer and the most common type of non-alcoholic beer.

  The word *lager* is German for "to store."

- **Pale ale:** Brewed using mainly pale malt and ale yeast; usually amber colored. These ales often taste fruity and floral.
- **Pilsner:** A light, hoppy, dry lager.
- **Stout:** An ale produced from heavily roasted barley. It's darker in color and has a slightly bitter flavor. You get notes of coffee and chocolate in this style.
- **Sour:** Tart and fruity. Also . . . sour. (Would you have guessed?)
- **Wheat beer:** Typically fruity and spicy, this beer is made, as you may expect, by using wheat. It's usually garnished with a lemon or an orange.

## Storing and Serving Non-Alcoholic Beer

In the United States, beer is served cold (around 45 degrees Fahrenheit). Lower temperatures tend to dull the taste, so consider 40 degrees the lower limit. Like beer that contains alcohol, store non-alcoholic beer away from sunlight to avoid *skunked* beer (meaning that it has a funky, unpleasant smell. This happens when beer is exposed to light) — never pleasant. The fridge is usually the best place for beer.

Most beers now have labels that say when they were brewed or when to remove them from the shelf, so keep an eye out for those dates.

Although most people drink beer on its own, guests might request some beer cocktails and beer mixes. Here are the most common ones (worth trying as a non-alcoholic beer cocktail if you feel experimental):

- Beer-mosa
- Beer-tita
- Michelada
- Summer shandy or grapefruit shandy

Check out Chapter 12 for even more recipes.

# Trying a Few Non-Alcoholic Beer Brands

You can find over 100 non-alcoholic beers on the market. After you find the style of beer that you like, try a variety of that style's non-alcoholic offerings. Here are some of my suggestions:

- Athletic Brewing Co. Upside Dawn (golden ale)
- Athletic Lite (light beer)
- Athletic Wild Run (IPA)
- Beck's Blue (pilsner)
- Blue Moon (wheat beer)
- Brooklyn Brewery Special Effects (IPA)
- Budweiser Zero (lager)
- Carlsberg 0.0 (pilsner)
- Clausthaler Dry Hopped (IPA)
- Coors Edge (lager)
- Corona Cero (lager)
- Free Damm (lager)
- Guinness 0.0 (stout)
- Heineken 0.0 (lager)
- Lagunitas IPNA (IPA)
- O'Doul's (lager)
- Original Sin Widow's Tea (cider)
- Paulaner Weizen-Radler (wheat beer)
- Sam Adams Just the Haze (IPA)
- Sierra Nevada Trail Pass (IPA)
- St. Pauli Girl (pilsner)
- Stella Artois (lager)
- Ted Segers (lager)
- Tsingtao (lager)
- IPAs
  - Athletic Wild Run
  - Brooklyn Brewery Special Effects

- Clausthaler Dry Hopped
- Lagunitas IPNA
- Sam Adams Just the Haze
- Sierra Nevada Trail Pass

» Lagers
- Budweiser Zero
- Coors Edge
- Corona Cero
- Free Damm
- Heineken 0.0
- O'Doul's
- Stella Artois
- Ted Segers
- Tsingtao

» Pilsners
- Beck's Blue
- Carlsberg 0.0
- St. Pauli Girl

» Wheat beers
- Blue Moon
- Paulaner Weizen-Radler

» Miscellaneous
- Athletic Brewing Co. Upside Dawn (golden ale)
- Athletic Lite (light beer)
- Guinness 0.0 (stout)
- Original Sin Widow's Tea (cider)

You can also find a few non-alcoholic hard teas and seltzers on the market, but those categories are still growing.

**IN THIS CHAPTER**

» Discovering how non-alcoholic wine is made

» Exploring current styles

» Reviewing brands to sip and savor

# Chapter 6
# Non-Alcoholic Wine

Wine, as you probably know, is made from fermented grapes, and non-alcoholic wine is made from grapes, but the alcohol content is reduced or fully removed. Non-alcoholic wine is also often called *dealcoholized* or *alcohol removed* wine.

Wine comes in red, white, rosé, and sparkling varieties. Winemaking dates back to roughly 3000 BC, making it one of the oldest fermented drinks in the world!

You can find whole books dedicated to types of wine; I don't even pretend to give a comprehensive overview in this chapter. The focus of this book, after all, is getting to know non-alcoholic drinks and their recipes.

TIP

A great introduction to buying, serving, and drinking wine is *Wine For Dummies*, by Ed McCarthy and Mary Ewing-Mulligan (Wiley). It's full of useful and interesting information that can help you better understand wine and its various styles.

## How Non-Alcoholic Wine Is Made

Just like non-alcoholic beer (which you can read about in Chapter 5), non-alcoholic wine is dealcoholized by using a process such as vacuum distillation or reverse osmosis. Another

CHAPTER 6 Non-Alcoholic Wine   51

process called *fermentation cessation* (meaning you stop the fermentation process before it even begins) can be used to make non-alcoholic wine.

Additionally, brands such as FRE use the *spinning cone* process, which uses a centrifugal force to separate the alcohol from the wine. This contraption looks very similar to a cone and spins very quickly to remove the alcohol.

## Current Styles of Non-Alcoholic Wine

Non-alcoholic wine is still a growing category, which comes in red, white, rosé and sparkling varieties. The following sections discuss each of the styles, along with their flavor profiles.

### Red wines

Non-alcoholic red wines are made from regular grapes that tend to have flavors of dark fruit, like cherries, with additional spice notes.

Table 6-1 lists a few styles of red grapes, their flavors, and where they're typically produced.

**TABLE 6-1 Red Wine Grapes**

| Name | Style | Produced in |
| --- | --- | --- |
| Bordeaux | Dry | France |
| Burgundy | Dry | France |
| Cabernet Sauvignon | Full body | France, United States, Australia, Chile |
| Grenache | Full body | Australia |
| Malbec | Full body | Argentina |
| Merlot | Full body | Chile |
| Shiraz (or Syrah) | Full body | Australia |
| Zinfandel | Dry | United States |

## Rosé wines

Non-alcoholic rosé wines are made from red grapes (see the preceding section), such as Zinfandel. For rosé wines, the grapes have minimal skin contact with the grape skins to achieve the light pink color. Rosé can include strawberry and watermelon. Rosé wines typically come from France, Spain, or the U.S.

## White wines

Non-alcoholic white wines are made from white grapes and are typically lighter and crisper than red wines. These wines have flavors such as citrus and apples and floral notes.

Table 6-2 presents a few styles of white grapes, their flavors, and the countries that typically produce them.

**TABLE 6-2 White Wine Grapes**

| Name | Style | Produced in |
| --- | --- | --- |
| Chardonnay | Dry | France, United States, Argentina, Australia, South Africa, New Zealand, Italy |
| Chenin Blanc | Light, dry or sweet | France, United States, South Africa |
| Pinot Grigio | Dry or sweet | Trentino, Italy |
| Riesling | Sweet | Germany, United States, France, Austria |
| Sauvignon Blanc | Dry | France, United States, New Zealand, South Africa, Chile |

## Sparkling wines

My personal favorite is non-alcoholic sparkling wine. This type of wine is so versatile when you make cocktails, and it's hard (but, of course, possible) not to have fun with some bubbles in your hand!

This style of non-alcoholic wine uses the same grape base as non-alcoholic white or rosé wines, but it's carbonated to create bubbles. These wines are often light and crisp, with citrus flavors to help bring taste profiles similar to Champagne or Prosecco.

**REMEMBER**

In order for a sparkling wine to be called Champagne, it must be made in the Champagne region of France. Otherwise, it's called sparkling wine. Prosecco is an Italian sparkling wine usually made from glera grapes. In order to be officially called Prosecco, the wines must come from this region of Italy.

A monk whose name many people know — Dom Pérignon — developed the first sparkling wine in the 1600s in the Champagne region of France.

## Popular Brands

Like the other categories of non-alcoholic drinks, non-alcoholic wine is still growing. Table 6-3 lists some of the most popular brands at the time of writing and some of their offerings.

**TABLE 6-3  Non-Alcoholic Wine Brands**

| Brand Name | Offerings |
| --- | --- |
| Ariel | Chardonnay, Cabernet Sauvignon |
| Carl Jung | Riesling, Merlot |
| FRE | Pinot Grigio, Sauvignon Blanc, sparkling Brut, Chardonnay, Moscato, rosé, White Zinfandel, red blend, Merlot, Cabernet Sauvignon |
| Lussory | Red, White, sparkling rosé |
| Noughty | Sparkling Chardonnay, sparkling rosé, Rouge, Blanc, and rosé |
| Oddbird | Sparkling rosé, Blanc de Blancs, Spumante Rosé, Domaine De La Prade Chardonnay |
| Proxies | Gold Crush, Blanc Slate, Red Amber |
| Society De La Rassi | Neue Brut Vintage 2023 |

> **IN THIS CHAPTER**
>
> » **Exploring how non-alcoholic spirits are made**
>
> » **Discovering popular brands**
>
> » **Handling your non-alcoholic spirits**

# Chapter 7
# Non-Alcoholic Spirits

Non-alcoholic spirits are the newest and soon to be, in my opinion, largest of the non-alcoholic options on the marketplace. In the past, people made most non-alcoholic cocktails from just a mix of juices or whatever they found in the fridge. Now, with the introduction of non-alcoholic spirits, bartenders can add in layers of flavors that they previously couldn't. This opportunity also opens up exciting possibilities for creating twists on classic cocktails — by using non-alcoholic spirits as the base.

At the time of writing, the non-alcoholic spirits category is rapidly expanding, with many products undergoing proprietary production processes. However, production of nearly all non-alcoholic spirits still uses some form of distillation. Producers have a wide variety of options, ranging from those inspired by the flavor profiles of alcoholic spirits such as bourbon or tequila to brands such as Seedlip (www.seedlipdrinks.com), which are botanical-forward and offer a unique flavor profile that differs from a more traditional spirit.

TIP

Personally, I believe you should have both styles available at your home bar because they cater to different preferences and cocktail applications.

CHAPTER 7 Non-Alcoholic Spirits     55

# How Non-Alcoholic Spirits Are Made

You can craft non-alcoholic spirits in various ways by using different techniques:

» **Remove the alcohol.** Many brands that offer non-alcoholic versions of traditional spirits, such as bourbon or tequila, follow similar processes to their alcoholic counterparts. For example, non-alcoholic bourbons might begin with fermenting and then distilling corn and other grains, but the alcohol is later removed. This technique helps preserve the intended flavor profile while still creating a quality, non-alcoholic option.

» **Create the flavor by using essences and extracts.** Other brands, such as Lyre's (www.1yres.com), take a different approach. Instead of distilling, Lyre's creates their non-alcoholic spirits by blending natural essences and extracts, recreating the flavors of classic spirits. This process has enabled Lyre's to produce well-known spirits and liqueurs that are unique as non-alcoholic products. For example, you can use their Coffee Originale, a coffee-inspired non-alcoholic liqueur, in a non-alcoholic espresso martini.

» **Use a blend of botanicals to develop distinctive flavor profiles.** Seedlip Grove 42, for instance, combines citrus fruit essences such as blood orange, lemon, and mandarin to create a bright, citrus-forward, non-alcoholic spirit. This kind of non-alcoholic spirit helps to create non-alcoholic cocktails such as a cosmopolitan, which traditionally calls for citrus vodka.

Each brand has its own approach to crafting non-alcoholic spirits, but they all have the same goal: to provide complex, flavorful options for people to use in cocktails (and beyond!) without the alcohol.

# Popular Brands

Here are some of the most popular options for non-alcoholic spirits at the time of writing. All of these brands do an excellent job of creating high quality products that work well in any non-alcoholic cocktail creation:

- **Atopia:** Rhubarb & Ginger, Hedgerow Berry, and Spiced Citrus
- **BARE Zero Proof:** Bourbon whiskey, modern classic gin, reposado-style tequila, rum blanco, and Caribbean Gold spiced rum
- **Ceder's:** Fresh & Floral, Light & Refreshing, Aromatic & Spicy, and Soft & Sweet
- **Cut Above:** Zero-proof whiskey, gin, agave blanco tequila, and mezcal
- **Everleaf:** Forest, Mountain, and Marine
- **Fluère Drinks:** Botanical Blend, Raspberry Blend, Spiced Cane, Smoked Agave, Bitter, and Anatolia Blend
- **Ghia:** Aperitif
- **Lumette:** Bright Light, London Dry, and Lumrum
- **Lyre's:** American Malt, Dry London Spirit, Pink London Spirit, Italian Spritz, Italian Orange, Agave Blanco, Dark Cane, Orange Sec, White Cane, Amaretti, Coffee Originale, and Apéritif Rosso.
- **Martini:** Vibrante and Floreale
- **Philters:** Jynn, Mezkahl, Ruhm, and Wiski
- **Seedlip:** Grove 42, Spice 94, Garden 108, and Notas de Agave
- **Ritual:** Tequila, rum, whiskey, gin, and aperitif
- **Wilfred's:** Aperitif

# Storing and Serving Suggestions

When storing non-alcoholic spirits, treat them like traditional spirits that contain alcohol. Keep them away from direct sunlight and in a cool, dry space. That said, although nearly all non-alcoholic spirits contain a small amount of preservative, they don't contain alcohol and so don't get the benefit from alcohol's broadly preservative effect. As a result, they do have a shelf life. Be sure to check expiration dates before serving to any of your guests or mixing in a cocktail.

After opening a non-alcoholic spirit, use it within two to three months because exposure to air starts to change the flavors of the spirits. Also, read all the labels of each of the products that you have because some may suggest storing the open bottle in the refrigerator.

TIP

You can make tons of fun and delicious non-alcoholic cocktails. From classics to new and modern drinks, the world is truly your oyster. Some of my favorites include the virgin piña colada, Arnold Palmer, and the no-jito (a spiritless mojito); flip to Chapter 11 for those recipes. Check out Part 3 for hundreds of great recipes.

REMEMBER

Stock at least one of these non-alcoholic spirit options at your home bar for your guests to enjoy!

> **IN THIS CHAPTER**
>
> » Giving options to your guests at home
>
> » Developing NA drink menus at your bar or restaurant
>
> » Taking a look at future trends

# Chapter 8
# Serving Non-Alcoholic Drinks at Home and at the Bar

Whether you're hosting a gathering at home or running a professional bar, offering non-alcoholic drink options is about more than just having something to offer for the non-drinkers — it's about inclusion, hospitality, and elevating the entire guest experience. This chapter explores why non-alcoholic drinks deserve a permanent place on your menu, covers how to name and cost them, and discusses what the future holds for zero-proof options.

## Offering Options at Home

When you're hosting a party, variety is key, which includes offering non-alcoholic options. A thoughtful selection of zero-proof drinks helps guests feel welcome, included, and respected, no matter their reason for skipping alcohol. It also encourages more mindful and responsible drinking overall.

Think of it this way: For every Negroni a guest enjoys, they might alternate with a non-alcoholic version. The same goes for beer or wine: Having spirit-free alternatives on hand makes it easier for guests to pace themselves without feeling like they're missing out.

As the host, it's your role to set the tone. Promoting responsible drinking means giving people choices with just as much flavor, care, and presentation as their alcoholic counterparts.

REMEMBER

Guests who choose not to drink, for whatever reason, will welcome the variety of non-alcoholic cocktails, beer, and wine that you offer.

You can easily create non-alcoholic punches (I give you some recipes in Chapter 11) and then have both non-alcoholic and alcoholic spirits near the bowl so that guests can add whatever they want. (I talk about more about non-alcoholic spirits in Chapter 7.)

TIP

Stock at least six cans or bottles of a non-alcoholic beer and a bottle of non-alcoholic wine (sparkling or not) to get your party started. If you have a lot of guests coming to your party, refer to Chapter 4, which can help you get a more accurate count of the drinks you should have available.

## Working Behind the Bar

I'm a firm believer in the value of offering non-alcoholic options on your bar or party menu. Continuing to create a safe and inclusive environment for all guests is fundamental to running a successful bar (or having a successful party).

The people working your bar need to understand the significance of respecting a guest's choice to order a non-alcoholic drink. Everyone should feel comfortable ordering a non-alcoholic cocktail — or a non-alcoholic beer or wine — without any judgment or pressure.

REMEMBER

Creating this respectful atmosphere helps make sure that all your guests have a positive experience.

Personally, I feel most at home behind the bar, and your guests should feel just as comfortable, whether they're sipping something spirit-free at your kitchen counter or ordering from your bar's cocktail list. In fact, nearly 70 percent of people check out a menu online before choosing where to go. Highlighting a dedicated section for non-alcoholic cocktails not only signals thoughtfulness, but can win over guests before they ever walk in the door. It also takes the pressure off everyone, eliminating any hesitation or awkwardness someone might feel about asking for a non-alcoholic option.

## What's in a name?

Have fun (and use some creativity) when you name your cocktails, whether they're alcoholic or non-alcoholic. Using the same names for non-alcoholic drinks as their alcoholic counterparts can create confusion for both guests and bartenders. To avoid this problem, give your non-alcoholic cocktails unique names. For example, label your non-alcoholic margarita clearly, with names such as Zero-Proof Margarita, Zero-Rita, or something playful that ties in with the name of your bar, such as Greg's Zero-Percent Margarita. These names not only make it clear that the drink is alcohol-free, but also keep things fun and engaging for your guests.

## Considering costs

Having non-alcoholic drinks on your menu can bring in big profits to your bar or restaurant if you're running such a business.

Because costs vary by location, I use some general numbers in this section to demonstrate the potential value. But feel free to adjust the figures based on your own expenses to see how much these drinks could help increase your profits. Table 8-1 shows cost breakdowns of coffee and tea, which patrons commonly order at a bar or restaurant.

**TABLE 8-1 Costs for a 12 Oz Coffee or Iced Tea**

| Drink | Cost Per Oz | Total Cost | Retail Price | Cost Percentage | Margin |
|---|---|---|---|---|---|
| Coffee | $0.10 | $1.20 | $4 | 30% | $2.80 |
| Iced Tea | $0.02 | $0.80 | $4 | 20% | $3.20 |

Most bars and restaurants have both coffee and tea options on their menus, which makes sense considering how profitable those beverage options are.

Similarly, when you create non-alcoholic drinks for your menu, you can still charge the same sort of premium that you do when you use alcoholic spirits. Again, these prices are for example purposes only: But generally, non-alcoholic spirits cost a bit less than the alcoholic version. Table 8-2 gives an example of the difference in cost of an alcoholic and non-alcoholic margarita, both of which contain the same amount of lime juice and agave syrup.

**TABLE 8-2 Costs for Alcoholic and Non-Alcoholic Margaritas**

| Drink | Cost per Oz of Tequila | Total Cost of Drink | Retail Price | Cost Percentage | Margin |
|---|---|---|---|---|---|
| Alcoholic Margarita | $1.77 | $3.78 | $16 | 23.62% | $12.22 |
| Non-Alcoholic Margarita | $1.34 | $2.92 | $16 | 18.25% | $13.08 |

As long as you keep all cocktails (alcoholic and non-alcoholic) around an 18 to 20 percent cost of goods, these cocktails not only sell, but also make money for you.

REMEMBER

Non-alcoholic spirits take the same amount of effort as — and sometimes more than — traditional alcoholic spirits do to produce. The lack of alcohol doesn't mean your non-alcoholic drink offerings require a lower price, or a lesser degree of creative and careful construction, compared to your alcoholic cocktails. Non-alcoholic cocktails are still cocktails!

# Looking at the Future of Non-Alcoholic Drinks

The future of non-alcoholic drinks is bright—and getting brighter. As drinkers become more adventurous and mindful, the demand for thoughtful, well-crafted zero-proof options continues to grow. Just like their alcoholic counterparts, non-alcoholic beverages are evolving with trends, seasonal ingredients, and global influences.

## New products

Expect a lot of new non-alcoholic products to come to market. At the time I'm writing, there are a few major brands currently leading the space, and many exciting newcomers are emerging with innovative zero-proof spirits, wines, and functional beverages. The following list gives you just a taste:

- **Beer:** Expect changes both big and small in the non-alcoholic beer market:
  - *More offerings from larger suppliers:* Larger brands such as Heineken and Budweiser have non-alcoholic beers, but more larger name brands will be offering non-alcoholic beers, if they haven't already.
  - *Craft breweries moving in:* Some smaller breweries have non-alcoholic beers already, but more will join while the non-alcoholic beer space grows.
- **Wine:** Non-alcoholic wines will blossom:
  - *More varietals:* Expect to see more styles of non-alcoholic wines.
  - *Vintages:* At the time of writing, you can already find some vintage non-alcoholic wines popping up, but more will come.
- **Seltzers:** Hard seltzers and teas really have boomed over the years, and the larger brands, such as White Claw, already have a non-alcoholic product. I expect other brands to do the same.
- **Spirits:** More and new brands, as well as more premium offerings. New variants are also coming. Brands such as Seedlip continue to evolve and expand their offerings.
- **New mixers:** For example, Fever-Tree's Espresso Martini Mix and others allow you to easily make non-alcoholic drinks. These mixers will continue to pop up while demand grows.
- **Ready-to-drink (RTD) non-alcoholic drinks:** The RTD market is another booming industry at the time of writing. Non-alcoholic spirits brands can move into this space and make drinks such as some RTD espresso martinis or cosmopolitans.

## Alcohol-free bars, stores, and events

Although many bars offer non-alcoholic cocktails, more and more alcohol-free bars are opening, and I expect that to continue.

Also, a lot of alcohol-free bottle shops are opening across the U.S. My friends in Chicago started a non-alcoholic drink shop called In Good Spirits (www.ingoodspirits.online), which hosts fun events for the community. I expect to see more of these stores coming soon.

Also, the number of non-alcoholic brands at trade shows and food-focused events continues to grow every year. I anticipate that a few events around the country will focus solely on brands in the category.

## Celebrity-backed brands

It is no surprise that celebrities are taking notice of the non-alcoholic space and getting involved. Their influence is helping to reshape the image of sober or mindful drinking, making it aspirational and accessible.

Lewis Hamilton co-founded *Almave*, a premium, non-alcoholic blue agave spirit crafted in Jalisco, Mexico. Blake Lively launched *Betty Buzz*, a line of sparkling mixers designed to stand alone or pair with spirits. Katy Perry's *De Soi* offers a line of sparkling non-alcoholic aperitifs focused on wellness and relaxation.

With such high-profile figures championing non-alcoholic alternatives, you would imagine that many more follow suit.

## Food pairings

You often see pairing suggestions on menus for food items with a certain wine, spirit, or cocktail. For example, you might see a pairing of steak with a recommended red wine or a burger with a beer from a local brewery. While the market for non-alcoholic cocktails grows, bars and restaurants will probably begin noting some fun food pairings with non-alcoholic cocktails.

# 3

# Sip & Savor: Non-Alcoholic Drink Recipes

**IN THIS PART . . .**

Play around with non-alcoholic variations of the most popular drinks.

Browse through over 300 recipes listed alphabetically.

Try out punches, holiday recipes, and drinks for each season.

Experiment with non-alcoholic drink recipes from some of the best bartenders.

Make non-alcoholic drinks whose recipes come from bars all over the globe.

**IN THIS CHAPTER**

» Classic non-alcoholic drinks

» Non-alcoholic twists on classic cocktails

» Fun facts along the way

Chapter **9**

# Classics & Riffs on Classic Cocktails

And now for my next number, I would like to return to the classics! You may have picked up this book for that exact reason.

This chapter starts with tried-and-true non-alcoholic drinks, such as the Arnold Palmer and Shirley Temple. Then things get more interesting when we dive into non-alcoholic twists on classic cocktails for you to enjoy.

Some of these recipes use non-alcoholic spirits and wines to help create similar flavor profiles of the classic cocktails that they mirror.

## Classic Non-Alcoholic Drinks

The drinks that follow are some of the most popular NA drinks that we have been enjoying for years. Ironically, most of these now have similar versions that include alcohol!

CHAPTER 9 Classics & Riffs on Classic Cocktails   **67**

## Arnold Palmer

3 oz. Iced Tea
1 oz. Lemonade
Lemon Wedge

Add tea and lemonade into a highball glass with ice and stir. Garnish with lemon wedge.

## Berry Smash

½ cup Berries (of your choice)
1 oz. Lime Juice
1 tbsp. Honey
Soda Water

Add honey and lime juice into a shaker with some of your favorite berries, and then muddle the mix. Add in ice and shake. Strain into a rocks glass filled with ice cubes or crushed ice. Top with soda water and garnish with 3 fresh berries.

## Fruit Punch

2 cups Orange Juice
2 cups Pineapple Juice
1 cup Cranberry Juice
½ cup Lime Juice
2 cups Ginger Ale or Soda

Add all ingredients into a punch bowl and stir. Serve in highball glasses.

## Iced Tea

4 cups Water
½ cup Sugar (can also use Agave or Honey)
4–6 Tea Bags
Lemon Slices

Bring water to a boil and add in tea bags. Steep tea bags for around 5 minutes, then discard the bags. Add in sugar and stir until dissolved. Bring tea to room temperature and add into a glass with ice. Garnish with lemon slices and serve. Store remaining tea in fridge.

## Lemonade

3 cups Cold Water
8–10 Lemons
½ cup Sugar
Pinch of Salt
Ice
Lemon Slice

Juice around 8–10 lemons until you have 1 cup of fresh lemon juice. In a pitcher, add in all ingredients and give it a nice stir. Once mixed, pour into a Collins glass with ice and a slice of lemon.

## Pina Colada

1 oz. Coco Lopez Cream of Coconut
2 oz. Pineapple Juice
1 cup Ice

Mix in a blender until smooth. Pour into glass.

## Roy Rogers

1 oz. Grenadine
6 oz. Cola
Maraschino Cherry

Pour grenadine and cola over ice in a tall glass. Garnish with the maraschino cherry.

## Shirley Temple

1 oz. Grenadine
6 oz. Lemon-Lime Soda or Ginger Ale
Maraschino Cherry

Pour grenadine and soda over ice in a tall glass. Garnish with a maraschino cherry.

# Twists on Classic Cocktails

To make this section easier to navigate, I use these drinks' classic cocktails names instead of adding in Zero, Non-Alcoholic (NA), or Virgin. As I mention in Chapter 9, if you choose to feature these non-alcoholic classics to your guests, make sure to specify that the drink is non-alcoholic in the name that you call it.

Feel free to add in some seasonal ingredients or adjust the recipes to make them your own!

TIP

## Bee's Knees

2 oz. NA Gin
¾ oz. Lemon Juice
½ oz. Honey Simple Syrup
Lemon Twist

Add all liquid ingredients into a shaker with ice and shake. Strain into a chilled coupe glass and garnish with a lemon twist.

## Bloody Mary

3 oz. Tomato Juice
½ oz. Lemon Juice
1 dash Worcestershire Sauce
1–2 dashes Hot Sauce
1 tsp. Celery Salt
1 pinch Pepper
1 pinch Salt
Celery Stick

Add all the ingredients (minus the celery stick) into a glass with ice and stir. Garnish with the celery stick.

*People have come up with hundreds, if not thousands, of ways to garnish this drink, so have some fun!*

## Clover Club

2 oz. NA Gin
1 oz. Lemon Juice
½ oz. Raspberry Syrup
1 Egg White or ½ oz. Aquafaba
4–5 Fresh Raspberries

Add all ingredients into a shaker (other than the fresh raspberries) and *dry shake* (shake without ice) for 30 seconds. Then, add in ice and shake again. Strain into a chilled coupe glass and garnish with a fresh raspberry skewer.

## Cosmopolitan

2 oz. NA Gin
½ oz. Cranberry Juice
½ oz. Lime Juice
¼ oz. Simple Syrup
Lime Wheel

Add all ingredients (except the lime wheel) into a shaker with ice and shake. Strain into a chilled coupe glass and garnish with the lime wheel.

## Daiquiri

2 oz. Lyre's Dry White Cane Spirit
1 oz. Simple Syrup
1 oz. Lime Juice
Lime Wedge

Add all ingredients (besides the lime wedge) into a shaker with ice and shake. Strain into a chilled coupe glass. Garnish with the lime wedge and serve.

*Find other NA Daiquiri recipes, such as a Strawberry Daiquiri, in Chapter 10.*

## Dark 'n' Stormy

2 oz. Philters Ruhm
6 oz. Ginger Beer
Lime Wedge

Fill a Collins glass with ice, then pour the ginger beer and float the rum on top. Garnish with the lime wedge.

## East Side

2 oz. Seedlip Garden 108
¾ oz. Simple Syrup
½ oz. Lime Juice
3 Cucumber Slices
5 Mint Leaves
Cucumber Ribbon

Add simple syrup, mint leaves, and cucumber slices into a shaker and muddle. Then add in all remaining ingredients (except for the cucumber ribbon) into a shaker with ice and shake. Strain into a chilled coupe glass. Garnish with the cucumber ribbon and serve.

## Espresso Martini

2 oz. Seedlip Spice 94
2 oz. Cold Brew Concentrate
¼ oz. Simple Syrup
Three Coffee Beans

Add all ingredients (other than the coffee beans) into a shaker with ice and shake. Strain into a chilled coupe glass. Garnish with the coffee beans and serve.

*The three coffee beans are meant to represent health, wealth, and happiness.*

## French 75

1½ oz. NA Gin
½ oz. Lemon Juice
½ oz. Simple Syrup
3 oz. NA Sparkling Wine/Prosecco
Lemon Twist

Add all ingredients except NA sparkling wine (and lemon twist) into a champagne flute. Top with NA sparkling wine, garnish with the lemon twist, and serve.

## Gibson

2 oz. NA Gin
⅓ oz. NA Dry Vermouth
Cocktail Onion

Add NA Gin and NA Dry Vermouth into a mixing glass with ice and stir. Strain into a chilled martini glass and garnish with a cocktail onion.

## Gin & Tonic

2 oz. NA Gin
Tonic
Lime Wedge

Add the gin into a highball glass with ice. Top with your favorite tonic and garnish with the lime wedge.

## Gin Rickey

2 oz. NA Gin
½ oz. Lime Juice
Club Soda
Lime Wheel

Fill a highball glass with ice, add in gin and lime juice. Top with club soda and stir. Garnish with the lime wheel.

## Gin Fizz

2 oz. NA Gin
1 oz. Lemon Juice
¾ oz. Simple Syrup
½ oz. Aquafaba
Club Soda

Add all ingredients except club soda into a shaker and dry shake. Then add ice and shake again. Double strain into a Collins glass with ice and top with club soda.

## Hot Toddy

1½ oz. NA Whiskey
3 oz. Hot Water
¼ oz. Lemon Juice
1 tsp. Honey or Sugar
Cinnamon Stick

Pour all ingredients (other than the cinnamon stick) into a mug and stir. Garnish with the cinnamon stick.

## Irish Coffee

2 oz. NA Whiskey
4 oz. Coffee
2 tsp. Brown Sugar
Whipped Cream

Add all ingredients (except for whipped cream) into a coffee mug and stir. Top with the whipped cream.

PART 3 Sip & Savor: Non-Alcoholic Drink Recipes

## Mai Tai

1½ oz. NA White Rum
¾ oz. NA Dark Rum
½ oz. Orange Juice or NA Triple Sec
½ oz. Fresh Lime Juice
½ oz. Orgeat Syrup
Mint Leaves
A Maraschino Cherry
Pineapple Fronds

Shake all the liquid ingredients and strain. Garnish with the mint, cherry, and pineapple fronds.

## Manhattan

1½ oz. NA Whiskey
1½ oz. NA Sweet Vermouth
3 dashes NA Bitters
Orange Peel
Cherry

Add all liquid ingredients into a mixing glass with ice and stir. Garnish with the orange peel and cherry.

## Margarita

2 oz. Ritual Tequila Alternative
¾ oz. Lime Juice
½ oz. Agave Syrup
Lime Wedge
Sugar or Salt (optional)

Add all ingredients (except for lime wedge and sugar/salt) into a cocktail shaker with ice and shake. Rim the glass with sugar or salt (optional). Strain drink into glass. Garnish with the lime wedge and serve.

## Mimosa

3 oz. NA Champagne
2 oz. Orange Juice

Combine ingredients in a champagne flute and stir.

*The Mimosa was created around 1925 at the Ritz Hotel Bar in Paris, France. It took its name from the mimosa flowering plant, whose color it resembles.*

CHAPTER 9  Classics & Riffs on Classic Cocktails

## Mint Julep

2 oz. NA Bourbon
¼ oz. Simple Syrup
8 Mint Leaves
Mint Sprig
2–3 Dashes of Angostura Bitters

In your julep or rocks glass, muddle mint leaves with simple syrup. Add in bourbon and top with crushed ice. Stir, garnish with the mint sprig and Angostura bitters, and serve.

*Horse racing fans love this classic drink at the racetrack!*

## Mojito

4 oz. Club Soda
½ oz. Simple Syrup
1 oz. Lime Juice
4–5 Mint Leaves

Muddle 4 to 5 mint leaves with simple syrup in a cocktail shaker. Add in ice and shake. Strain into a highball glass with ice and add in club soda.

*This drink is sometimes called a no-jito.*

## Mule

2 oz. NA Spirit (your choice; optional)
½ oz. Lime Juice
4 oz. Ginger Beer
Lime Wheel

Add NA spirit and lime juice into a mule mug with ice. (You don't need to include NA spirits, but they add in extra flavor.) Top with ginger beer, garnish with the lime wheel, and serve.

*You can add in any NA spirits that you want in your mule, such as rum, whiskey, or gin. Vodka was originally the spirit in this cocktail. Mules made with Bourbon are usually called "Kentucky Mules."*

## Negroni

1½ oz. Lyre's Dry London Spirit
1½ oz. Lyre's Apéritif Rosso
1½ oz. Lyre's Italian Orange
Orange Peel

Add all ingredients (besides orange peel) into a mixing glass with ice and stir. Strain into chilled rocks glass and garnish with the orange peel.

*Sometimes also called a Nagroni (for non-alcoholic) or No-groni.*

## Old Fashioned

2 oz. Ritual Whiskey Alternative
¼ oz. Simple Syrup
1-2 dashes NA Orange Bitters
1-2 dashes NA Aromatic Bitters
Orange Slice
Maraschino Cherry

Add all ingredients (except orange slice and cherry) into a mixing glass with ice and stir. Strain into a rocks glass and garnish with the orange slice and cherry.

## Paloma

1½ oz. NA Blanco Tequila
½ oz. Lime Juice
4 oz. Grapefruit Juice
1 pinch Salt
Lime Wheel

Add all ingredients (except the lime wheel) into a highball glass with ice and stir. Garnish with the lime wheel and serve.

## Pina Colada

1½ oz. NA Rum
1 oz. Coco Lopez Cream of Coconut
2 oz. Pineapple Juice
1 cup Ice

Mix ingredients in a blender until smooth. Pour into glass and serve.

## Revolver

2 oz. NA Bourbon
½ oz. NA Coffee Liqueur
2 dashes NA Orange Bitters
Orange Peel

Add all ingredients into a mixing glass with ice and stir. Strain into a chilled coupe glass. Garnish with the orange peel and serve.

## Spicy Margarita

2 oz. Ritual Tequila Alternative
¾ oz. Lime Juice
½ oz. Agave Syrup
1-2 Jalapeno Pepper Slices
Lime Wedge
Sugar or Salt (optional)

Add jalapeno slices to the cocktail shaker with lime juice and muddle. Add the tequila and agave syrup into the cocktail shaker with ice and shake. Rim the glass with sugar, salt or your own salt blend (optional). Pour drink into glass, garnish with the lime wedge, and serve.

*Try mixing other fun ingredients to create spice, such as hot honey or other spicy peppers.*

## Tequila Sunrise

2 oz. NA Tequila
4 oz. Orange Juice
¼ oz. Grenadine
Soda Water (optional)
Cherry
Orange slice

Add tequila and orange juice into a highball glass with ice. Top with grenadine and let sit until the grenadine floats to the bottom. Top with soda water (optional). Serve.

## Tom Collins

2 oz. NA Gin
1 oz. Lemon Juice
1¼ oz. Simple Syrup
Soda Water
Lemon Wheel
Maraschino Cherry

Add gin, lemon juice, and simple syrup into a Collins glass with ice. Top with soda water and garnish with the lemon wheel and maraschino cherry.

## Whiskey Sour

2 oz. NA Whiskey
½ oz. Simple Syrup
¾ oz. Lemon Juice
1 Egg White or Aquafaba (optional)
Lemon Slice or dashes of NA Bitters

Add egg white or aquafaba (optional) into a shaker with other liquid ingredients and dry shake. Then add in ice and shake again. If you're not using egg white or aquafaba, add in all liquid ingredients into a shaker with ice and shake. Strain into rocks or coupe glass and garnish with either the lemon slice or bitters.

> **IN THIS CHAPTER**
> » Recipes from A to Z
> » Tips on how to make these recipes

# Chapter 10
# Non-Alcoholic Drink Recipes from A to Z

This largest chapter of the book includes over 300 recipes for you to test, try, and enjoy! Try to come up with your own recipes and see what you can create. (Who knows? Maybe your recipe will appear in the next version of this book.) These recipes appear in alphabetical order to help you easily reference back to them.

## Agave Amargo

1 oz. NA Tequila
1 oz. Wilderton Bittersweet Aperitivo
1 oz. Martini Floreale
3 dashes All The Bitter Orange Bitters
Orange Peel

Express the orange peel. Stir all other ingredients in a mixing glass until chilled. Strain into a coupe glass and garnish with the orange peel.

*Shared by Ian James Blessing*

## Agave Espresso Martini

2 oz. Seedlip Notas de Agave NA Spirit
2 oz. Cold Brew Coffee Concentrate
¼ oz. Simple Syrup
3 Coffee Beans

Add all ingredients (except coffee beans) into a shaker with ice and shake. Strain into a chilled coupe glass. Garnish with the coffee beans and serve.

## Agave Royal Hawaiian

1½ oz. Cut Above Agave Blanco
¾ oz. Lemon Juice
½ oz. Pineapple Juice
½ oz. Orgeat Syrup
Lemon Wedge

Add all ingredients (except pineapple fronds and lemon wedge) into a cocktail shaker with ice and shake. Strain into a rocks glass filled with pebble ice. Garnish with the pineapple fronds and lemon wedge.

## Apple & Ginger

4 oz. Apple Cider
1 oz. Ginger Syrup
Apple Slice
Cinnamon Stick

Add all ingredients (except apple slice and cinnamon stick) into a rocks glass with ice and stir. Garnish with the apple slice and cinnamon stick, and serve.

## Apple Cider Whiskey Smash

2 oz. Cut Above Bourbon
3 oz. Apple Cider
½ oz. Lemon Juice
¼ oz. Pumpkin Pie Simple Syrup
Cinnamon Stick

Add all ingredients (besides cinnamon stick) into a cocktail shaker with ice. Shake and strain into a rocks glass with ice. Garnish with the cinnamon stick.

## Aviation

2 oz. Philters Jynn
½ oz. Luxardo Cherry Syrup
¼ oz. Lavender Syrup
¼ oz. Lemon Juice
Luxardo Cherry

Add ingredients in a shaker with ice. Shake and double strain into a coupe glass. Add the Luxardo cherry for garnish.

## Avocado Margarita

2 oz. Ritual Tequila Alternative
¾ oz. Lime Juice
½ oz. Agave Syrup
½ Avocado (peeled)
Sugar or Salt (optional)

Add all ingredients (other than lime wedge, and sugar or salt) into a blender and blend. Rim a rocks glass with salt/sugar (optional). Pour mixture into the rocks glass and garnish with the lime wedge.

## Beer at the Orchard

4 oz. NA Beer (Pale Ale or Wheat)
1 oz. Apple Cider
1 oz. Ginger Syrup
Apple Slice

Add all ingredients (except apple slice) into a pint glass and stir. Garnish with the apple slice and serve.

## Beer-Mojito

4 oz. NA Beer (Lager or Wheat)
1 oz. Lime Juice
1 oz. Simple Syrup
6-8 Mint Leaves
Lime Wedge
Mint Sprig

In a cocktail shaker, add mint leaves, lime juice, simple syrup, and ice; muddle. Shake and strain into a Collins glass with ice. Add in NA beer and stir. Garnish with the lime wedge and mint sprig.

## Beer-Mojito Mule

4 oz. NA Beer (Lager or Wheat)
1 oz. Lime Juice
1 oz. Simple Syrup
6-8 Mint Leaves
Club Soda
Lime Wedge
Mint Sprig

In a cocktail shaker, add ice, mint, lime, and simple syrup; muddle. Shake and strain into a Collins glass with ice. Add in NA beer and top with club soda. Garnish with lime wedge and mint sprig.

## Beer-Mosa

12 oz. NA Beer
4 oz. Orange Juice
Orange Slice

Pour your favorite NA beer in a pint glass. Then, add in orange juice and garnish with the orange slice.

## Beer-Paloma

2 oz. Grapefruit Juice
1 oz. Lime Juice
1 oz. Agave Syrup
4 oz. NA Beer (Grapefruit or Pale Ale)
2 tbsp. Salt or Sugar (Optional)
Grapefruit Slice

Rim your rocks glass with salt or sugar by rubbing a lime wedge around the rim of the glass and dipping it into the salt or sugar (optional). Add grapefruit juice, lime juice, agave syrup, and ice into a cocktail shaker; shake. Strain drink into the rocks glass and top with chilled NA beer. Stir and garnish with a grapefruit slice.

## Beer-Rita

1 oz. Lime Juice
1 oz. Agave Syrup
1 oz. Orange Juice
4 oz. NA Beer (Lager or Wheat)
2 tbsp. Salt or Sugar (Optional)
Lime Wedge

Rim your glass with salt or sugar by rubbing a lime wedge around the rim of your rocks glass and dipping it into the salt or sugar (optional). Add all ingredients (except NA beer and lime wedge) into a cocktail shaker. Shake and strain into rocks glass and top with chilled NA Beer. Give a quick stir and garnish with the lime wedge.

## Beer-Sour

1 oz. Lemon Juice
1 oz. Simple Syrup
4 oz. NA Beer (Wheat or Ale)
Lemon Wheel

Add lemon juice and simple syrup into a glass with ice and shake. Strain into a rocks glass with ice and top with NA beer. Garnish with the lemon wheel.

*A beer twist on a whiskey sour*

## Bee's Kiss

2 oz. NA Dark Rum
1 oz. Heavy Cream
¾ oz. Honey Syrup
1 tsp. of Grated Nutmeg

Add all ingredients (except nutmeg) into a cocktail shaker with ice and shake. Strain into a chilled coupe glass and sprinkle nutmeg on top for garnish.

*This drink first debuted in Trader Vic's Book of Food and Drink (Doubleday & Company) in 1946.*

## Bee's Knees

2 oz. NA Gin
¾ oz. Lemon Juice
½ oz. Honey Simple Syrup
Lemon Twist

Add all ingredients (except lemon twist) into a shaker with ice and shake. Strain into a chilled coupe glass and garnish with the lemon twist.

## Bellini

1½ oz. White Peach Puree
4 oz. NA Prosecco
Peach Slice

Add white peach puree into the champagne flute. Top with NA Prosecco and garnish with peach slice.

*Invented at Harry's Bar in Venice, Italy, by Giuseppi Cipriani on the occasion of an exhibition of the work of Venetian painter Bellini.*

## Berry Lemonade & Beer

2 oz. Lemonade
½ oz. Simple Syrup
8–10 of your favorite berries
4 oz. NA Beer (Lager or Wheat)
Lemon Wedge or Berry

In a cocktail shaker, add in simple syrup and a mixture of your favorite berries and muddle. Add in ice and lemonade; shake. Double Strain into a Collins glass with ice and top with NA beer. Garnish with a lemon wedge or your favorite berry.

## Bitter Sweet Moment

1½ oz. NA Sparkling Wine
2 oz. Clearer Twist Premium French Pink Mixer
¾ oz. Lemon Juice
Lemon Coin

Add ingredients (except lemon coin) into a flute glass and stir. Garnish with the lemon coin.

## Blackberry Bramble

2 oz. Cut Above Whiskey
1 oz. Lemon Juice
½ oz. Simple Syrup
4 Blackberries
1 Basil Sprig
2 Basil leaves

Gently muddle basil and blackberries in a cocktail shaker. Add whiskey, lemon juice, and simple syrup. Shake well with ice and then strain into a rocks glass filled with fresh ice. Garnish with basil sprig and blackberries.

## Blackberry Lemonade

3 oz. Lemonade
½ oz. Blackberry Syrup
2 Blackberries
2 Mint leaves

In a cocktail shaker, add in lemonade, blackberry syrup, and ice; shake. Strain into a rocks glass with ice and garnish with fresh blackberries and mint.

## Blackberry Mojito

6 Blackberries
4 oz. Club Soda
½ oz. Simple Syrup
1 oz. Lime Juice
4–5 Mint Leaves

Muddle blackberries and 4–5 mint leaves with simple syrup in a cocktail shaker. Add in ice and shake. Strain into a highball glass with ice and add in club soda.

## Blood Orange Daiquiri

2 oz. NA Rum
1 oz. Blood Orange Juice
1 oz. Simple Syrup
1 oz. Lime Juice
Lime Wedge

Add all ingredients (besides lime wedge) into a shaker with ice and shake. Strain into a chilled coupe glass. Garnish with the lime wedge and serve.

## Bloody Maria

1½ oz. NA Tequila
3 oz. Tomato Juice
½ oz. Lemon Juice
1 dash Worcestershire Sauce
1–2 dashes Hot Sauce
1 tsp. Celery Salt
1 pinch Pepper
1 pinch Salt
Celery Stick

Add all ingredients (except celery stick) into a highball glass with ice and stir. Garnish with the celery stick.

## Blueberry-Banana Slushie

1 cup Blueberries
Banana
½ cup of Ice
Dehydrated Banana Slice

Add all ingredients (besides dehydrated banana) into a blender and blend. Pour into a glass and garnish with the dehydrated banana slice.

## Blueberry Cream Dirty Soda

8 oz. Soda (Lemon-Lime or Cola)
2 tbsp. Blueberry Syrup
1 oz. Heavy Cream
5-6 Blueberries

Add all ingredients (other than blueberries) into a glass with ice and stir. Garnish with the blueberries.

## Blueberry Daiquiri

2 oz. NA Rum
1 oz. Blueberry Puree
1 oz. Simple Syrup
1 oz. Lime Juice
Lime Wedge

Add all ingredients (except lime wedge) into a shaker with ice and shake. Strain into a chilled coupe glass. Garnish with the lime wedge and serve.

## Blueberry Smash

½ cup Blueberries
1 oz. Lime Juice
1 tbsp. Honey
Soda Water
Mint Sprig
4-5 Fresh Berries

Add honey and lime juice into a shaker with blueberries and muddle. Add in ice and shake. Strain into a rocks glass filled of ice or crushed ice. Top with soda water and garnish with fresh blueberries and a mint sprig.

## Blueberry-Lemon Slushie

Lemon
1 cup Blueberries
½ cup Water
Lemon Slice

Juice the lemon into the blender. Add the lemon juice, blueberries, water, and ice into a blender and blend. Pour into a glass and garnish with the lemon slice.

## Blueberry Mojito

6 Blueberries
4-5 Mint Leaves
½ oz. Simple Syrup
1 oz. Lime Juice
4 oz. Club Soda

Muddle blueberries and mint leaves with simple syrup and lime juice in a cocktail shaker. Add in ice and shake. Strain into a highball glass with ice and add in club soda.

CHAPTER 10  Non-Alcoholic Drink Recipes from A to Z

## Brave Bull

2 oz. Cut Above Mezcal
2 oz. Chilled Coffee
Lemon Twist
3 Coffee Beans

Pour mezcal and coffee into a shaker or glass; stir. Strain into a coupe glass and add a twist of lemon and coffee beans as garnish.

## Breakfast in Oaxaca

1 oz. NA Mezcal
3 oz. Cold Brew Coffee
2 dashes Aztec Chocolate Bitters
Orange Twist

Add all ingredients (except orange twist) to a mixing glass with ice and stir. Pour into a rocks glass with ice and garnish with the orange twist.

## Brooke Bravely

1 oz. Orange Juice
1 oz. Pineapple Juice
½ oz. Cranberry Juice
4 oz. NA Sparkling Wine
Orange Twist

Add all juices into a shaker with ice and shake. Strain into a chilled flute glass and top with sparkling wine. Garnish with the orange twist and serve.

*Inspired by Brooke Marren in New Jersey*

## Brown Derby

2 oz. Philters Wiski
1 oz. Grapefruit Juice
1 oz. Honey
2 Cherries skewered on cocktail pick

Add Wiski, juice, and honey to a shaker tin with ice. Shake and double strain into a coupe glass. Garnish with the cherry pick and serve.

## Brown Derby #2

2 oz. Philters Wiski
1 oz. Grapefruit Juice
1 oz. Lime Juice
½ oz. Honey
Cherry skewered on cocktail pick

Add ingredients (except cherry pick) to a shaker with ice. Shake and double strain into a coupe glass. Garnish with the cherry pick and serve.

**84** PART 3 Sip & Savor: Non-Alcoholic Drink Recipes

## Bruce the Hairdresser

1 oz. NA Whiskey
½ oz. Lemon Juice
¼ oz. Raspberry Simple Syrup
4 oz. Raspberry Iced Tea
Lemon Wedge

Add all ingredients (except lemon wedge) into a highball glass with ice and stir. Garnish with the lemon wedge and serve.

*Created by R. Foley from BARTENDER Magazine*

## Café con Rhum

2 oz. Philters Ruhm
4 oz. Coffee
¾ oz. Half-and-Half
½ oz. Vanilla Syrup
1 tsp. of Grated Cinnamon
1 tsp. Grated Nutmeg

Brew coffee and warm the half-and-half in a small pot until warm, do not boil. Combine all ingredients (except cinnamon and nutmeg) in a mug and stir. Garnish with the cinnamon and nutmeg, and serve.

## Catching Smoke

1½ oz. NA Mezcal
1½ oz. Lapsang Souchong Tea
¾ oz. Lime Juice
½ oz. Cinnamon Syrup
2 oz. Ginger Beer
Lime Wheel

Chill the tea. Combine all ingredients (besides the ginger beer and lime wheel) in a shaker with ice and shake until chilled. Gently add ginger beer to the shaker tin, then strain into a highball glass over fresh ice. Garnish with the lime wheel.

*Shared by Ian James Blessing*

## Candy Cane Crush

2 oz. Sobrii 0-Gin
1 oz. Candy Cane Syrup
3 oz. Coconut Milk
½ oz. Lemon Juice
2 Candy Canes

In a shaker, combine all ingredients (except candy cane) with ice and shake well. Crush the candy canes, and then rim a coupe glass with them. Strain the shaker contents into the coupe glass. Garnish with a small candy cane and serve.

## Cantaloupe Crush

2 oz. Cut Above Mezcal
½ oz. Simple Syrup
¾ oz. Lime Juice
3 oz. Cantaloupe Juice
6 Basil Leaves
Topo Chico
Melon Slice

Combine syrup, lime juice, and 5 basil leaves into shaker and muddle. Add cantaloupe juice and mezcal with ice and shake vigorously. Double strain into a rocks glass with fresh ice. Top with Topo Chico. Garnish with remaining basil leaf and the melon slice.

## Chemin de Pamplemousse

1½ oz. The Pathfinder NA Spirit
2 oz. Grapefruit Juice
½ oz. Lemon Juice
½ oz. Simple Syrup
2 oz. Soda Water
Grapefruit Wedge

Place everything (except soda water and grapefruit wedge) into a shaker with ice and shake until chilled. Gently add soda water to the shaker tin, then strain into a highball glass over fresh ice. Garnish with the grapefruit wedge.

*Shared by Ian James Blessing*

## Cherry Daiquiri

2 oz. NA Rum
1 oz. Cherry Puree
1 oz. Simple Syrup
1 oz. Lime Juice
Lime Wedge

Add all ingredients (except lime wedge) into a shaker with ice and shake. Strain into a chilled coupe glass. Garnish with the lime wedge and serve.

## Cherry Dark 'N' Stormy

2 oz. Philters Ruhm
6 oz. Cherry Cola
Lime Wedge

Fill a Collins glass with ice, then pour in the cherry cola and float the rum on top. Garnish with lime wedge.

## Cherry Vanilla Dirty Soda

8 oz. Cherry Vanilla Cola
2 tbsp. Vanilla Syrup
2 oz. Half-and-Half
Maraschino Cherry

Add all ingredients (except cherry) into a glass with ice and stir. Garnish with the cherry and serve.

## Chinese 5 Spice Dark 'N' Stormy

2 oz. Philters Ruhm
½ oz. Chinese 5 Spice Simple Syrup*
6 oz. Ginger Beer
Lime Wedge

Fill a Collins glass with ice, then pour in the ginger beer and Chinese 5 spice simple syrup and stir. Float the rum on top. Garnish with lime wedge.

*Chinese 5-Spice Simple Syrup:*
1 cup water
1 cup cane sugar
1½ tsp. Chinese 5-spice powder (or a blend of star anise, cinnamon, fennel, cloves, and Sichuan peppercorns)
In a small saucepan, combine the water and sugar. Stir over medium heat until the sugar is fully dissolved. Add the Chinese 5-spice powder, and bring to a gentle simmer for 5–10 mins. Remove from heat and let steep for another 10–15 minutes for fuller flavor. Strain through a fine mesh strainer or cheesecloth to remove sediment.

## Chocolate Almond Negroni

2 oz. Cut Above Gin
¾ oz. NA Aperitivo
¾ oz. NA Sweet Vermouth
¼ oz. Lyre's Amaretti
4 dashes Chocolate Bitters
1 large Ice Cube
Cinnamon Stick
Star Anise

Add the ingredients (other than cinnamon stick and star anise) together in mixing glass and stir until chilled. Pour over fresh cube ice. Garnish with the cinnamon stick and whole star anise.

## Chocolate Avocado Smoothie

Banana
½ Avocado
½ cup Chocolate Milk

Add all ingredients into a blender and blend until smooth. Pour mixture into a glass and serve.

## Chocolate Banana Colada Shake

⅓ cup Coco Lopez Cream of Coconut
½ cup Milk
1 tbsp. Chocolate Syrup
1½ cups Chocolate or Vanilla Ice Cream
½ cup Sliced Banana

Mix all ingredients in a blender until smooth and serve.

CHAPTER 10  Non-Alcoholic Drink Recipes from A to Z

## Chocolate Colada Shake

⅓ cup Coco Lopez Cream of Coconut
½ cup Milk
1 tbsp. Chocolate Syrup
1½ cups Chocolate or Vanilla Ice Cream

Mix all ingredients in a blender until smooth and serve.

## Chili-Lime Pineapple Soda

4 tbsp. Tajin
½ cup of Lime Juice
1 cup Pineapple Juice
3 cups Club Soda

Rim four glasses with Tajin and fill the glasses with ice. In a pitcher, add in lime juice, then add pineapple juice and club soda; stir. Pour mixture into glasses and serve.

*Makes 4 servings*

## Citrus Beer Spritz

4 oz. NA Wheat Beer
2 oz. Orange Juice
2 oz. Lemon Juice
1 oz. Soda Water
Orange Slice
Mint Sprig

Add all ingredients (except orange slice and mint sprig) into a pint glass and stir. Garnish with the orange slice and mint sprig; serve.

## Citrus Seltzer

8 cups Unflavored Seltzer Water or Still Water
Lemon
Lime
Orange
½ Grapefruit
8-10 Basil Leaves

Cut the lemon, lime, orange, and grapefruit half into slices. In a pitcher, add water with ice. Add in citrus slices and basil leaves and let sit for about an hour to infuse. Pour water into a glass with ice and garnish with your favorite citrus slice.

## Clamato Cocktail

1 oz. Lime Juice
6 oz. Clamato Juice

Stir ingredients together in a highball glass filled with ice.

## Clover Club

2 oz. NA Gin
1 oz. Lemon Juice
½ oz. Raspberry Syrup
Egg White or ½ oz. Aquafaba
4-5 fresh raspberries

Add all ingredients (besides raspberries) into a shaker and dry shake first. Then add in ice and shake again. Strain into a chilled coupe glass. Skewer the raspberries on a toothpick and garnish with them.

## Coco Lopez Shake

2½ oz. Coco Lopez Cream of Coconut
1 scoop Vanilla Ice Cream
1 cup Ice

Mix all ingredients in a blender until smooth. Pour into margarita glass.

## Coconut Margarita

2 oz. Ritual Tequila Alternative
¾ oz. Coconut Milk
¾ oz. Lime Juice
½ oz. Agave Syrup
Lime Wedge
Sugar or Salt (Optional)

Add all ingredients (except lime wedge, and sugar or salt) into a cocktail shaker with ice and shake. Rim a rocks glass with sugar or salt (optional). Pour drink into glass. Garnish with the lime wedge and serve.

## Coconut Bay Breeze

1 oz. NA Dark Rum
½ oz. Coconut Syrup
3 oz. Pineapple Juice
1 oz. Cranberry Juice
Pineapple Wedge

Add all ingredients (except pineapple wedge) into a shaker with ice and shake. Pour into a highball glass with ice. Garnish with the pineapple wedge and serve.

## Coconut Dirty Soda

8 oz. Soda (Lemon-Lime or Cola)
1 tbsp. Coconut Syrup
1 tbsp. Lime Juice
2 oz. Coconut Milk
Lime Wedge

Add all ingredients (besides lime wedge) into a glass and stir. Garnish with the lime wedge and serve.

## Coconut Limeade

2 Limes
4 cups Water
1½ oz. Simple Syrup
5 oz. Coconut Condensed Milk
½ cup of Pebble Ice

Cut your limes in quarters and place them into a food processor with water, simple syrup, and coconut condensed milk. Blend for around 30 seconds and fine strain (or strain twice) into a glass with pebble ice. Garnish with lime wedge and serve.

## Coconut Nog Margarita

2 oz. Sobrii 0-Tequila
2½ oz. Coconut Milk
2½ oz. Almond Milk
½ oz. Agave Syrup
1 tsp. Nutmeg
1 tsp. Coconut Flakes

In a shaker, add all ingredients (other than coconut flakes) with ice and shake well. Rim a rocks glass with the coconut flakes. Strain drink into the rocks glass over ice.

## Coconut Mango Sunrise

4 oz. Vita Coco Original Coconut Water
2 oz. Mango Nectar
3 dashes Angostura Bitters
½ oz. Grenadine
Maraschino Cherry

Add coconut water, mango nectar, bitters, and ice to shaker. Shake vigorously until outside of shaker is cold. Fill a highball or Collins glass with ice and pour in the mango mixture. Hover an upturned teaspoon over the drink near the rim of the glass and slowly drizzle the grenadine over the back of the spoon so it travels down the side of the glass. Do not stir. Serve garnished with the maraschino cherry.

## Coconut Mojito

10 Mint Leaves
4 Thin Lime Slices
1 tbsp. White Granulated Sugar
2 oz. Vita Coco Original Coconut Water
Club Soda

In a tumbler or Collins glass, combine the mint, lime, and sugar. Muddle until the mint is fragrant and the lime releases some of its juice. Fill the glass with ice and add coconut water. Stir vigorously to dissolve the sugar and chill the coconut water. Top with club soda.

## Coconut Watermelon Cooler

3 cups Fresh Seedless Watermelon Cubes
¾ cup Vita Coco Original Coconut Water
2 tbsp. Lime Juice
3–4 Lime Slices

Cut the watermelon into 1-inch cubes. In a blender, combine the watermelon, coconut water, and lime juice. Purée until smooth. Place a mesh strainer over a pitcher and strain the mixture to remove any remaining pulp (optional). Fill 2 Collins glasses with ice and divide the mixture among them. Garnish with the lime slices.

*Makes 2 servings*

## Cold-Brew Negroni

1½ oz. Lyre's Dry London Spirit
1½ oz. Coffee Infused Lyre's Apéritif Rosso*
1½ oz. Lyre's Italian Orange
Orange Peel

Add all ingredients (besides orange peel) into a mixing glass with ice and stir. Strain into a chilled rocks glass and garnish with the orange peel.

**\*Coffee-Infused Lyre's Apéritif Rosso*
1½ oz. Lyre's Apéritif Rosso
1 tbsp. of Coffee Grounds
Add the coffee grounds to the Lyre's Apéritif Rosso in a sealed jar or container. Let sit at room temperature or in the refrigerator for 24 hours to infuse. Strain through a fine mesh strainer or coffee filter to remove all grounds.

## Cold-Brew Old Fashioned

1½ oz. Cut Above Whiskey
¾ oz. Cold Brew Coffee Concentrate
¼ Simple Syrup
Orange Twist

Add all ingredients (except orange twist) into a mixing glass with ice. Stir and strain into a rocks glass. Garnish with the orange twist.

## Cool Coffee Club

1 oz. NA Coffee Liqueur
2 scoops Coffee Ice Cream
3 oz. Whole Milk
1 tsp. Coffee Grounds

Add all ingredients (except coffee grounds) into a blender and blend. Pour into a glass and dust with coffee grounds.

CHAPTER 10  Non-Alcoholic Drink Recipes from A to Z

## CosNOpolitan

2 oz. Seedlip Grove 42 NA Spirit
1 oz. Cranberry Juice
½ oz. Lime Juice
½ oz. Simple Syrup
Orange Peel

Combine all ingredients (besides orange peel) into a shaker with ice. Shake, and then strain into a chilled coupe glass. Garnish with the orange peel.

## Cracked Coffee

1 cup Milk (of your choice)
2 oz. Espresso
¼ oz. Simple Syrup (or your favorite sweetener)
¼ cup of Melted Chocolate (dark or white)

Coat the entire inside of a plastic cup with the melted chocolate. Place in freezer for around 10–15 minutes. Take the cup out and add in your espresso, sweetener, and choice of milk. Stir with a straw and place the lid on. Squeeze your cup to crack the chocolate, and give the drink another stir. Serve in a highball glass.

## Cranberry Collins

½ cup Cranberry Juice
½ tbsp. Lime Juice
1 cup Club Soda
1 cup of Ice Cubes
4–5 Lime Slices

Mix club soda, cranberry juice and lime juice in a pitcher. Add 1 cup of ice cubes and 4–5 lime slices and stir. Pour into a glass with ice and top with a lime slice.

## Cranberry Smash

½ cup Cranberries
1 oz. Lime Juice
1 tbsp. Honey
Soda Water
Mint Sprig
¾ cup of Fresh Cranberries

Add honey and lime juice into a shaker with ½ a cup of cranberries and muddle. Add in ice and shake. Strain into a rocks glass filled with ice or crushed ice. Top with soda water and garnish with the remaining fresh cranberries and a mint sprig.

## Cranberry Spritz

2 oz. Cranberry Juice
4 oz. Soda Water or NA Sparkling Wine
4–5 Cranberries

Add cranberry juice and soda water (or sparkling wine) into a white wine glass with ice and stir. Garnish with cranberries and serve.

## Crisp Stinger

2 oz. Ceder's Crisp NA Spirit
2/3 oz. Lemon Juice
2/3 oz. Agave
12–14 Mint Leaves

Add all ingredients (except for a single mint leaf) into a shaker with ice and shake. Fine strain into a chilled coupe glass. Garnish with a mint leaf.

## Crisp Valley Spritz

2 oz. Ceder's Crisp NA Spirit
1.5 oz. Cloudy Apple Juice
1.5 oz. Cucumber Juice
¼ oz. Lavender Syrup
Tonic Water
4 Apple Half-Moons
Sprig of Lavender

Pour ingredients (except tonic water, apple half-moons, and lavender) into Collins glass with ice and stir to combine. Add ice cubes and tonic water and stir gently. Garnish with the apple half-moons and sprig of lavender.

## Cucumber Apple Smoothie

1 Cucumber
1 Green Apple
¼ cup Mint Leaves
1 tbsp. Honey
Cucumber Slice

Peel the cucumber and cut into slices. Slice the green apple into wedges. Add all ingredients (other than cucumber slice) into a blender and blend until smooth. Pour mixture into a glass and garnish with the cucumber slice.

## Cucumber Cooler

5 Cucumber slices
1 oz. Lime Juice
½ oz. Simple Syrup or Agave
2–3 oz. Soda Water
Lime Wedge or Cucumber Slice

Muddle slices of cucumber in a Collins glass with agave or simple syrup. Add in remaining lime juice and soda water; stir. Add in ice and garnish with lime wedge or cucumber slice, then serve.

## Daiquiri

2 oz. Lyre's Dry White Cane Spirit
1 oz. Simple Syrup
1 oz. Lime Juice
Lime Wedge

Add all ingredients (except lime wedge) into a shaker with ice and shake. Strain into a chilled coupe glass. Garnish with the lime wedge and serve.

## Dark 'N' Stormy

2 oz. Philters Ruhm
6 oz. Ginger Beer
Lime Wedge

Fill a Collins glass with ice, then pour in the ginger beer and float the rum on top. Garnish with lime wedge.

## Desert Rose

2 oz. Philters Mezkahl
1 oz. Rose Water Syrup
¾ oz. Lemon Juice
2 Dried Rose Petals

Add all ingredients (except rose petals) into a shaker with ice and shake. Strain into a coupe glass and garnish with the dried rose petals.

## Dirty Soda

8 oz. Soda (Cola or Lemon-Lime)
2 tbsp. Coconut Syrup
2 oz. Half-and-Half
Lime Wedge

Add all ingredients (other than lime wedge) into a glass with ice and stir. Garnish with the lime wedge.

## Dragon Fruit Margarita

2 oz. Sobrii 0-Tequila
4 oz. Dragon Fruit Juice
¾ oz. Lime Juice
Bay Leaf

Add all ingredients (besides bay leaf) into a shaker with ice and shake. Strain into a rocks glass with ice and garnish with the bay leaf.

## Dust Cutter

¾ oz. Lime Juice
6 oz. Tonic Water
Lime Wedge

Combine all ingredients in a Collins glass with ice and stir. Garnish with a lime wedge.

## Eggnog

½ cup NA Bourbon
¼ cup Sugar (for egg yolks)
2 tbsp. sugar (for egg whites)
1½ cups Whole Milk
½ cup Heavy Cream
2 Eggs
1 tbsp. Grated Nutmeg

Separate the egg yolks and whites into two bowls. Mix egg yolks with ¼ cup of sugar until fluffy. Mix the egg whites with 2 tablespoons of sugar in other bowl. In the bowl that contains the egg yolks, stir in the milk, heavy cream, and bourbon. Then, fold in the beaten egg whites. Do one more stir and pour into rocks glasses; garnish with grated nutmeg.

*Makes 4-6 servings*

## Espresso Martini

2 oz. Seedlip Spice 94 NA Spirit
2 oz. Cold Brew Coffee Concentrate
¼ oz. Simple Syrup
3 Coffee Beans

Add all ingredients (except coffee beans) into a shaker with ice and shake. Strain into a chilled coupe glass. Garnish with the coffee beans and serve.

## Euphoric Spritz

1½ oz. Three Spirit Livener
2½ oz. Sparkling Lemonade
2½ oz. Kombucha (Original, or Lemon or Ginger Flavored)
½ cup Cubed Ice
1 Cucumber Ribbon*
Mint Leaf

Place your cucumber ribbon around the inside of your wine glass and hold in place with cubed ice. Add Three Spirit Livener and top with sparkling lemonade and kombucha. Garnish with the mint leaf.

***Cucumber Ribbon:*** *Using a potato peeler or mandoline, slice thin, even strips lengthwise along the cucumber. Continue peeling until you reach the seeds. Then rotate and repeat on the other sides.*

## Falling For You

1½ oz. NA Bourbon
½ oz. Apple Syrup
3 oz. Chai (Hot)

Add all ingredients into a coffee or tea mug and stir.

## Fancy Sorbet

2 scoops Sorbet
4 oz. NA Sparkling Wine

Add your favorite sorbet into a glass and top with sparkling wine.

## Fool's Gold

2 oz. Cut Above Whiskey
¾ oz. Lemon Juice
¾ oz. Honey Simple Syrup
Lemon Wheel
Sage Leaf

Fill cocktail shaker with ice, then add simple syrup, lemon juice, and whiskey. Shake well and then strain into a coupe glass. Garnish with lemon wheel and sage.

## Freddy Bartholomew

6 oz. Ginger Ale
¾ oz. Sweetened Lime Juice
Lime Wedge

Add ginger ale and lime juice into a highball glass with ice and stir. Garnish with lime wedge.

## French 05

1¼ oz. Seedlip Grove 42 NA Spirit
½ oz. Lemon Juice
½ oz. Simple Syrup
3½ oz. Kombucha
Lemon Peel

Add all ingredients (except kombucha and lemon peel) into a shaker with ice and shake. Strain into a chilled champagne flute and top with kombucha. Garnish with the lemon peel.

## French 75

1½ oz. NA Gin
½ oz. Lemon Juice
½ oz. Simple Syrup
3 oz. NA Sparkling Wine
Lemon Twist

Add all ingredients (except sparkling wine and lemon twist) into a champagne flute. Top with sparkling wine and garnish with the lemon twist; serve.

## Frosé

1 bottle or 3 cups of NA Rosé
½ cup Sugar
2½ oz. Lemon Juice
8 oz. Strawberries
1 cup of ice

Cut strawberries into chunks. Add all ingredients into a large blender. Blend and pour into a chilled martini glass.

*Makes 6 servings*

## Frozen Daiquiri

2 oz. NA Rum
¾ oz. Simple Syrup
1½ oz. Lime Juice
1 cup of ice
Lime Wheel

Add all ingredients (except lime wheel) into a blender and blend. Garnish with the lime wheel.

## Frozen Margarita

2 oz. NA Tequila
¾ oz. Orange Juice
1 oz. Lime Juice
1 cup of Ice
2 tbsp. Salt
Lime Wheel

Add tequila, orange juice, lime juice, and ice into a blender and blend. Rim a rocks glass with salt. Pour drink into the rocks glass and garnish with lime wheel.

## Frozen Negroni

1½ oz. Lyre's Dry London Spirit
1½ oz. Lyre's Apéritif Rosso
1½ oz. Lyre's Italian Orange
1 cup of ice
Orange Peel

Add all ingredients (except orange peel) into a blender and blend. Pour into a rocks glass and garnish with the orange peel.

## Fruit Bowl

1 oz. Orange Juice
1 oz. Pineapple Juice
1 oz. Grape Juice
1 oz. Grapefruit Juice

Add all ingredients into a shaker with ice and shake. Pour into a Collins glass and serve.

## Garden Jynn

2 oz. Philters Jynn
½ oz. Vanilla Syrup
½ oz. Lemon Juice
3 oz. Carrot Juice
2 Thyme Sprigs
Lemon Wheel

Scrape thyme leaves off one sprig into a shaker. Add other ingredients (besides second thyme sprig and lemon wheel) into the shaker. Shake hard and double strain into a Collins glass. Garnish with the lemon wheel and second thyme sprig.

## The Garnet

4 Mint Sprigs
4 oz. Pomegranate Juice
2 cubes Frozen Orange Juice*
6 oz. Perrier

Crush one sprig of mint in each of two rocks glasses. Add pomegranate juice and orange juice ice cube. Top with Perrier and garnish with an additional mint sprig.

*Makes 2 servings*
***Frozen Orange Juice***
1 cup of Orange Juice
Pour orange juice into an ice cube tray and place in freezer overnight. After frozen, remove cubes from tray.

## Gin & Tonic

2 oz. NA Gin
4 oz. Tonic
Lime Wedge

Add gin and tonic into a Collins glass with ice and stir. Garnish with lime wedge and serve.

## Gold Minded

2 oz. NA Gin
¾ oz. Lemon Juice
¾ oz. Honey Simple Syrup
Lemon Wheel

Add all ingredients (except lemon wheel) into a cocktail shaker with ice and shake. Strain into a coupe glass. Garnish with the lemon wheel and serve.

## Grape Dirty Soda

8 oz. Soda (Lemon-Lime or Cola)
2 tbsp. Grape Syrup
1 oz. Half-and-Half
5–6 Grapes

Add all ingredients (except grapes) into a glass with ice and stir. Garnish with the grapes and serve.

## Grapefruit Cooler

8 oz. Grapefruit Juice
3 dashes NA Aromatic Bitters

Pour grapefruit juice into a Collins glass filled with ice. Add bitters and stir.

## Green Tea Highball

2 oz. NA Bourbon or Rum
½ oz. Honey Simple
3 oz. Green Tea
Lemon Wheel

Add all ingredients (except lemon wheel) into a highball glass with ice and stir. Garnish with the lemon wheel and serve.

## Grilled Lemonade

3 cups Cold Water
8–10 Lemons
1 cup Sugar
Pinch of salt
4 Grilled Lemon Slices*

Juice lemons to get about 1 cup fresh lemon juice. In a pitcher, add in all ingredients (except lemon slices) and stir. Pour lemonade into Collins glasses, and then garnish with grilled lemon slices.

*Makes about 4 servings*
**\*Grilled Lemon Slices**
2 Lemons
½ cup of Sugar
Cut the lemons into slices. Sprinkle sugar on the lemon slices and place the slices on a heated grill. Grill until the down side receives a nice char, and then flip and char the other side.

## Gunner

8 oz. Ginger Ale
8 oz. Ginger Beer
¼ oz. Sweetened Lime Juice
2 dashes Angostura Bitters
Lime Wedge

Add all ingredients (except lime wedge) into a highball glass with ice and stir. Garnish with the lime wedge.

## Hazelnut Italian Soda

1½ oz. Hazelnut Soda
1 oz. Half-and-Half
4 oz. Sparkling Water

Add all ingredients into a highball glass with ice and mix.

## Hibiscus Cooler

1½ oz. NA Reposado Tequila
1 oz. Fresh Lemon Juice
¾ oz. Hibiscus Raspberry Syrup

Add all ingredients into a shaker with ice and shake. Strain into a rocks glass.

*Created by V. Leon, Miami, FL*

## Hibiscus Sour

2½ oz. Hibiscus Tea
¾ oz. Grapefruit Juice
¾ oz. Lime Juice
½ oz. Agave Nectar
7 dashes All The Bitter New Orleans Bitters
1 Egg White

Brew and place the hibiscus tea in the fridge to chill it. Dry shake all ingredients (without ice) for 20 seconds. Add ice and shake until chilled. Fine strain into a coupe glass.

*Shared by Ian James Blessing*

## High Tea

2 oz. Philters Wiski
¼ oz. Honey
½ oz. Simple Syrup
3 oz. Hot Earl Grey Tea
Lemon Wheel

Add all ingredients (except lemon wheel) into a coffee mug with ice. Stir and garnish with the lemon wheel.

## Hole-in-One

2 oz. Grape Juice
¼ oz. Lime Juice
X Ginger Ale
Lime Wedge
3–4 Frozen Grapes

Add all ingredients (except lime wedge and frozen grapes) into a highball glass with ice and stir. Garnish with the lime wedge and grapes.

## Honey & Fig G&T

2 oz. Cut Above Gin
½ oz. Honey Fig Syrup*
1 cup of Cubed Ice
3 oz. Tonic Water

Shake the ingredients together (except tonic water) in a shaker with ice. Strain and pour over fresh cubed ice and top with tonic water.

***Honey Fig Syrup*
½ cup dried figs (about 4–6, chopped)
1 cup water
½ cup honey
Optional: 1 small strip lemon zest for added complexity
Chop the figs into small pieces to help release flavor. In a saucepan, combine the water and chopped figs. Bring to a simmer over medium heat. Simmer for 10–15 minutes or until the figs are softened and the water is infused. Remove from heat and stir in the honey until fully dissolved. Let steep for an additional 10–15 minutes off heat and strain through a fine mesh strainer or cheesecloth, pressing to extract all the syrup. Let cool and then bottle and refrigerate for up to 2 weeks.

## Honey Limeade

3 oz. Lemonade
1 oz. Lime Juice
½ oz. Honey or Honey Syrup
Lime Wheel

Add all ingredients (except lime wheel) into a highball glass with ice and stir. Garnish with the lime wheel and serve.

## Hot Apple & Ginger

4 oz. Hot Apple Cider
1 oz. Ginger Syrup
Apple Slice
Cinnamon Stick

Add apple cider and ginger syrup into your favorite mug with ice and stir. Garnish with apple slice and cinnamon stick.

## Hot Toddy

1½ oz. NA Whiskey or NA Rum
3 oz. Hot Water
¼ oz. Lemon Juice
1 tsp. Honey or Sugar
Cinnamon Stick

Pour all ingredients (besides cinnamon stick) into mug and stir. Garnish with the cinnamon stick.

## Hugo Spritz

½ oz. Elderflower Syrup
4 oz. NA Sparkling Wine or Champagne
1 oz. Soda Water
2 Mint Sprigs
Lemon Wheel

In wine glass, add in elderflower syrup and a mint sprig; muddle gently (to prevent breaking the glass). Then add in sparkling wine or champagne with soda and stir. Garnish with second mint sprig and the lemon wheel, and serve

## Isaac's Apple

2 oz. Philters Ruhm
3 oz. Apple Cider
½ oz. Spiced Syrup
½ oz. Lemon Juice
Cinnamon Stick

Add all ingredients (except cinnamon stick and ice) into a shaker tin with ice. Shake, and then strain into a rocks glass over ice.

## J & T

2 oz. Philters Jynn
4 oz. Tonic Water
Lime Wedge

Add Jynn and tonic water into a Collins glass with ice and stir. Garnish with lime wedge and serve.

## Jack of Clubs

2 oz. NA Gin
1 oz. Lemon Juice
½ oz. Blackberry Syrup
Egg White or ½ oz. Aquafaba
4–5 Blackberries

Add all ingredients (except ice and blackberries) into a shaker and dry shake. Then add in ice and shake again. Strain into a chilled coupe glass. Skewer blackberries on a toothpick and use as garnish.

*Inspired by J. Muskett, Hoboken, NJ*

## John Collins

2 oz. NA Bourbon
1 oz. Lemon Juice
1⅕ oz. Simple Syrup
Club Soda
Lemon Wheel
Maraschino Cherry

Add bourbon, lemon juice, and simple syrup into a Collins glass with ice. Top with soda water and garnish with lemon wheel and maraschino cherry.

## Josh Cellars Sparkling Italian Spritz

3 oz. Josh Cellars NA Sparkling Wine
2 oz. NA Italian Orange Liqueur
1 oz. Club Soda
Orange Slice
2 Mint Leaves

Fill a large wine glass with ice. Add in Josh Cellars NA Sparkling and NA Italian Orange Liqueur; stir gently. Top with club soda and garnish with orange slice and mint leaves.

## Jumping Jack

1¼ oz. NA Rum
4 oz. Pineapple Juice
½ oz. Lime Juice
1 dash NA Bitters

Add all ingredients into a cocktail shaker with ice. Shake and strain into a Collins glass and serve.

## Kath's Clocking In

1 oz. NA Dark Rum
2 scoops Vanilla or Chocolate Ice Cream
½ oz. Chocolate Syrup

Add all ingredients into a blender and blend. Pour into a margarita glass and serve.

*Inspired by K.B. Fallon*

## Kiwi Cooler

2 oz. NA Tequila
½ Kiwi
½ oz. Lime Juice
½ oz. Agave Nectar
1 oz. Cucumber Juice
1 cup of Cubed Ice
Kiwi Disc

Muddle peeled kiwi in a shaker. Add all other ingredients (except kiwi disc) and fill with cubed ice. Shake and then strain into a Collins glass over cubed ice. Garnish with the kiwi disc.

## Kiwi Seltzer

8 cups Unflavored Seltzer Water or Still Water
2 cups of Peeled Kiwi
Lemon
Kiwi Slice

In a pitcher add in seltzer or still water with ice. Peel and cut the kiwi. Slice the lemon. Add kiwi and lemon to seltzer and let sit for about an hour to infuse. Pour infused seltzer into a glass with ice and garnish with a kiwi slice.

## Kona Coast

1 oz. Lime Juice
¼ oz. Grenadine
5 oz. Apple Juice
2 oz. Ginger Ale

Stir all ingredients, except grenadine, together in a Collins glass with ice. Add grenadine on top and serve.

## Lady Nora

1½ oz. NA Tequila
1 oz. NA Rose Wine
½ oz. Lime Juice
4 oz. Grapefruit Soda
1 tbsp. Salt

Rim a rocks glass with salt. Combine tequila, wine, and lime juice into a cocktail shaker with ice and shake. Strain into the rimmed rocks glass and top with grapefruit soda.

*Inspired by Miss Nora Foley*

## Lavender Lemonade

¾ oz. Lemon Juice
½ oz. Plain or Lavender Simple Syrup
5–7 dashes All The Bitter Lavender Bitters
5 oz. Sparkling Water
Lemon Wedge

Add all ingredients (other than lemon wedge) into a highball glass with ice. Stir and garnish with the lemon wedge.

## Lavender Non-Collins

2 oz. Philters Jynn
1 oz. Lemon Juice
1 oz. Lavender Syrup
Soda Water
Lemon Wheel
Lavender Sprig

Add Jynn, lemon juice, lavender syrup, and ice into a shaker with ice. Shake and strain into a Collins glass. Top with soda water. Garnish with lemon wheel and lavender sprig.

## Lemon-Lime Seltzer

8 cups Unflavored Seltzer Water or Still Water
1 cup of ice
Lemon
2 Limes

Slice the lemon and limes. In a pitcher, add seltzer and ice. Add in lemon and lime slices (saving one of each) and let sit for about an hour to infuse. Pour seltzer into a glass with ice and garnish with the saved lemon and lime slices.

## Lemonade

3 cups Cold Water
8–10 Lemons
½ cup Sugar
Pinch of Salt
Lemon Slice

Juice lemons until you have 1 cup of fresh juice. In a pitcher, add in all ingredients (except lemon slice) with ice and stir. Pour into a Collins glass with ice and garnish with the slice of lemon.

## Lime Dirty Soda

8 oz. Lemon-Lime Soda
2 tbsp. Lime Syrup
2 oz. Half-and-Half
Lime Wedge

Add all ingredients (except lime wedge) into a glass with ice and stir. Garnish with the lime wedge and serve.

## Livener XS Picante

2 oz. Livener XS NA Spirit
1 oz. Lime Juice
½ oz. Agave Syrup
1 cup of Cubed Ice
4 Basil Leaves
Slice of Jalapeño

Add all liquid ingredients into a cocktail shaker. Slap 3 of the basil leaves between your hands to release the aroma; add them to the shaker, along with cubed ice. Shake. Pour through a strainer into a rocks glass with cubed ice. Garnish with the remaining basil leaf and slice of jalapeño.

## Mai Tai

1½ oz. NA White Rum
¾ oz. NA Dark Rum
½ oz. Orange Juice or NA Triple Sec
½ oz. Fresh Lime Juice
½ oz. Orgeat Syrup
1 cup of crushed ice
¼ oz. Simple Syrup (Optional)
Mint Leaf
Maraschino Cherry
2 Pineapple Fronds

Combine rums, orange juice (or triple sec), lime juice, orgeat syrup, and simple syrup (optional) into a shaker with ice and shake. Strain into a Collins glass with crushed ice and garnish with mint leaf, cherry, and pineapple fronds.

## Mango Daiquiri (Frozen)

¾ oz. Lemon-Lime Soda
¼ cup Sugar
1 tbsp. Lime Juice
2 Mangos
1 cup of Ice

Peel and cut mangos, reserving a slice for garnish. Add all other ingredients into a blender and blend. Strain into a margarita glass, top with the mango slice, and serve.

## Mango Margarita

1½ oz. Ritual Tequila Alternative
1 oz. Mango Puree
½ oz. Lime Juice
½ oz. Agave Syrup
Lime Wedge
1 tbsp. Sugar or Salt (Optional)

Rim a rocks glass with either salt or sugar (optional). Add all ingredients (except lime wedge) into a cocktail shaker with ice and shake. Pour drink into rocks glass. Garnish with the lime wedge and serve.

## Mango Mule

2 oz. NA Rum
1 oz. Mango Puree
½ oz. Lime Juice
3 oz. Ginger Beer
Lime Wheel

Add rum, mango puree, lime juice, and ice into a cocktail shaker with ice and shake. Strain into a mule mug with ice and top with ginger beer. Garnish with the lime wheel and serve.

## Mango-Pineapple Slushie

½ cup Sliced Mangos
½ cup Pineapple Wedges
½ cup Water
1 cup of Ice

Add all ingredients (except for one pineapple wedge) into a blender and blend until smooth. Pour into a glass and garnish with the remaining pineapple wedge.

## Manhattan

1½ oz. NA Whiskey
1½ oz. NA Sweet Vermouth
3 dashes NA Bitters
Orange Peel
Maraschino Cherry

Add whiskey, vermouth, bitters, and ice into a mixing glass and stir. Pour into a martini glass and garnish with orange peel and maraschino cherry.

## Maple Old Fashioned

2 oz. NA Bourbon
½ oz. Maple Simple Syrup*
2 dashes Bitters
Orange Peel

In a mixing glass, add in maple simple syrup, bourbon, ice and bitters; stir. Strain into a rocks glass with ice and garnish with orange peel.

**\*Maple Simple Syrup*
1 cup Maple Syrup
1 cup Water
In a small saucepan, combine the water and maple syrup. Stir over medium heat until the mixture is fully combined, usually takes 5–10 minutes. Remove from heat and let cool. Store in a clean jar or bottle in the refrigerator for up to 2 weeks.

## Margarita

2 oz. Ritual Tequila Alternative
¾ oz. Lime Juice
½ oz. Agave Syrup
Lime Wedge
1 tbsp. Sugar or Salt (Optional)

Rim a rocks glass with either salt or sugar (optional). Add all ingredients (except lime wedge) into a cocktail shaker with ice and shake. Pour drink into rocks glass and garnish with the lime wedge; serve.

## Martino

½ oz. Seedlip Garden 108 NA Spirit
1½ oz. Æcorn Dry NA Aperitif
1 oz. Green Olive Juice

Add all ingredients into a mixing glass with ice and stir. Strain into a chilled martini glass.

## Matcha Highball

2 oz. NA Bourbon
½ oz. Lemon Juice
½ oz. Honey Syrup
¼ tsp. Matcha Powder
Club Soda
Lemon Wheel

Add all ingredients (except club soda and lemon wheel) into a shaker with ice. Shake and strain into highball glass with ice. Top with club soda and garnish with lemon wheel.

## Matcha Tonic

½ cup Hot Water
2 tsp. Matcha Powder
4 oz. Tonic Water

In a bowl or glass, add hot water and matcha powder and stir to create a matcha mixture. Add into a highball glass with ice and top with tonic water. Stir and serve.

## Maverick's Caddy

2 oz. Lemon-Lime Soda
¼ oz. Lime Juice
1 oz. Grape Syrup
Lime Wedge

Add all ingredients (except lime wedge) into a highball glass with ice and stir. Garnish with the lime wedge and serve.

*Inspired by C. Mackey, Fayetteville, AR*

## Mexican Hot Tea

1½ oz. NA Tequila
4 oz. Hot Water
½ tsp. Sugar
1 pat Butter
Cinnamon Stick
1 tsp. Grated Nutmeg

Pour tequila into a coffee mug and add Hot Water. Stir in sugar and then butter. Garnish with cinnamon stick and nutmeg.

## Mezcal Bramble

1½ oz. Cut Above Mezcal
¾ oz. Lemon Juice
½ oz. Island Oasis Wildberry Mix
Blackberry
Lemon Wedge

Add all ingredients (except blackberry and lemon wedge) into a cocktail shaker with ice and shake. Strain into a rocks glass filled with pebble ice. Garnish with the blackberry and lemon wedge, and serve.

## Mezcal Gilda

1½ oz. Philters Mezkahl
½ oz. Pineapple Juice
½ oz. Lime Juice
½ oz. Cinnamon Syrup
Dehydrated Lime Wheel

Add all ingredients (besides lime wheel) into a shaker with ice. Shake and double strain into a coupe glass. Garnish with the lime wheel and serve.

## Mezcal Mole Martini

2 oz. Cut Above Mezcal
2 oz. Cold Brew Coffee Concentrate
½ oz. Maple Syrup
2 dashes Mole Bitters
3 Coffee Beans

Add all ingredients (except coffee beans) into a shaker with ice. Shake and strain into a martini glass. Garnish with the coffee beans.

## Mezcal Mule

2 oz. NA Mezcal
½ oz. Lime Juice
4 oz. Ginger Beer
Lime Wheel

Add mezcal and lime juice into the mule mug with ice. Top with ginger beer and garnish with lime wheel.

## Mezcal Passion Mule

2 oz. NA Mezcal
1 oz. Passion Fruit Puree
½ oz. Lime Juice
4 oz. Ginger Beer
Lime Wheel

Add all ingredients (except ginger beer and lime wheel) into a shaker with ice and shake. Strain into a mule mug with ice. Top with ginger beer and garnish with lime wheel.

## Mezkahl Chiller

2 oz. Philters Mezkahl
¾ oz. Lime Juice
1 oz. Mint Iced Tea
¾ oz. Simple Syrup
1 slice Cucumber
Lime Wedge
Mint Sprig

Add cucumber slice and simple syrup into a cocktail shaker and muddle. Add remaining ingredients (besides lime wedge and mint sprig) with ice and shake. Strain into a Collins glass with ice and garnish with the lime wedge and mint sprig.

## Miami Vice

5 oz. of NA Strawberry Daiquiri
5 oz. of NA Pina Colada
Pineapple Wedge

Pour the strawberry daiquiri into the bottom of a margarita glass and top with pina colada. Garnish with pineapple wedge and serve.

*See recipes for Strawberry Daiquiri and Piña Colada in this chapter*

## Michelada

6 oz. NA Beer
1 oz. Lime Juice
2 dashes Hot Sauce
1 dash Worcestershire Sauce
1 pinch Salt
1 tsp. Tajín
Lime Wedge

Rim your pint glass with Tajín. Then, add all ingredients (except lime wedge) to pint glass and stir. Garnish with the lime wedge and serve.

## Mimosa

3 oz. NA Champagne
2 oz. Orange Juice

Combine champagne and orange juice in a champagne flute and stir.

## Mionetto Spritz

2 oz. Mionetto Aperitivo Alcohol Free
3 oz. Mionetto Alcohol-Removed Sparkling Wine
Soda Water
Orange Slice or Orange Twist

Add ice to a wine glass. Combine aperitivo and sparkling wine in the wine glass with ice. Top with soda water and garnish with an orange slice or orange twist.

## Mint Berry Smash

¼ cup Raspberries
¼ cup Blueberries
1 oz. Lime Juice
1 tbsp. Honey
3–4 Mint Leaves
Soda Water
2 Fresh Berries of your choice (Raspberries or Blueberries)

Add honey and lime juice into a shaker with mint, raspberries, and blueberries; muddle. Add in ice and shake. Strain into a rocks glass filled with ice or crushed ice. Top with soda water and garnish with fresh berries and a mint leaf.

## Mojito

2 oz. NA Rum
4 oz. Club Soda
½ oz. Simple Syrup
1 oz. Lime Juice
4–5 Mint Leaves

Muddle mint leaves with simple syrup in a cocktail shaker. Add in ice and shake. Strain into highball glass with ice and add in club soda.

## The Moonraker

½ oz. NA Bourbon
1/¼ oz. Hazelnut Coffee Creamer
3 oz. Iced Coffee
Whipped Cream (Optional)

Add all ingredients (except whipped cream) into a shaker. Strain into a rocks glass with crushed ice. Top with whipped cream (optional).

## Mule

2 oz. NA Spirit (of your choice)
½ oz. Lime Juice
4 oz. Ginger Beer
Lime Wheel

Add spirit and lime juice into a mule mug with ice. Top with ginger beer and garnish with the lime wheel.

## New Orleans Day

2 oz. Coco Lopez Cream of Coconut
1 oz. Butterscotch Topping
1 oz. Half-and-Half
1 cup Ice

Put all ingredients in a blender and blend until smooth. Pour into a margarita glass.

## NONA Ginger & Pink Grapefruit

1.25 oz. NONA Ginger NA Spirit
2 oz. Pink Grapefruit Juice
½ oz. Honey Syrup
Egg White
Sprig of Thyme

Fill a shaker with all ingredients (except ice and thyme sprig) and dry shake. Add ice and shake again. Strain into a chilled coupe glass and garnish with the sprig of thyme.

## NONA June Collins

1.5 oz. NONA June NA Spirit
1 oz. Lemon Juice
⅔ oz. Simple Syrup
Soda Water
½ tsp. Lemon Zest
1 Thyme Sprig

Fill a highball glass with ice and add in all ingredients (except lemon zest and thyme). Top with soda water and stir. Garnish with lemon zest and thyme, and serve.

## Nora's Tiger Lilly

2 oz. Orange Juice
1 oz. Mango Puree
2 oz. NA Sparkling Wine

Add all ingredients except sparkling wine into a cocktail shaker with ice. Shake and then strain into a chilled coupe glass. Top with sparkling wine and serve.

*Inspired by Nora Foley*

## Notorious F.I.G.

2 oz. Cut Above Whiskey
½ oz. Fig Syrup
½ oz. NA Aperitivo
½ oz. Lemon Juice
2 dashes NA Lemon Bitters
Lemon Slice
Sprig of Thyme

In a shaker, add ice, Cut Above whiskey, aperitivo, fig syrup, lemon juice, and bitters. Shake vigorously for about a minute. Double strain into a cocktail glass and garnish with slice of lemon and sprig of thyme.

CHAPTER 10  **Non-Alcoholic Drink Recipes from A to Z**    111

## Oaxacan Old Fashioned

2 oz. Philters Mezkahl
½ oz. Agave Syrup
2 dashes Angostura Bitters
2 dashes Aztec Chocolate Bitters
Large Ice Cube
Orange Twist

Add all ingredients (besides orange twist) into a mixing glass with ice and stir. Strain into a rocks glass over a large ice cube and garnish with the orange twist.

## Old Cuban

1½ oz. NA Rum
¾ oz. Fresh Lime Juice
1 oz. Simple Syrup
2 dashes NA Aromatic Bitters
2 oz. NA Sparkling Wine
4 Mint Leaves

In a cocktail shaker, muddle mint with simple syrup and fresh lime juice. Add in rum and bitters with ice, and then shake. Double strain into a cocktail glass and top with sparkling wine.

## Orange Margarita

1½ oz. NA Tequila
½ oz. NA Triple Sec
3 oz. Orange Juice
½ oz. Sweet & Sour Mix
Orange Wedge

Combine all ingredients (except strawberries) in a blender with ice and blend until smooth. Pour into margarita glass and garnish with an orange wedge.

## Orange Smoothie

2½ oz. Coco Lopez Cream of Coconut
3 oz. Orange Juice
1 scoop Vanilla Ice Cream
1 cup Ice
1 tsp. Grated Nutmeg

Blend all ingredients (except nutmeg) in a blender with ice until smooth. Pour into a margarita glass and sprinkle with nutmeg.

## Orchard Sour

1½ oz. Seedlip Garden 108 NA Spirit
1 tbsp. Pear Jam
½ oz. Lemon Juice
¾ oz. Egg White
1 tsp. Lemon Zest

Add all ingredients (except ice and lemon zest) into a shaker and dry shake. Add ice and shake again. Strain into a chilled coupe glass and garnish with the lemon zest.

## P.G.'s Tea

1½ oz. NA Rum
¼ oz. NA Orange Liqueur
¼ oz. Lemon Juice
4 oz. Iced Tea

Add all ingredients (except iced tea) to shaker and shake. Pour into a highball glass with ice and top with iced tea.

*Inspired by P. Getzow*

## Pa-Faux-Ma

2 oz. Philters Mezkahl
¾ oz. Grapefruit
¾ oz. Lime Juice
1 oz. Agave Syrup
2 slices Jalapeno
Lime Wheel

Add lime juice and jalapeno slices into a shaker and muddle. Add in remaining ingredients (except lime wheel) and shake with ice. Strain into a Collins glass and garnish with the lime wheel.

## Paloma

1½ oz. NA Blanco Tequila
½ oz. Lime Juice
4 oz. Grapefruit Juice
1 pinch Salt
Lime Wheel

Add all ingredients (except lime wheel) into a highball glass with ice and stir. Garnish with lime wheel and serve.

## Painkiller

2 oz. NA Rum
4 oz. Pineapple Juice
1 oz. Orange Juice
1 oz. Coco Lopez Cream of Coconut
½ cup of Crushed Ice
1 tsp. Grated Nutmeg
Pineapple Wedge

Blend all ingredients (except nutmeg and pineapple wedge) until smooth and pour into a chilled highball glass with crushed ice. Garnish with nutmeg and pineapple wedge.

## Peach Daiquiri

2 oz. NA Rum
1 oz. Peach Puree
1 oz. Simple Syrup
1 oz. Lime Juice
Lime Wedge

Add all ingredients (except lime wedge) into a shaker with ice and shake. Strain into a chilled coupe glass. Garnish with the lime wedge and serve.

CHAPTER 10  Non-Alcoholic Drink Recipes from A to Z

## Peach Dirty Soda

8 oz. Soda (Lemon-Lime or Cola)
2 tbsp. Peach Syrup
2 oz. Half-and-Half
Lime Wedge

Add all ingredients (besides lime wedge) into a glass with ice and stir. Garnish with the lime wedge and serve.

## Peach Fizz

2 oz. Peach-Infused NA Bourbon*
½ oz. Orange Juice
4 oz. NA Sparkling Wine
Mint Sprig

Combine bourbon, orange juice, and sparkling wine in a champagne flute and garnish with mint sprig.

*\*Peach Infused NA Bourbon*
*8 oz. NA Bourbon*
*5–6 Peaches*
*Add peach slices to a clean jar or container. Pour in the non-alcoholic bourbon. Seal and refrigerate for 24–48 hours, shaking gently once or twice per day. Strain out the peaches and store in the fridge for about a week.*

## Peaches & Cream

3 oz. Coco Lopez Cream of Coconut
2½ oz. Pineapple Juice
1 oz. NA Rum
1 cup of Crushed Ice

Combine all ingredients in a blender and blend until smooth. Pour into a margarita glass and serve.

## Pear Vanilla

2 oz. Vanilla-Infused NA Bourbon*
½ oz. Simple Syrup
½ oz. Fresh Lemon Juice
Pear Slice

Combine all ingredients (except pear slice) in a Collins glass with and stir. Garnish with the pear slice.

*\*Vanilla-Infused NA Bourbon*
*2 Vanilla Bean Pods*
*2 oz. NA Bourbon*
*Add vanilla bean pods and bourbon in a jar and let sit for 24 hours to infuse in the refrigerator. Strain out the vanilla and store bourbon for about a week.*

## PEEPStini

4 oz. Wild Berry Tea
2 oz. Coconut Milk
PEEPS Candy

Brew wild berry tea and set aside to chill. Pour cooled tea into a mug with ice, add in coconut milk, and stir. Garnish with a PEEP candy and serve.

## Perfect Storm (Rum Mule)

2 oz. NA Rum
½ oz. Fresh Lime Juice
2 dashes NA Bitters
3 oz. Ginger Beer
Lime Wedge

Add all ingredients into a rocks or mule glass with ice and stir. Garnish with a lime wedge.

## Perrier Mimosa

⅓ cup Orange Juice
1½ cups Perrier
4 Raspberries or Grapes

Chill the orange juice and Perrier in the fridge. Divide the orange juice between two champagne flutes and top each with Perrier. Garnish with two raspberries or grapes in each glass.

*Makes 2 servings*

## Piña Colada

1½ oz. NA Rum
1 oz. Coco Lopez Cream of Coconut
2 oz. Pineapple Juice
1 cup Ice

Blend all ingredients with ice in a blender until smooth. Pour into margarita glass and serve.

## Piña Colada Shake

½ cup Unsweetened Pineapple Juice
⅓ cup Coco Lopez Cream of Coconut
1½ cups Vanilla Ice Cream

Blend all ingredients in a blender until smooth. Pour into margarita glass. Serve immediately.

## Pineapple Coconut Dirty Soda

8 oz. Soda (Lemon-Lime or Cola)
2 tbsp. Pineapple Syrup
1 tbsp. Coconut Syrup
2 oz. Coconut Milk
Lime Wedge

Add all ingredients (except lime wedge) into a glass with ice and stir. Garnish with the lime wedge and serve.

## Pineapple Daiquiri

2 oz. Lyre's Dry White Cane Spirit
1 oz. Pineapple Puree
1 oz. Simple Syrup
1 oz. Lime Juice
Lime Wedge

Add all ingredients (except lime wedge) into a shaker with ice and shake. Strain into a chilled coupe glass. Garnish with the lime wedge and serve.

## Pineapple Princess

2 oz. NA Tequila
1 oz. Pineapple Juice
½ oz. Lime Juice
Soda Water
Pineapple Wedge

Add all ingredients (except club soda and pineapple wedge) into a highball glass with ice and stir. Top with soda water, garnish with the pineapple wedge, and serve.

*Inspired by C. Fallon Foley*

## Pineapple Seltzer

8 cups Unflavored Seltzer Water or Still Water
2 cups Fresh Pineapple Slices
8 Basil Leaves

In a pitcher, add water and ice. Add in pineapple slices (except for one) and basil leaves, and let sit for about an hour to infuse. Pour seltzer into a glass with ice and garnish with remaining pineapple slice.

## Pink Lemonade

½ cup Simple Syrup
4 cups Water
1 cup Cranberry Juice
1 cup Lemon Juice
3–4 Lemon Wheels

Add all ingredients (except lemon wheels) into a pitcher with ice and stir. Pour into a Collins glass with ice and garnish with the lemon wheels.

*Makes about 4 servings*

## Pink Rose Garden

Slice of Lemon Peel
2 sprigs Thyme
1 oz. Honey Syrup
2 oz. Ceder's Pink Rose NA Spirit
1 oz. Pink Grapefruit Juice
2 oz. Soda Water
1 tsp. of Lemon Zest
Dehydrated Orange Wheel

In a rocks glass gently muddle together lemon peel, 1 sprig of thyme, and honey syrup. Add the Ceder's Pink Rose and pink grapefruit juice; stir. Add ice and top with soda water. Garnish with remaining sprig of thyme, lemon zest, and dehydrated orange wheel.

## Playful Punch

1½ oz. Philters Ruhm
2 oz. Pineapple Juice
½ oz. Lime Juice
¼ oz. Grenadine
Soda Water
Maraschino Cherry
Pineapple Leaf

Add Ruhm, pineapple and lime juice, and grenadine to a shaker with ice. Shake and strain into a Collins glass over fresh ice. Top with soda water and garnish with maraschino cherry and pineapple leaf.

## Pop-in-Prosecco

4 oz. NA Prosecco
1 Frozen Popsicle

Pick a frozen popsicle flavor (you choose the flavor) and place directly into a white wine glass. Make sure the stick is face up. Add NA prosecco and serve.

## Prickly Pear

2 oz. NA Tequila
1 oz. Lime Juice
¾ oz. Prickly Pear Syrup
1 tbsp. Tajín
Cucumber Slice

Rim a rocks glass with Tajín and set aside. Add all other ingredients (besides cucumber slice) into a cocktail shaker with ice and shake. Strain into Tajín-rimmed glass and garnish with the cucumber slice.

## Pumpkin Old Fashioned

2 oz. NA Bourbon
1 tbsp. Pumpkin Puree
½ tbsp. Maple Syrup
¼ tsp. Pumpkin Pie Spice
¼ tsp. Vanilla
Orange Peel

Place all ingredients (except for orange peel) in a mixing glass with ice and stir. Strain into a rocks glass with ice. Garnish with the orange peel.

*Great drink for the fall!*

## Pumpkin Patch

2 oz. Philters Ruhm
½ oz. Pumpkin Spice Syrup
½ oz. Cream of Coconut
¼ oz. Lime Juice
1 oz. Orange Juice
1 oz. Pineapple Juice
Lime Wheel
Orange Wheel

Add all ingredients (besides lime and orange wheels) to a shaker with ice. Shake and strain into a large white wine glass over ice and garnish.

## Raspberry Champagne

¼ oz. Simple Syrup
½ oz. Grenadine
4 oz. NA Champagne
2 Raspberries

Add simple syrup and grenadine into flute. Add in champagne and drop in raspberries.

## Raspberry Daiquiri

2 oz. NA Rum
1 oz. Raspberry Puree
1 oz. Simple Syrup
1 oz. Lime Juice
Lime Wedge

Add all ingredients (except lime wedge) into a shaker with ice and shake. Strain into a chilled coupe glass. Garnish with the lime wedge and serve.

## Raspberry Dirty Soda

8 oz. Soda (Lemon-Lime or Cola)
2 tbsp. Raspberry Syrup
1 oz. Cream of Coconut
2-3 Raspberries

Add all ingredients (except raspberries) into a glass with ice and stir. Garnish with the raspberries and serve.

## Raspberry Lemonade

½ cup Simple Syrup
5 cups Water
¾ cup Fresh Raspberries
1 cup Lemon Juice
4 Lemon Slices

In a blender, add in raspberries (keeping 4 raspberries for garnish) and puree them. Pour the puree over a fine mesh strainer into a pitcher. Add in remaining ingredients to the pitcher and stir. Pour into 4 glasses and garnish each with a fresh raspberry and lemon slice.

*Makes 4 servings*

## Raspberry Mojito

9 Raspberries
4–5 Mint Leaves
4 oz. Club Soda
½ oz. Simple Syrup
1 oz. Lime Juice

Muddle 6 raspberries and the mint leaves with simple syrup in a cocktail shaker. Add in ice and shake. Strain into highball glass with ice and add in club soda. Put remaining raspberries on a toothpick to create a skewer and garnish drink.

## Ranch Water

2 oz. NA Tequila
1 oz. Lime Juice
2 oz. Topo Chico
Lime Wedge

Add all ingredients (except lime wedge) into a glass with ice and stir. Garnish with the lime wedge and serve.

## Red Racket

½ cup Cranberry Juice
½ cup Grapefruit Juice
10 Ice Cubes

Chill the cranberry and grapefruit juice in the fridge. In a blender, combine the juice and ice cubes. Blend on high speed till frothy. Pour into a Collins glass and serve.

## Revolver

2 oz. NA Bourbon
½ oz. Lyre's Coffee Originale NA Coffee Liqueur
2 dashes NA Orange Bitters
Orange Peel

Add all ingredients into a mixing glass with ice and stir. Strain into a chilled coupe glass. Garnish with orange peel and serve.

## Root Beer Dark 'N' Stormy

2 oz. Philters Ruhm
6 oz. Root Beer
Lime Wedge

Fill a Collins glass with ice, then pour the root beer and float the rum on top. Garnish with lime wedge.

## Root Beer Dirty Soda

8 oz. Root Beer
2 tbsp. Vanilla Syrup
2 oz. Half-and-Half
Whipped Cream
Maraschino Cherry

Add root beer, vanilla syrup, and half-and-half into a highball glass with ice and stir. Garnish with whipped cream and the cherry.

## Rosemary Gin Fizz

2½ oz. Cut Above Gin
1 oz. Lemon Juice
¾ oz. Rosemary Syrup
2 oz. Club Soda

Add all ingredients together into shaker with ice and shake. Strain over fresh ice and top with the club soda.

## Roy Rogers

6 oz. Cola
½ oz. Grenadine
Maraschino Cherry

Pour cola into a highball glass with ice and top with grenadine; stir. Garnish with maraschino cherry and serve.

## Ruby Cooler

4 oz. Cranberry Juice
2 oz. NA Gin
Ginger Ale
2 Raspberries

In a Collins glass with ice, add in Cranberry Juice and NA Gin and stir. Top with ginger ale and garnish with raspberries.

## Ruby Slippers

2 oz. Philter Jynn
4 oz. Pomegranate Juice
¼ oz. Orange Juice
2 dashes Fee Brothers
Orange Bitters
Orange Peel

Add ingredients (except orange peel) in a shaker with ice. Shake and double strain into a coupe glass. Garnish with orange peel.

## Ruhm With a View

2 oz. Philters Ruhm
3 oz. Coconut Water
½ oz. Lime Juice
½ oz. Simple Syrup
1 tsp. of Grated Cinnamon
Mint Sprig

Add ingredients (other than cinnamon and mint sprig) to a shaker with ice. Shake and strain over fresh ice in a Collins glass. Garnish with the cinnamon and mint, and serve.

## Rum Flip

2 oz. NA Dark Rum
½ oz. Heavy Cream
1 tsp. Granulated Sugar
Egg
1 tsp. Grated Nutmeg

Add all ingredients (except ice and nutmeg) into a shaker and hard dry shake. Add in ice and shake again. Strain into a chilled coupe glass and garnish with the nutmeg.

## Rum Madras

1½ oz. NA Dark Rum
2 oz. Cranberry Juice
2 oz. Orange Juice

Combine ingredients in a shaker with ice and shake. Strain into a Collins glass.

## Rum Raspberry Lemonade

1 cup NA Rum
6 cups Raspberry Lemonade
1 cup Fresh Raspberries

In a blender, combine all ingredients and blend until smooth. Pour into a large pitcher. Pour into highball glasses with ice when ready to serve.

*Makes 2-plus servings*

## Rum Old Fashioned

2 oz. NA Dark Rum
¼ oz. Demerara Syrup
2 dashes NA Aromatic Bitters
2 dashes NA Orange Bitters
Orange Peel

Add all ingredients (except orange peel) into a rocks glass with one large ice cube and stir. Garnish with the orange peel.

## See No Evil

1½ oz. Philters Mezkahl
¾ oz. Orgeat Bitters
¾ oz. Lime Juice
3 dashes Tabasco
4 dashes Angostura Bitters
½ tsp. of Grated Nutmeg
2 Mint Leaves

Add all ingredients (except for bitters, nutmeg, and mint leaves) to a shaker tin. Shake and *dirty pour* (without straining) into a chilled rocks glass. Add more crushed ice on top. Add the Angostura bitters on top and garnish with the nutmeg and mint leaves.

## Shandy

6 oz. NA Beer
3 oz. Lemonade
2 Lemon Slices

In a pint glass, add beer. Top with lemonade and stir. Garnish with lemon slices.

## Softcore Martini

1 oz. Passion Fruit Puree
½ oz. Lime Juice
½ oz. Vanilla Simple Syrup
¼ oz. Apple Cider Vinegar
4 oz. NA Sparkling Wine
½ Passion Fruit

Add all ingredients (except sparkling wine and passion fruit half) into a cocktail shaker with ice. Shake, and then strain into a chilled martini glass. Top with the sparkling wine and garnish with the passion fruit half.

*A non-alcoholic riff on the Porn Star Martini*

## Spa Water

9–10 cups Water
Lemon
Cucumber
Mint Sprig

Slice the lemon and cucumber. Add water into a pitcher with ice. Add in lemon and cucumber slices (reserving some for garnish), and mint sprig; let sit for an hour to infuse. Pour into highball glasses with ice and garnish with lemon or cucumber slices.

*Makes 4 servings*

## Spiced Wild

1.5 oz. Ceder's Wild NA Spirit
1.5 oz. Pineapple Juice
1/3 oz. Ginger Syrup
Dash of NA Bitters
Sage Leaf or Orange Zest

Combine all ingredients (besides sage leaf or orange zest) in a shaker; dry shake. Add ice and shake again. Fine strain into a chilled coupe glass. Garnish with the sage leaf or orange zest.

**Shirley Temple**

**Piña Colada**

**No-Maro Swizzle**

**Cold Brew Martini**

**Cucumber Cooler**

**Raspberry Lemonade**

**Petit Llama**

**Eliza's Hymns**

**Espresso Martini**

**Negroni**

**Peppermint "Irish" Coffee**

**Blackberry Lemonade**

**Strawberry Daiquiri**

**Maple Old Fashioned**

**Gin Free and Tonic**

**Spicy Margarita**

**Caprese Spritz**

**Disco Dust**

**Cosmopolitan**

**Mimosa**

**Eye See You**

**Turkey Trot**

**Midnight Kiss**

**Shake Those Shamrocks**

**Bee's Knees**

**Bloody Mary**

**Fresca Tonic**

**Lush and Locks**

**Dirty Soda**

**Pop-in-Prosecco**

**Puppy Pose**

**Featherweight Smash**

## Spicy Cucumber Margarita

2 oz. Philters Mezkahl
1 oz. Lime Juice
1 oz. Agave Syrup
3 Cucumber Slices
2-3 Jalapeño Slices
1 tbsp. Tajin

Rim a rocks glass with Tajin. Add 2 cucumber slices and 1-2 jalapeno slices to shaker tin and muddle. Add in all remaining ingredients (except for remaining cucumber and jalapeño slices) into the shaker with ice. Shake, and then strain into the rocks glass with fresh ice. Garnish with the remaining cucumber and jalapeño slices.

## Spicy Margarita

2 oz. Ritual Tequila Alternative
¾ oz. Lime Juice
½ oz. Agave Syrup
1-2 Jalapeño Slices
Lime Wedge
2 tbsp. Sugar or Salt (optional)

Rim rocks glass with sugar or salt (optional). Add jalapeño slices and lime juice to a cocktail shaker and muddle. Add in remaining ingredients (except lime wedge) to the cocktail shaker with ice and shake. Garnish with the lime wedge and serve.

*Try using other ways to create spice like replacing the jalapeño slices with hot honey or different spicy peppers.*

## Spicy Paloma

1½ oz. NA Tequila
1½ oz. Grapefruit Juice
2 Jalapeño Slices
Club Soda
Lime Wedge or Grapefruit Slice

Add tequila and jalapeño slices into a shaker and muddle. Add in grapefruit juice and ice and shake. Strain into a Collins glass with ice. Top with club soda and stir. Garnish with lime wedge or grapefruit slice; serve.

## Spicy Raspberry Margarita

2 oz. Ritual Tequila Alternative
¾ oz. Lime Juice
½ oz. Agave Syrup
1-2 Jalapeño Slices
3-4 Raspberries
Lime Wedge
2 tbsp. of Sugar or Salt (Optional)

Rim a rocks glass with sugar or salt (optional). Add raspberries and jalapeño slices to a cocktail shaker with lime juice and muddle. Add in remaining ingredients (except lime wedge) with ice and shake. Pour into rocks glass. Garnish with the lime wedge and serve.

## Spring Sunrise

2 oz. Carrot Juice
¼ oz. Monin Pistachio Syrup
¼ oz. Lemon Juice
Ginger Beer

Add all ingredients (except ginger beer) into a cocktail shaker with ice and shake. Strain into a rocks glass and top with ginger beer.

## Spritzer

3 oz. NA White Wine
Club Soda
Lemon Twist

Pour wine in a glass and top with club soda. Garnish with a lemon twist.

## Sobrii Peach Bellini

2 oz. Sobrii 0-Gin
2 Peaches
2 oz. Peach Nectar
1 oz. Soda Water
3 Peach Slices
Mint Sprig

Slice and pit peaches, place in a blender, and blend until smooth. Add gin and peach nectar to the blender and blend again. Fill a rocks glass with crushed ice, then fill it just less than halfway with soda water. Pour in peach mixture to top of glass. Garnish with 3 peach slices and mint sprig.

## Southside

4 Mint Leaves
1 oz. Lemon Juice
2 oz. NA Gin
1 oz. Simple Syrup

In a shaker, muddle two mint leaves and lemon juice. Add in gin and ice; shake. Strain into a coupe glass and garnish with the remaining two mint leaves.

## Stillman

2 oz. Blood Orange Juice
6 oz. Soda Water
2 dashes Angostura Bitters

Add all ingredients into a highball glass with ice and stir.

*Inspired by S. Troullos, Philadelphia, PA*

## Strawberry Daiquiri

¾ oz. Lemon-Lime Soda
¼ cup Sugar
1 tbsp. Lemon Juice
3 Large Strawberries
1 cup of ice

Add all ingredients (except one strawberry) into a blender with ice and blend. Strain into a margarita glass, top with the remaining strawberry, and serve.

*Try this recipe with other fruits for fun combinations!*

## Strawberry-Kiwi Slushie

½ cup sliced Strawberries
½ cup Peeled Kiwi
½ cup Water
½ cup of Ice
Strawberry Slice

Add all ingredients (except for a strawberry slice) into a blender and blend until smooth. Pour into a glass and garnish with the strawberry slice.

## Strawberry Lemonade

2 oz. Strawberry Juice
2 oz. Lemonade
Lemon Wedge
Strawberry

Add juice and lemonade into a Collins glass with ice. Garnish with lemon wedge and strawberry; serve.

## Strawberry Mule

2 oz. Strawberry Juice
1 oz. Fresh Lime Juice
4 oz. Ginger Beer
Strawberry

Add strawberry and lime juice into a mule mug with ice. Top with ginger beer and stir. Garnish with fresh strawberry and serve.

## Strawberry-Watermelon Slushie

½ oz. Lemon Juice
½ oz. Simple Syrup
3-4 Large Strawberries
2 Large Watermelon Chunks
1 cup Ice

In a blender, add all ingredients (except for one strawberry or watermelon slice) and blend. Pour into a rocks glass and garnish with the strawberry or watermelon slice.

CHAPTER 10  Non-Alcoholic Drink Recipes from A to Z

## Strawberry Gin Collins

2 oz. Cut Above Gin
¾ oz. Lemon Juice
¾ oz. Giffard Aperitif
½ oz. Strawberry Syrup
Club Soda
Lemon Wedge

Add all ingredients (except club soda and lemon wedge) in a cocktail shaker with ice and shake. Strain into a Collins glass with ice and top with the club soda. Garnish with the lemon wedge.

## Sweet Peach Tea

4 oz. Sweet Tea
½ oz. Peach Syrup
Peach Slice

Add all ingredients (except peach slice) into a highball glass with ice. Stir and garnish with the peach slice.

## Symbole d'Espoir

1 oz. Seedlip Garden 108 NA Spirit
½ oz. Lemon Juice
5 drops Stevia Extract
3 oz. Topo-Chico Sparkling Water
Lemon Twist

Add Seedlip, lemon juice, and Stevia to a shaker with ice and shake. Strain into a chilled flute and top with Topo Chico. Garnish with a lemon twist and serve.

## Takeaway

2 oz. NA Bourbon
1½ oz. Cold Brew Coffee
2 oz. Tonic Water

Add all ingredients into a highball glass with ice and stir.

## Tea & T

4 oz. Green Tea
4–6 Basil Leaves
4–6 Mint Leaves
½ oz. Lime Juice
¼ oz. Simple Syrup
Clearer Twist Premium Tonic Water

Add cooled tea, basil, lime, and simple syrup to a shaker and shake. Fine strain into a rocks glass and top with Clearer Twist Premium tonic water. Garnish with mint leaves.

## Tequila & Soda

1½ oz. NA Tequila
3 oz. Soda Water
Lime Wedge

Stir ingredients (except lime wedge) in a Collins glass with ice. Garnish with the lime wedge

## Tequila Julep

3 Mint Leaves
1 tsp. Superfine Sugar
1½ oz. NA Tequila
Club Soda
Mint Sprig

Crush mint leaves with sugar in a chilled highball glass and add ice. Add tequila and top with club soda. Garnish with a mint sprig.

## Tequila Sunrise

2 oz. NA Tequila
4 oz. Orange Juice
¼ oz. Grenadine
Soda Water (Optional)
Maraschino Cherry
Orange Slice

Add tequila and orange juice into a highball glass with ice. Top with grenadine and let sit until the grenadine floats to the bottom. Top with soda water (optional). Garnish with maraschino cherry and orange slice.

## That's-a-CoCo

1½ oz. NA Tequila
3 oz. Coconut Water
¼ oz. Lime Juice
Lime Wedge

Add all ingredients (except lime wedge) into a rocks glass with ice. Stir and garnish with the lime wedge.

*Inspired by CoCo Foley*

## Tiger Lily

1½ oz. Cut Above Mezcal
1½ oz. Pineapple Juice
2 oz. Ginger Beer
Pineapple Slice

Combine all ingredients (except pineapple slice) in a highball glass with ice. Garnish with the pineapple slice and serve.

## JOHN OR TOM COLLINS?

The story goes that John Collins, a waiter at Limmer's Old House (on Conduit Street, by Hanover Square, in London, England), invented the drink known as the Tom Collins. John used the name Tom (instead of John) because he made the drink with Old Tom Gin. Today, bartenders make a John Collins with whiskey, rather than the Tom Collins' gin.

## Tom Collins

2 oz. NA Gin
1 oz. Lemon Juice
1⅛ oz. Simple Syrup
Club Soda
Lemon Wheel
Maraschino Cherry

Add gin, lemon juice, and simple syrup into a Collins glass with ice. Top with club soda and garnish with lemon wheel and maraschino cherry.

## Tommy's Margarita

2 oz. NA Blanco Tequila
1 oz. Fresh Lime Juice
½ oz. Agave Nectar
1 tbsp. Salt

Rim a rocks glass with salt. Shake tequila, lime juice, and agave nectar in a cocktail shaker with ice. Strain into the rimmed rocks glass with ice.

## Tranquilita

1 oz. Cut Above Agave Blanco
1 oz. Ocho Verde Spirit
1 oz. Lime Juice
1 oz. Cucumber Puree
1 oz. Agave Syrup
2 Pineapple Fronds

Add all ingredients (besides pineapple fronds) into a shaker with ice. Shake and double strain into a rocks glass with ice. Garnish with the pineapple fronds and serve.

## Tropical Dirty Soda

8 oz. Pineapple Soda
1 tbsp. Coconut Syrup
2 tbsp. Mango Syrup
1 oz. Cream of Coconut
Pineapple Wedge

Add all ingredients (except pineapple wedge) into a glass with ice and stir. Garnish with the pineapple wedge.

## Valhalla

¾ oz. Lyre's Italian Orange
¾ oz. Seedlip Garden 108 NA Spirit
¾ oz. Lime Juice
Soda Water
Lime Wheel

Add all ingredients (besides soda water and lime wheel) into a highball glass with ice. Top with the soda water and stir. Garnish with the lime wheel and serve.

*Inspired by S. Troullos, Brooklyn, NY*

## Vanilla Dark 'N' Stormy

2 oz. Philters Ruhm
6 oz. Vanilla Cola
Lime Wedge

Fill a Collins glass with ice, then pour in the vanilla cola and float the rum on top. Garnish with lime wedge.

## Vanilla Pop

½ oz. Vanilla Simple Syrup
5 oz. Cola

Pour syrup and cola over ice in a Collins glass. Stir and serve.

## Very Peachy

2 oz. NA Bourbon
1 tbsp. Peach Jam
½ oz. Lemon Juice
Lemon Twist

Add all ingredients (except lemon twist) into a cocktail shaker with ice and shake. Strain into a coupe glass and garnish with the lemon twist.

## Violette Lady

2 oz. Philters Jynn
¾ oz. Lemon Juice
¾ oz. Lavender Syrup
Egg White
¼ Simple Syrup
2 Dried Rose Petals

Add all ingredients (except ice and rose petals) to a shaker tin and dry shake. Then add the ice and shake again. Double strain into a coupe glass. Garnish with the dried rose petals.

## VIP Welcome

2 oz. Ritual Whiskey Alternative
1 oz. Pineapple Juice
¾ oz. Orange Juice
¾ oz. Lemon Juice
¼ oz. Grenadine
½ oz. Honey Syrup
½ cup Crushed Ice

Add all ingredients into a shaker with ice and shake. Strain into a highball glass with crushed ice and serve.

## Walter

2 oz. Pineapple Juice
4 oz. Soda Water
¼ oz. Tamarindo Syrup
Tamarind Stick

Add all ingredients (except tamarind stick) into a highball glass with ice and stir. Garnish with the tamarind stick.

*Inspired by S. Troullos, Brooklyn, NY*

## Water Rush

2 oz. NA Dark Rum
½ oz. Raspberry Syrup
6 oz. Vanilla Cola
Lime Wedge

Fill a Collins glass with ice, then pour in the raspberry syrup and vanilla cola; float the rum on top. Garnish with lime wedge.

## Watermelon Daiquiri

6 oz. Watermelon Juice
2 oz. NA Rum
1 oz. Lime Juice
½ oz. Simple Syrup
½ oz. Orange Juice
Watermelon Wedge

Add all ingredients (except watermelon slice) into a cocktail shaker with ice and shake. Strain into a coupe glass, garnish with the watermelon wedge, and serve.

*Makes about 2 servings*

## Watermelon Iced Tea

4 cups Water
½ oz. Watermelon Simple Syrup
4-6 Tea Bags
2 Lemon Slices

Bring water to a boil and add in tea bags. Steep tea bags for around 5 minutes and then discard the bags. Add watermelon simple syrup into the freshly brewed tea. Bring to room temperature and pour into a glass with ice. Garnish with watermelon and lemon slices, and serve.

*Makes 2 servings*

## Watermelon Paloma

2 oz. Sobrii 0-Tequila
½ oz. Lime Juice
½ oz. Agave Syrup
5 oz. Watermelon Juice

To make the watermelon juice, blend 5-6 watermelon pieces with some water. Strain out pulp with a fine mesh strainer. Add tequila, agave syrup, and lime and watermelon juice to a shaker with ice. Shake well. Strain into a highball glass over fresh ice.

## Watermelon Seltzer

8 cups Unflavored Seltzer Water or Still Water
2 cups Fresh Watermelon Slices
10 Mint Leaves

In a pitcher, add water with ice. Add in watermelon slices (reserving one for garnish) and mint leaves; let sit for about an hour to infuse. Pour water into a highball glass with ice and garnish with a watermelon slice.

## Watermelon Slushie

1 cup Watermelon Slices
Lime
½ cup Water
½ cup of Ice

Juice the lime and pour into a blender. Add all other ingredients (except for one watermelon slice) and blend until smooth. Pour into a glass and garnish with the watermelon slice.

CHAPTER 10  Non-Alcoholic Drink Recipes from A to Z    131

## Whiskey Collins

2 oz. Cut Above Whiskey
1 oz. Lemon Juice
½ oz. Simple Syrup
Club Soda
Lemon Wheel
Maraschino Cherry

Add whiskey, lemon juice, and simple syrup to a highball glass and stir gently. Add ice, top with club soda, and stir again. Garnish with lemon wheel and maraschino cherry.

## Whiskey Peach Lemonade

1 cup Cut Above Whiskey
6 cups Peach Lemonade
1 cup Peach Slices
2 Thyme Sprigs

In a blender, combine whiskey, peach lemonade, and peach slices (reserving two peach slices for garnish) and blend until smooth. Pour into a large pitcher. Fill two highball glasses with ice and garnish each with a peach slice and thyme sprig.

*Makes 2-plus servings*

## Whiskey Tea

1½ oz. NA Whiskey
4 oz. Iced Tea
1 oz. Lemon Juice
½ oz. Simple Syrup
Lemon Wedge

Add all ingredients into a highball glass with ice and stir. Garnish with lemon wedge and serve.

## Winter Bee

2 oz. Philters Jynn
¾ oz. Lemon Juice
¾ oz. Honey Syrup
1 dash Cardamom Bitters
Lemon Wheel
Rosemary Sprig

Add all ingredients (except lemon wheel and rosemary sprig) into a shaker with ice. Shake, then double strain into a coupe glass. Garnish with the lemon wheel and rosemary sprig.

## Yeehaw, Beebaw!

2 oz. NA Tequila
1 oz. Lime Juice
½ oz. Strawberry Simple Syrup
4 oz. Lime Topo Chico
Lime Wedge
Strawberry Slice

Add all ingredients (except lime wedge and strawberry slice) into a glass with ice and stir. Garnish with the lime wedge and strawberry slice; serve.

*Inspired by Beebaw Getzow*

## Zing Zang Iced Tea-Rita

4 oz. Zing Zang Classic Margarita Mix
4 oz. Brewed Tea (black, green or hibiscus)

Combine all ingredients (besides lemon wedge) into a highball glass with ice and stir. Garnish with the lemon wedge.

## Zing Zang Mango Fizz

4 oz. Zing Zang Mango Margarita Mix
4 oz. Club Soda
Lime Slice, Mango Slice, or Mint Sprig

Pour margarita mix and club soda over ice in a Collins glass and garnish with the lime slice, mango slice, or mint sprig.

## Zing Zang Strawberry Fizz

4 oz. Zing Zang Strawberry Margarita-Daiquiri Mix
4 oz. Club Soda
Lime Wheel

Pour margarita-daiquiri mix and club soda into a Collins glass, over ice and stir. Garnish with lime wheel

## Zing Zang Piñita Colada

4 oz. Zing Zang Piña Colada Mix
1 oz. NA Rum
3 pieces of Fresh Fruit

Pour Zing Zang piña colada mix and Rum into highball glass over ice. (Alternatively, you can put the mix and rum with 1 cup of ice in a blender and blend until smooth, then pour into highball glass.) Garnish with fresh fruit.

CHAPTER 10  Non-Alcoholic Drink Recipes from A to Z

# Zing Zang Lemon Fizz

4 oz. Zing Zang Sweet & Sour Mix
4 oz. Club Soda
Mint Leaf

Pour sweet & sour mix and club soda into a highball glass over ice and garnish with mint leaf.

> **IN THIS CHAPTER**
> » Punches for parties
> » Holiday and seasonal drinks

# Chapter 11
# Drinks for Special Occasions

You're bound to have a few parties throughout the year, and some of those parties probably fall on holidays. This chapter offers some non-alcoholic punch recipes that guests at any gathering will love, and you can make them with either alcoholic or non-alcoholic spirits! This chapter also gives you a sampling of holiday drinks, as well as drinks for the seasons of the year. Try them with your friends.

## Party Punches

The name *punch* to describe a kind of drink may have come from the word *puncheon*, a cast made to hold liquids, such as beer. British expatriates in India in the 17th century made a beverage consisting of five ingredients: tea, water, sugar, lemon juice, and a fermented sap called *arrack*.

Regardless of the history or origin, guests expect punches of all kinds at many of today's social gatherings. If you want to be a good host (and the life of the party), you need at least a few of the following punches in your repertoire.

## Apple Cider

4 cups Apple Cider
2 cups Water
½ cup Brown Sugar
1 tsp. Ground Cinnamon
½ tsp. Grated Nutmeg
¼ tsp. Ground Cloves
3-4 Orange Slices
2 Cinnamon Sticks

Bring water to a simmer over medium heat. Add in all ingredients (except orange slices and cinnamon sticks) and bring back to a simmer. Stir and garnish with orange slices and cinnamon sticks.

*Makes 6-8 servings*

## Ambrosia Punch

20 oz. Crushed Pineapple
15 oz. Coco Lopez Cream of Coconut
2 cups Apricot Nectar
2 cups Orange Juice
1½ cups NA Rum (optional)
1 L Club Soda, chilled

Chill the apricot nectar and orange juice in the fridge. In a blender, purée the pineapple and cream of coconut until smooth. In a punch bowl, combine the pureed mixture, apricot nectar, orange juice, and rum (if desired). Mix well. Just before serving, add club soda and serve over ice.

*Makes about 24 servings.*

## Berry Punch

1 cup Raspberry Juice
1 cup Blueberry Juice
2 cups Cranberry Juice
1 cup Apple Juice
2 cups Sparkling Water
4-5 Strawberries
4-5 Raspberries

Add all ingredients (besides berries) into a large punch bowl with ice and stir. Garnish with the fresh strawberries and raspberries.

*Makes 4 servings.*

## Brunch Punch

1 L of Strawberry Lemonade
1 L of Club Soda
1 cup Rhubarb Simple Syrup
Lemon Slices
Sliced Strawberries

Add all ingredients (other than lemon and strawberry slices) into a large punch bowl with ice and stir. Garnish with the strawberries and lemon slices.

*Makes 4 servings.*

# Confetti Punch

6 oz. Frozen Lemonade Concentrate
6 oz. Frozen Grapefruit Juice Concentrate
6 oz. Fruit Cocktail
2 L Club Soda

Chill the club soda in the fridge. Drain the fruit cocktail and discard the liquid. Combine all ingredients except club soda in a large container and chill for two hours in the fridge, stirring occasionally. Before serving, pour the mixture over ice in a punch bowl and add club soda. Stir gently.

*Makes 8 servings.*

# Citrus Serenade

8 oz. Ocean Spray Cranberry Juice Cocktail
½ Banana
½ cup Low-Fat Vanilla Yogurt
¼ cup Red Grapefruit Sections
½ cup Crushed Ice

Cut the banana half into slices. Remove the membranes from the grapefruit sections by cutting or slicing. Put all ingredients in a blender. Blend for a few seconds on high speed or until ingredients are thoroughly combined. Pour into a large glass.

*Makes 1 serving.*

# Coral Paradise

10 oz. Ocean Spray Ruby Mango Grapefruit Juice Cocktail
4 oz. Orange Juice
¼ cup Crushed Pineapple
¼ cup Crushed Ice

Drain the pineapple and discard the liquid. Put all ingredients in a blender. Blend for a few seconds on high speed or until ingredients are thoroughly combined.

*Makes 1 serving.*
*Variation: Substitute 1 scoop or ½ cup of Vanilla Yogurt for Crushed Ice.*

# Cranberry Punch

4 cups Cranberry Juice
2 cups Orange Juice
1 cup Pineapple Juice
2 cups Sparkling Water
5–6 Fresh Cranberries
3–4 Orange Slices

Add all ingredients (except for cranberries and orange slices) into a large punch bowl and stir. Garnish with the cranberries and orange slices.

*Makes 4 servings.*

## Double Berry Coco Punch

20 oz. Frozen Strawberries in Syrup
15 oz. Coco Lopez Cream of Coconut
48 oz. Cranberry Juice Cocktail
2 cups NA Rum (optional)
1 L Club Soda

Thaw the frozen strawberries in syrup in the fridge (usually takes 1–2 hours), and chill the cranberry juice and club soda in the fridge. In a blender, purée the strawberries and cream of coconut until smooth. In a large punch bowl, combine the pureed mixture, cranberry juice, and rum (if desired). Just before serving, add club soda and serve over ice.

*Makes about 32 servings.*

## NA Eggnog

1 qt. Vanilla Ice Cream
1 cup Half-and-Half
1 cup Whole Milk
1½ tsp. Ground Cinnamon
1½ tsp. Grated Nutmeg
1½ tsp. Vanilla Extract
¼ tsp. Ground Cloves
1 cup NA Whiskey or NA Dark Rum (optional)
¼ tsp. Salt
Grated Cinnamon

In a blender, add all ingredients (except grated cinnamon) — including the optional non-alcoholic (NA) whiskey or NA rum, if you want — and blend until smooth. Add into a bowl and garnish with grated cinnamon.

*Makes about 6 servings.*
*Variation: Try adding in other ice cream flavors for different taste profiles, such as coffee ice cream.*

## Fall Symphony Punch

1½ oz. Cut Above Agave Blanco Tequila
½ oz. Apple Juice
½ oz. Cranberry Juice
½ oz. Allspice-Infused Demerara Syrup*
¼ oz. NA Orange Liqueur
2–3 oz. NA Champagne
Orange Zest Twist
¼ tsp. Demerara Sugar

Shake all the ingredients (except the champagne, orange zest twist, and demerara sugar) in a shaker with ice. Pour into a coupe glass and top with champagne. Garnish with the demerara sugar and orange zest twist.

*Makes 2 servings.*
***Allspice-Infused Demerara Syrup**
½ tsp. Ground Allspice
3 cups Demerara Syrup

Add ground allspice and demerara syrup to a saucepan and simmer over medium heat for 10 minutes. Remove from heat and rest for 5 minutes. Strain the mixture through a cheesecloth to remove excess spices.

## Fruit Punch

4 oz. Pineapple Juice
6 oz. Orange Juice
6 oz. Lemon or Lime Juice
1 qt. Ginger Ale or Club Soda
6–8 oz. NA Rum or NA Whiskey (optional)
2–3 Pineapple Slices
2–3 Orange Slices

Chill ginger ale or club soda in the fridge. Mix pineapple juice, orange juice, and lemon or lime juice in a large container. Chill for 2 hours in the fridge. Pour mixture over a block of ice in a bowl. Add ginger ale or club soda. If you want, add in NA rum or NA whiskey. Decorate with fresh pineapple and orange slices.

*Makes about 9 servings.*

## Grapefruit Banana Shake

4 oz. Ocean Spray White Grapefruit Juice
2 oz. Pineapple Juice
¼ cup Fat-Free Vanilla Yogurt
½ Banana

Cut the banana half into slices. Put all ingredients in a blender. Blend for a few seconds on high speed or until ingredients are thoroughly combined. Pour into a glass with crushed ice.

*Makes 1 serving.*

## Holiday Bourbon Punch

½ cup NA Bourbon
1 cup Pomegranate Juice
½ cup Orange Juice
1 bottle NA Sparkling Wine

Put all ingredients in large pitcher and stir. Allow to chill. Bring out when party is about to start!

*Makes 8 servings.*

## NA Planter's Punch

3 oz. NA Dark Rum
1 oz. Simple Syrup
¾ oz. Lime Juice
1 tsp. Grenadine
3 dashes Bitters
1 splash Club Soda

Add all ingredients (except the club soda) into a shaker with ice. Shake, and then strain into a rocks glass.

*Makes 1 serving.*

## Orange Coconut Frost

15 oz. Coco Lopez Cream of Coconut
12 oz. Frozen Orange Juice Concentrate
1 tsp. Vanilla Extract
4 cups Ice Cubes
Mint Leaves
Orange Slices

Thaw the orange juice concentrate in the fridge (should take about 2-3 hours). In a blender, combine cream of coconut, juice concentrate, and vanilla; blend well. Gradually add ice, blending until smooth. Garnish with mint and orange slices. Serve immediately.

*Makes about 5 servings.*

## Party Punch

2 cups Cranberry Juice
2 cups Pineapple Juice
2 cups Orange Juice
2 cups Sparkling Apple Cider
2 cups Ginger Beer
2 Cinnamon Sticks
2 Star Anise
2 Fresh Rosemary Sprigs
2-3 Orange Slices
4-5 Cranberries

Mix ingredients in a large bowl with ice. Serve in rocks glasses with ice and garnish with fresh cranberries.

*Makes about 4 servings.*

## Poinsettia Punch

1 L Orange Juice
1 L Club Soda
1 L Cranberry Juice
750 mL NA Sparkling Wine
½ cup Cranberries

Mix ingredients and add ice. Serve from a punch bowl or pitcher. You can mix the first three ingredients in advance and refrigerate them. Add the sparkling wine right before serving or top each glass with the sparkling wine. Garnish with fresh cranberries.

*Makes about 8 servings.*

## Pomegranate Punch

3 cups Pomegranate Juice
2 cups Ginger Ale
1 cup Club Soda
½ cup Lime Juice
6-8 Pomegranate Seeds
3-4 Lime Slices

Add all ingredients (except pomegranate seeds and lime slices) into a punch bowl with ice and stir. Garnish with the pomegranate seeds and lime slices.

*Makes 6-8 servings.*

## Scorpion Bowl

6 oz. NA Rum
1 oz. NA Brandy
6 oz. Orange Juice
4 oz. Lemon Juice
1½ oz. Orgeat Syrup

Combine all ingredients into a bowl. Add in shaved or pebble ice and serve.

*Makes about 6 servings.*

## Shower Punch

2 qt. Orange Juice
2 qt. Grapefruit Juice
750 mL NA Rum
3 Thin Orange Slices

Mix ingredients in a large container. Chill for 2 hours in the fridge. Pour mixture over a block of ice just before serving. Add the orange slices.

*Makes about 4–6 servings.*

## Snow Blower

6 oz. Cran-Apple Juice
1 tsp. Lemon Juice
1 pinch Cloves or Nutmeg
1 oz. NA Rum (optional)
Lemon Slice

Heat cran-apple juice, lemon juice, and cloves or nutmeg in a small saucepan over medium heat. Pour into a mug and stir in NA rum, if desired. Garnish with the lemon slice.

*Makes 1 serving.*

## Tennessee Punch

4 cups Sweet Tea
2 cups Pineapple-Orange Juice
3–4 Orange Slices

Mix tea and juice in a large bowl with ice. Serve in rocks glasses with ice and garnish with the orange slices.

*Makes 2 servings.*

## Tropical Fruit Smoothie

15 oz. Coco Lopez Cream of Coconut
Banana
8 oz. Crushed Pineapple
1 cup Orange Juice
1 tbl. Lemon or Lime Juice from Concentrate
2 cups Ice Cubes

In a blender, combine all ingredients except ice; blend well. Gradually add ice, blending until smooth. Garnish as desired. Serve immediately. Refrigerate leftovers.

*Makes about 5 servings.*

## Watermelon-Basil Sweet Tea

3 cups Sweet Tea
1 bunch Fresh Basil
¾ cup Watermelon Syrup
3 Basil Leaves

Mix ingredients (besides basil leaves) in a large bowl with ice. Serve in rocks glasses with ice and garnish with one basil leaf per cocktail.

*Makes about 2 servings.*

## Watermelon NA Tequila Punch

1¼ cup Cut Above Agave Blanco Tequila
¼ cup Simple Syrup
¼ cup Lime Juice
¾ cup Mint Leaves
8 cups Diced Seedless Watermelon
1¾ cups Blueberries

In a blender, puree the watermelon until smooth. Set a fine-mesh strainer over a bowl and strain the watermelon juice, pressing gently on the solids to extract as much juice as possible. Discard the pulp.

In a large pitcher, combine the syrup with the lime juice, blueberries and mint leaves. Using a wooden spoon, lightly muddle the blueberries and mint. Add the watermelon juice and tequila. Refrigerate until chilled, about 2 hours.

Pour the cocktail into tall ice-filled glasses and serve.

*Makes about 2 servings.*

## Vanilla-Rosemary Lemonade

3 cups Water
3 cups Lemon Juice
1 cup Vanilla Rosemary Syrup*
2 Rosemary Sprigs
3-4 Lemon Slices

Mix water, juice, and syrup in a large bowl with ice. Serve in rocks glasses with ice and garnish with a rosemary sprig and lemon slice per drink.

*Makes about 2 servings.*
**Vanilla Rosemary Syrup**
1 cup Sugar
1 cup Water
1 Rosemary Sprig
1 Vanilla Bean
*Combine ingredients in a pan and bring to a boil over medium heat. Set aside to cool.*

# Holiday Recipes

Sure, you could have a non-alcoholic Irish Coffee on St. Patrick's Day or non-alcoholic sparkling wine on New Year's Eve, but these cocktails offer a fun and delicious alternative! You can serve these drinks on holidays throughout the calendar year.

## New Year's Eve: Midnight Kiss

4 oz. NA Champagne
2 Strawberry Slices

Fill a champagne flute with chilled NA champagne and add in strawberry slices.

## Valentine's Day: Secret Admirer

3 oz. Pineapple Juice
2 oz. NA Rum
4 oz. Coco Lopez Cream of Coconut
2 oz. Raspberry Syrup
2 Cups of Ice
Top with Whipped Cream

Add all ingredients (except whipped cream) into a blender and blend. Pour into a Mason jar and top with whipped cream as desired.

## St. Patrick's Day: Shake Those Shamrocks!

3 scoops Mint Chocolate Chip Ice Cream
½ cup Milk
⅛ tsp. Peppermint Extract
⅛ tsp. Green Food Coloring
1 cup of Ice
Top with Whipped Cream
1 tbsp. Green Sprinkles

Add all ingredients (besides whipped cream and sprinkles) into a blender and blend. Pour into a glass and top with whipped cream and sprinkles.

## Easter: Egg Hunt

1 cup Vanilla Ice Cream
2 oz. Milk
1 oz. Monin Desert Pear Syrup
Top with Cotton Candy

Add all ingredients (except cotton candy) into a blender and blend till smooth. Pour into mug and garnish with the cotton candy.

CHAPTER 11  Drinks for Special Occasions   143

## Cinco De Mayo: Spicy Pineapple Non-Alcoholic Margarita

2 oz. NA Blanco Tequila
½ oz. Fresh Lime Juice
½ oz. Agave Syrup
½ oz. Pineapple Juice
½ Jalapeno Pepper
½ cup of Spicy Salt

Combine jalapeno half in a shaker with lime juice and begin to muddle. Add in the remaining ingredients with ice and shake. Rim a rocks glass with spicy salt. Double strain the drink into the rocks glass and serve.

## Independence Day: Red, White, and Blueberry Blast

1½ oz. NA Bourbon
1 oz. Blueberry Simple Syrup*
¼ oz. Lemon Juice
Mint Sprig

In a cocktail shaker with ice, add the NA bourbon, simple syrup, and lemon juice; shake. Strain into a rocks glass with ice and garnish with the mint sprig.

**\*Blueberry Simple Syrup**
1 cup Blueberries
½ cup Water
½ cup Sugar
Combine blueberries, water, and sugar in a pan. Bring to a simmer over medium heat until the sugar dissolves. Allow to cool for 15–20 mins.

## Halloween: EYE See You Punch

3 cups
750 mL NA Red Wine
½ cup Pomegranate Juice
1 cup Apple Cider
12 oz. Lemon-Lime Soda
Lychee and Blueberry Eye*

In a punch bowl, add in all ingredients (other than lychee and blueberry eye) and stir. Ladle drink into a rocks glass and place the eye on top to serve.

**\*Lychee and Blueberry Eye**
Lychee
Blueberry
Peel the lychee and place the blueberry in the center to create the eye and secure with a toothpick.

## Thanksgiving: Turkey Trot

2 oz. Seedlip Grove 42
½ oz. Lemon Juice
¾ oz. Blood Orange Juice
¼ oz. Simple Syrup

Add all ingredients into a cocktail shaker with ice and shake. Strain into a coupe glass and serve.

## Hanukkah: Gelt Hot Chocolate

3 Chocolate Coins
2 oz. Cream
2 oz. Milk
¼ oz. Simple Syrup
½ tsp. Ground Cinnamon
Whipped Cream

Bring cream and milk (or if you don't want to use cream, 4 oz. of milk) to a boil. Take unwrapped chocolate coin and place it in a mug. Pour in the hot cream/milk, along with the simple syrup and ground cinnamon; stir until coin is fully melted. Top with whipped cream and serve.

## Christmas: Gingerbread Martini

1 cup Heavy Cream
6 oz. Vanilla Soda
¼ oz. Demerara Syrup
1 tsp. Molasses
⅛ tsp. Ground Allspice
⅛ tsp. Ground Cinnamon
2 Crushed Gingerbread Cookies

Add all ingredients (except crushed gingerbread cookies) into a mixing glass with ice and stir. Strain into a martini glass and sprinkle the crushed cookies on top for garnish.

# A Few for the Seasons

A few cocktails always stand out to me for certain seasons. I love having fresh palomas in the summer and hot buttered rums in the winter. What follows are a few cocktails that work great for the various seasons.

## Winter
## Cran-Rosemary Soda

1¼ cup Fresh Cranberries
½ cup Honey Syrup
2-3 Rosemary Leaves
3-4 oz. Soda Water
Rosemary Sprig

Add 1 cup cranberries into a food processor and blend into a puree. Add cranberry puree into a pan with honey syrup and chopped rosemary leaves. Bring mixture to a simmer until reduced; strain into a jar. Set aside to cool. After it's cool, add 2 tablespoons of mixture into a glass with ice and top with soda water. Garnish with the remaining fresh cranberries and the rosemary sprig.

## Peppermint Irish Coffee

2 oz. NA Whiskey
4 oz. Coffee
1 tsp. Brown Sugar
½ oz. Peppermint Simple Syrup
Top with Whipped Cream
Peppermint Candy

Add all ingredients (besides whipped cream and peppermint) into a coffee mug and stir. Crush the peppermint candy. Top your drink with the whipped cream and crushed peppermint for garnish.

## Spring
## Cherry Blossom

2 oz. Seedlip Spice 94
2 tsp. Cherry Syrup
1 oz. Cold Brew Jasmine Tea
Jasmine Flower

Add all ingredients (except flower) into a cocktail shaker with ice and shake. Strain into a wine glass. Garnish with the jasmine flower and serve.

## Spring Sunrise

2 oz. Carrot Juice
1 oz. Coconut Cream
1 tsp. Grated Ginger
½ oz. Maple Syrup
1 piece of Candied Ginger

Add all ingredients (except candied ginger) into a cocktail shaker with ice and shake. Strain into a rocks glass and garnish with the candied ginger.

## Summer
# Strawberry Margarita

2 oz. NA Tequila
¾ oz. Lime Juice
½ oz. Agave Syrup
1 oz. Strawberry Puree*
Fresh Strawberry
Lime Wedge
½ cup Sugar or Salt (optional)

Add tequila, lime juice, agave syrup, and strawberry puree into a cocktail shaker with ice and shake. Rim a rocks glass with a lime wedge and then place into the sugar or salt mixture to rim the glass (optional). Double strain the drink into the rocks glass with ice. Garnish with a lime wedge and serve. You can also blend this drink with ice to make a frozen strawberry margarita.

*Variation:* Strain the drink into a blender, add ice, and blend to make a frozen strawberry margarita.
*Strawberry Puree
6 Strawberries
Add strawberries into a food processor and blend into a puree.

# Sparkling Raspberry Lemonade

1 cup Raspberries
4 cups Sparkling Water
1 cup Lemon Juice
½ cup Honey
Fresh Raspberry

Add raspberries, lemon juice and honey to a blender and blend until smooth. Add mixture into a pitcher with ice, top with sparkling water, and stir. To serve, pour into a highball glasses with ice and garnish with fresh raspberry.

## Fall
# Maple Old Fashioned

2 oz. Vanilla Infused Ritual Whiskey Alternative*
¼ oz. Maple Syrup
2 dashes NA Aromatic Bitters
Cinnamon Stick

Add all ingredients (except for cinnamon stick) into a mixing glass with ice and stir. Strain into a rocks glass and garnish with the cinnamon stick.

***Vanilla Infused Ritual Whiskey Alternative***
2 oz. Ritual Whiskey Alternative
2 Vanilla Beans
Add vanilla beans to NA whiskey bottle and let sit for 24 hours, shaking every few hours to help infuse.

CHAPTER 11  Drinks for Special Occasions   **147**

# Fall Apples

1 oz. Apple Juice
1 oz. Ginger Beer
2 tsp. Lime Juice
1 tbl. Agave Syrup
1 Apple Slice
1 Sprig of Thyme

Add Apple juice, lime juice, and agave syrup into a shaker with ice. Strain into a rocks glass and top with Ginger Beer. Garnish with an apple slice and a sprig of thyme.

IN THIS CHAPTER

» Trying drinks from bartenders around the world

» Exploring interesting techniques

# Chapter 12
# Non-Alcoholic Drinks from Top Bartenders

One of the things I love most about the hospitality industry is the people. Working on BARTENDER Magazine (Foley Publishing), I have the privilege of connecting with bartenders from all over the globe who generously share their craft with the magazine. This chapter gives you the chance to meet these talented bartenders — and even try some of the signature non-alcoholic drinks that they pour at their bars or restaurants. Hopefully, this chapter (like others in this book) can spark your creativity and inspire you to craft your own non-alcoholic cocktails.

A big thank you to each of these incredible bartenders for taking the time to share their recipes with me and for highlighting just how inventive and delicious non-alcoholic drinks are.

## Age of Discovery

1 oz. Seedlip 94
¾ oz. Raspberry-Infused Lyre's Italian Spritz*
1 oz. Passion Fruit Vanilla Syrup**
¾ oz. Fresh Lemon Juice
5 drops AÉR (egg white replacement)
2 dashes Saline Solution (salt water)
Pinch of Powdered Dehydrated Raspberry

Add all the ingredients (besides the powdered raspberry) into a shaker filled with ice. Shake vigorously for 10–15 seconds. Strain into a coupe glass. Garnish with the powdered raspberry.

Shared by Lidiyanah "Yana" K at ATLAS in Singapore
*Raspberry-Infused Lyre's Italian Spritz
2 oz. Fresh Raspberries
16 oz. Lyre's Italian Spritz
Gently crush (muddle) the raspberries with Lyre's Italian Spritz in a bowl or container. Transfer the mixture to a vacuum-seal bag or airtight container. Use a double boiler or heatproof bag in a pot of water at a similar temperature. Strain the mixture to remove solids. Bottle and label.
**Passion Fruit Vanilla Syrup
1 capful Vanilla Essence
2⅓ Cup White Sugar
¾ cup Passion Fruit Purée
½ cup Water
Combine sugar, water, and passion fruit purée in a pot. Heat the mixture until it boils and the sugar fully dissolves. Stir in the vanilla essence. Let the syrup cool down completely. Transfer to a bottle and label.

## Aline sitoé Diatta

⅗ oz. Chef's Syrup (soumpe, vanilla, honey, and passion fruit)
⅗ oz. Ginger Juice
⅗ oz. Tamarind Juice
⅗ oz. Bouye Juice (from the baobab fruit)
Pineapple Slice
2 Pieces Tamarind Sprinkled with Cinnamon Powder

Add ice cubes and the homemade chef's syrup to a cocktail shaker, then add the natural ginger juice, then the tamarind juice, and finally the bouye juice. Shake everything for 2–3 minutes so that the mixture is homogeneous, then pour with an ice filter into a cocktail glass. Garnish with the pineapple slice and pieces of tamarind.

Shared by Cheikh Cissé Dakar Senegal, Head Barman at Noom Hotel Sea Plaza Dakar, in Dakar, Senegal, and the President of ASBAH, the Senegalese association of barmen and hotel industry players

# Amore

2 oz. Seedlip Grove
½ oz. Grapefruit Juice
½ oz. Simple Syrup
3 dashes Orange Blossom Water
1 Grapefruit Expression

Add all ingredients (except the grapefruit expression) into a cocktail shaker with ice and shake. Strain into a coupe glass and serve with the grapefruit expression, which is a strip of grapefruit peel and gently squeeze it over the drink to release its aromatic oils

*Shared by Joshua James, Bar Manager at Fellow Osteria in Scottsdale, AZ*

# Apple-Rol Spritz

1 oz. Ish Gin
½ oz. Lyre's Italian Orange Spirit
½ oz. Apple Demerara Syrup
1 oz. Soda Water

Combine the Ish Gin, Lyre's Italian Orange Spirit, and Apple Demerara in a shaker. Shake well, strain into a coupe glass, and top with soda water.

*Shared by Conrad C. Helms IV, Beverage Director of Lazy Betty in Atlanta, GA*

# baNAnana

1½ oz. Vanilla Chai
1½ oz. Fresh Pineapple Juice
1 oz. Verjus
½ oz. Banana Oleo*
2 dashes Fee Brothers Aztec Chocolate Bitters
2 Mint Sprigs

Brew and chill your vanilla chai. I recommend an overnight steep in cold water to keep all of the bright and delicate flavors intact. Combine all ingredients (except for mint sprigs) in a shaker and shake. Strain over fresh ice. Throw in a couple mint sprigs and enjoy!

*Shared by Jordan Milano from Caveau in Boston, MA*
***Banana Oleo***
*3 Banana Peels*
*1 Cup of Sugar (I prefer Demerara)*
*Put the banana peels into a container with an equal amount (by weight) of sugar. (I prefer Demerara sugar.) Let it sit overnight. Make sure that the banana peel oil has absorbed all of the sugar. If it hasn't, let it sit a little longer. If it has, strain the mixture into a bottle.*

CHAPTER 12  Non-Alcoholic Drinks from Top Bartenders

## Bitter Spritz

¾ oz. Martini & Rossi Vibrante L'Aperitivo
½ oz. Three Spirit Livener
½ oz. Giffard Aperitif Sirop
3 oz. Three Spirit Spark
Orange Coin on Ice Spear

Add all ingredients (except for orange coin) into a collins glass and stir. Add in the ice spear and place the orange coin on top.

*Shared by Stuart Weaver from Lady Jane in Denver, CO*

## Bodega Daiquiri

½ oz. Orange Juice
¾ oz. Pineapple Juice
¾ oz. Mango Oleo Saccharum
2 oz. Cold Brew Coffee

Add all ingredients into a shaker with ice and shake. Strain into a coupe glass and serve.

*Shared by Wilson Oliver of Ava's Kitchen & Bar in Kenilworth, NJ*

## Brown and Stormy

1 oz. NA Dark Rum
1 oz. Spiced Ginger Syrup*
Soda Water
Lime Wedge

Combine rum and syrup in a highball glass filled with ice. Top with soda water and garnish with the lime wedge.

*Shared by Yugnes Susela at The Elephant Room in Singapore*
***Spiced Ginger Syrup***
2 oz. Ginger
½ oz. Cumin Seed
10.5 oz. Sugar
5.25 oz. Water
5 Dried Arbol Chilies
Toast cumin and dried chili peppers. Add sugar, water, and ginger. Blend, strain through a cloth, and bottle.

# Butterfly Tea Lemonade

2¼ tsp. Coriander Seeds
2½ tbsp. Dried Butterfly Pea Flower Tea
½ cup Turbinado Sugar
6 cups Boiled Water
3 oz. Agave Nectar
3 tbsp. Lemon Juice
1 oz. Club Soda
Dehydrated Lemon slice

Toast the coriander seeds in a small sauté pan over medium-low heat. Stir for about 3 minutes (don't let them burn). Allow seeds to cool, and then crack them in a mortar. Combine dried flowers, sugar, and coriander seeds in a large heatproof bowl or pitcher. Pour boiling water over ingredients. Allow to steep for 30 minutes. Add in turbinado sugar. Fine strain and discard solids, then refrigerate the liquid for at least 2 hours. To serve, pour 1 oz. lemon juice and 1 oz. club soda over crushed ice. Use tea pot to pour tea over the top at the table so the guests can watch the color change.

*Shared by Alexa Delgado, Director of Bars at The Miami Beach EDITION in Miami Beach, FL*

# Caprese Spritz

1 oz. Bittersweet Aperitivo
¼ oz. Balsamic Vinegar
¼ oz. Simple Syrup
3 Cherry Tomatoes
Pinch of Salt
2½ oz. Fever-Tree Sicilian Lemon Soda
Mozzarella Ball and Cherry Tomato on a Toothpick
Basil Sprig

Add the first 5 ingredients to a tin and muddle until the cherry tomatoes have released all their juices. Add ice and shake vigorously for 10 seconds. Double strain into a wine glass, and add lemon soda. Add ice and garnish with the toothpick and basil bouquet.

*Shared by Nora Furst of West Bev Consulting*

# Celery Gimlet

2 oz. Amethyst Lemon
¾ oz. Celery Lemon Cordial
3 drops Chive Oil
Cucumber Slice

Shake the Amethyst Lemon and Celery Lemon Cordial. Strain into a coupe and garnish with chive oil drops and a cucumber slice.

*Shared by Conrad C. Helms IV, Beverage Director of Lazy Betty in Atlanta, GA*

## Celestial

2 oz. Seedlip Garden
2 oz. Celestial Batch*
½ can of Watermelon Redbull
1 Rock Candy

Combine Seedlip Garden and Celestial Batch into a Collins glass and top with Watermelon Redbull. Garnish with rock candy and serve.

*Shared by Nihat Cam, Director of Bars at The Tampa Edition in Tampa, FL*
**\*Celestial Batch: (Yields 2½ L)**
1½ quarts Watermelon Juice
½ quart Yuzu Juice
½ quart Simple Syrup
1 tsp. Edible Gold Glitter Dust
Mix all ingredients together in a food safe bucket such as a Cambro bucket and then strain into a bottle.

## Cham-Painless

1 oz. Dill-Infused Simple Syrup*
¾ oz. Fresh Lemon Juice
4 oz. Club Soda (chilled)
Lemon Peel

Add club soda to a champagne flute. Add syrup and lemon juice to a mixing glass, then add ice and shake well. Strain into the club soda flute and garnish with the lemon peel.

*Shared by Frank Caiafa, author of* The Waldorf Astoria Bar Book *(Penguin Random House)*
**\*Dill-Infused Simple Syrup**
8 oz. Water
1 cup Sugar
1 bunch Fresh Dill
Add water and sugar to a saucepan. Stir over medium heat until integrated, about 3 minutes. Remove from heat and add dill. Steep for 30 minutes. Fine strain into glass container. Refrigerate for up to 3 weeks.

## Coquito Lemonade

1½ oz. Coconut Cream
½ oz. Coconut Water
¼ oz. Simple Syrup
¼ oz. Fresh Lemon Juice
1 drop Lemon Oil
Pinch of Hibiscus Salt
Pinch of Coconut Flakes

Add all the liquid ingredients into a shaker. Add ice and shake vigorously, then pour into a cocktail glass with crushed ice. Garnish with the hibiscus salt and coconut flakes.

*Shared by Luis Villanueva, Beverage Director-Managing Partner at Casa Bond in New York City, New York*

## Crimson and Clover

1½ oz. Raspberry-Black Pepper Syrup*
1 oz. Orange Juice
¾ oz. Lemon Juice
4 drops Saline Solution**
Soda Water
Lemon Peel

Combine all ingredients except soda water and lemon peel in shaker tin. Fill with ice and shake hard for 20 seconds. Strain into a chilled coupe glass and top with soda. Garnish with lemon peel and serve.

*Shared by Colin Williams at Saffron in New Orleans, LA*
**\*Raspberry-Black Pepper Syrup (Makes 1½ cups)**
1 cup Frozen Raspberries
1 cup Sugar
1 cup Water
1 tbsp. Black Peppercorns
Toast the black peppercorns in s skillet over medium heat until fragrant and toasted. Lightly crush them in a mortar and pestle, or a spice grinder. Combine in a small sauce pot with sugar, water, and frozen raspberries. Bring to a boil, then take off the heat. Cover and allow to steep for 30 minutes. Strain through a fine strainer and cool. Store in fridge and use within 1 week.
**\*\*Saline Solution**
2 tbsp. Salt
⅔ cup Hot Water
Combine ingredients and stir until salt dissolves. Allow liquid to cool and store in fridge.

## Cucumber Cooler

3 oz. Strange-Water Sparkling Coconut Water
1 oz. Sweetened Aloe Vera Juice
2 dashes Bitter Truth Cucumber Bitters
Cucumber Ribbon

Combine all ingredients (other than cucumber ribbon) over ice in a Collins glass. Stir gently and serve garnished with the cucumber ribbon.

*Shared by Charles Hardwick, Portfolio Mixologist, Moet Hennessy*

## Cucumber Mule

1 oz. Lemon Amethyst
½ oz. Fermented Cucumber Juice
¼ oz. Lemon Juice
½ oz. Simple Syrup
½ oz. Ginger Beer
3 drops Shoyu
Cucumber Slice

Shake all ingredients except for the ginger beer and cucumber slice. Then strain into a rocks glass, and top with ginger beer. Garnish with the cucumber slice.

*Shared by Conrad C. Helms IV, Beverage Director of Lazy Betty in Atlanta, GA*

## Desert Bloom

1½ oz. Seedlip Notas de Agave
½ oz. Lemon Juice
1 oz. Pineapple Juice
½ oz. Cinnamon/Hot Honey Syrup*
2 oz. Peroni 0.0
Lemon Twist
Pineapple Frond

Pour Peroni 0.0 into Collins glass with ice. Add all other ingredients (besides the lemon twist and pineapple frond) into a shaker tin, shake hard, and strain into Collins glass. Garnish with the lemon twist and pineapple frond.

*Shared by Chris Cardone, Founder of Continuous Beverage Solutions in New York City, NY*
**\*Cinnamon/Hot Honey Syrup**
*1 cup Water*
*¾ cup Honey*
*¼ cup of Hot Honey*
*4 Cracked Pieces of Cinnamon*
*Add ingredients to a pot and heat over medium heat until the liquids become one. Remove from heat. Add the cinnamon to the honey syrup and allow to cool for 15 minutes. Remove the cinnamon and store the liquid in the refrigerator for up to 2 weeks.*

## Desert Rose

1½ oz. Seedlip Notas de Agave
1 oz. Agua de Jamaica*
½ oz. Lime Juice
½ oz. Simple Syrup
1 pipette Herbal Riot Root and Bloom Bitters
Ginger Beer
1 Dehydrated Lime slice

Combine all ingredients (other than the ginger beer and dehydrated lime) into your shaker with ice and shake. Strain into a Collins glass with fresh ice and top with ginger beer. Garnish with a dehydrated lime and serve.

*Shared by Jasmyne Colín, Head bartender at Pony Up in Denver, CO*
**\*Agua de Jamaica**
*4.25 oz. Hibiscus*
*1 cup Sugar*
*Half a Lemon Peel*
*Half an Orange Peel*
*88 oz. Water*
*In a pot, add lemon and orange peels, and half of the water. Bring to a boil. After the mixture boils, add hibiscus and let boil for 5 minutes. Remove from heat and cover for 2 hours or until completely cool. Strain and add the remaining water over the top of the strained hibiscus. Add sugar and then pour into an immersion blender and use it to fully combine the ingredients.*

## Dirty Spritz

1½ oz. Citrus Aperitivo
½ oz. Lemon Juice
¼ oz. Olive Brine
3 oz. Tonic Water
2 Olives
Sprig of Thyme

Add all ingredients (except olives and thyme) to a Collins glass, top with ice, and stir twice. Garnish with olives and thyme sprig.

*Shared by Nora Furst of West Bev Consulting*

## Dragon Fruit Highball

1½ oz. Dragon Fruit Cordiale*
½ oz. Lime Leaf Syrup**
Soda Water

Add all ingredients into a Collins glass and stir.

*Shared by Nathalie Durrieu, Head Bartender at Experimental Cocktail Club in New York City, NY*

**Dragon Fruit Cordiale*
2.2 pounds Frozen Dragon Fruit
1 quart Water
0.6 oz 3% Pectinex Ultra SP-L
17.6 oz. Sugar
0.7 oz. Tartaric Acid
0.07 oz. Citric Acid
0.25 oz. Kosher Salt
0.5 oz. Vegetal Glycerin
Combine the dragon fruit, water, and Pectinex Ultra in a food-safe bucket and blend. Strain through a very fine mesh strainer. Add remaining ingredients.

***Lime Leaf Syrup*
16 oz. Sugar
16 oz. Water
⅓ oz. Lime Leaf
Combine all ingredients in a saucepan on medium heat. When it starts to simmer, remove from heat. Allow to infuse for 24–36 hours in the refrigerator. Strain through a cheesecloth.

## FauxMelo

1½ oz. Almave
1 oz. Fauxmelo Syrup*
½ oz. Giffard NA Elderflower Liqueur
¾ oz. Lime Juice
2 dashes Black Lemon Bitters
¼ cup of Furikake Seasoning

Garnish the rim of a coupe glass with furikake. Shake all remaining ingredients together and double strain into the coupe glass.

*Shared by Mohammed Zagha*

CHAPTER 12  Non-Alcoholic Drinks from Top Bartenders

***FauxMelo Syrup***
32 oz. Pink Grapefruit Juice
½ oz. Kombu (edible kelp/seaweed)
½ oz. Rose Water
½ oz. Orange Blossom
32 oz. White Sugar
1 pinch Salt
Heat the grapefruit juice in a pan; add the kombu and bring to a boil. Turn the heat off, cover, and allow to infuse for 30 minutes. Strain into a bottle and refrigerate.

## Featherweight Smash

Half of a Lemon, quartered
½ oz. Simple Syrup
5–7 Fresh Mint Leaves
2 oz. The Pathfinder Hemp and Root
Lemon Wheel
Mint Sprig

Add the lemon half and simple syrup to a cocktail shaker and muddle gently. Add the mint leaves and The Pathfinder, and then fill the shaker with ice. Shake until cold and fine strain into a double rocks glass over crushed ice. Garnish with the lemon wheel and mint sprig, and serve.

Shared by Ivy Mix, Co-Founder of the Speed-Rack competition and co-author of A Quick Drink: The Speed Rack Guide to Winning Cocktails for Any Mood (Harry N. Abrams)

## Filipino Flip

2 oz. Calamansi Curd*
¾ oz. Green Curry Syrup**
½ tsp. of Lime Zest

Combine all ingredients (except lime zest) into your shaker and shake. Pour into tea cup and garnish with lime zest.

Shared by Nathalie Durrieu, Head Bartender at Experimental Cocktail Club in New York City, NY

***Calamansi Curd***
1 cup Granulated Sugar
3 Limes
6 Eggs
½ cup Calamansi Juice
½ cup Unsalted Butter
Zest the limes by using a microplane zester. Mix lime zest and sugar together. Rest the zest and sugar mixture for 2 hours to extract all the oils from the zest. Separate the egg yolks from the whites. Strain yolks into a pot and beat lightly with a wire whisk. Whisk in the lime zest sugar until the mix becomes lighter in color. Stir in the calamansi juice gradually. Heat on low while stirring constantly with a wire whisk until mixture thickens, just starts to bubble, and coats back of wooden spoon. Remove pot from heat, then add the cold, cubed butter, and mix until melted. Strain the final mixture to remove any bits of zest. Transfer the curd to a sealable container or bowl. If storing in a bowl, make sure to cover the surface with plastic wrap to prevent a skin from forming.

**\*\*Green Curry Syrup**
1 kg Demerara Sugar
500 g Water
80 g Green Curry Paste
Combine all ingredients in a saucepan on medium heat. When the mixture starts to simmer, remove from heat. Infuse overnight in the refrigerator. Strain through cheesecloth into a food-safe bucket. Add syrup into a bottle for use.

## Fresca Tonic

1 oz. Hibiscus Infused Almave Blue N/A
1 oz. Prickly Pear Aromatic Syrup
1 oz. Pomegranate Juice
2 oz. Club Soda
Dehydrated Nopal Diamond

Build in chilled highball glass. Add an ice spear and garnish with dehydrated nopal diamond

*Shared by Jose Ignacio "Nacho" Jimenez, Superbueno, NYC*

## Fun in the Sun

2 oz. Seedlip Grove 46
2 oz. Lemon Juice
1½ oz. Pineapple Juice
1 oz. Simple Syrup
Sparkling Water
4 Mint Leaves
Lime Wheel
Pineapple Frond

Add all ingredients (other than the lime wheel and pineapple frond) into a shaker with ice and shake. Double strain into a white wine glass with crushed ice. Top with sparkling water and garnish with lime wheel and pineapple frond.

*Shared by Gio Olivera of Sirenetta in Hoboken, NJ*

## Ginger Blossom

1 oz. Calpico
¾ oz. Pineapple Juice
½ oz. Lime Juice
½ oz. Ginger Syrup
2 oz. Cranberry Juice
Cucumber Ribbon
Luxardo Cherry

Combine Calpico, pineapple juice, lime juice, and ginger syrup in a shaker with ice. Shake well and strain into a chilled glass. Float the cranberry juice on top and garnish with the cucumber ribbon and Luxardo cherry.

*Shared by Mickey Stevenson, Lead Bartender at Four Walls in Nashville, TN*

## Golden Bloom

1.5 oz. Yuzu Juice
1.5 oz. Chamomile Tea
½ oz. Creamed Honey
3-5 Fresh Basil Leaves

Pour all the ingredients into a shaker, along with 3-5 basil leaves. Add ice and shake. Strain into a coupe glass and garnish with a fresh basil leaf.

*Shared by Jiawei Bai at White Shades in Singapore*

## Gold Mosey

2 oz. Ritual Zero Proof Non-Alcoholic Whiskey
¾ oz. Fresh Lemon Juice
¾ oz. Honey Syrup*
Lemon Twist

Pour the bourbon, honey syrup, and lemon juice into a cocktail shaker filled with ice. Shake until thoroughly chilled. Strain the mixture into a pre-chilled rocks glass over a large ice cube. Finish by garnishing with the lemon twist.

*Shared by Adrienne Smith*
**\*Honey Syrup**
*1 cup Pure Honey*
*1 cup Water*
*In a saucepan, mix the honey and water. Heat the mixture over medium heat, stirring constantly until the honey completely dissolves and the syrup becomes clear, with no residue left sticking to the pan. Remove from heat and cool. Transfer the syrup into a container and store in the fridge for up to two weeks. You can create a richer honey syrup by using twice as much honey or adjust the proportions to suit your personal preferences.*

## Going Green

2 oz. Optimist Fresh
1 oz. Cucumber Juice
1 oz. Simple Syrup
¾ oz. Lime Juice
3-4 Cucumber Slices
Mint Leaves
Mint Sprig

In a cocktail shaker, add mint leaves and all but one cucumber slice, along with simple syrup, and muddle. Add in remaining ingredients and ice. Shake and strain into a rocks glass with ice and garnish with a cucumber slice and the mint sprig.

*Shared by Laura Royer, New York City, NY*

## Granata

1½ oz. Seedlip Grove
½ oz. Grenadine
1½ oz. Pomegranate Juice
¾ oz. Lemon Juice
¾ oz. Egg Whites
Edible Flower

Combine all ingredients (except flower) in a shaker tin with ice and shake vigorously for 20 seconds. Strain the drink into a container on the side, then dump out the ice from the shaker. Return the drink to the shaker, and shake vigorously for another 10 seconds. Fine strain into a large coupe glass and garnish with the edible flower.

*Shared by Rachel Larsen at Cafe Riggs, Washington, D.C.*

## Green With Envy

1½ oz. Monday Zero Alcohol Gin
½ oz. Monin Green Apple Syrup
1 oz. Pineapple Juice
1¾ oz. Lime Juice
Edible Gold Star Glitter

Combine all ingredients (besides glitter) into a mixing shaker tin. Add ice, cap tin, and shake well. Strain cocktail into a coupe glass. Sprinkle edible gold star glitter on top to garnish.

*Shared by Inga Tantisalidchai*

## Iki

1 oz. Perfect Puree Yuzu Luxe Sour
½ oz. Lemon Juice
½ oz. Lemongrass Ginger Syrup
Moshi Sparkling Yuzu
Uji Matcha Soda
Flower Confetti

Add Perfect Puree Yuzu Luxe Sour, Lemon Juice, and Lemongrass ginger syrup into a shaker with ice. Strain over fresh ice. Top with Moshi Sparkling Yuzu Uji Matcha Soda and garnish with Flower confetti.

*Shared by Mariena Boarini, Resort Mixologist at Wynn Las Vegas in Las Vegas, NV*

## Illegal Backflip

2 oz. Pistachio Falernum (syrup)
½ oz. Three Spirit Social
½ oz. Heavy Cream
1 Egg
Garnish with Grated Nutmeg

Add all ingredients (except nutmeg) into a cocktail shaker and dry shake. Add ice and shake again. Fine strain into an Irish Coffee glass and garnish with grated nutmeg.

*Shared by Stuart Weaver from Lady Jane in Denver, CO*

## Indian Summer

1⅓ oz. Lyre's Italian Orange
1 oz. Nannari Syrup
1 oz. Lime Juice
Soda Water
1 Dehydrated Orange wheel

Measure Italian Orange, syrup, and juice with a jigger and add them to the glass. Fill the glass with ice cubes. Gently stir the mixture to combine the ingredients well. Add soda water to fill the glass. Add the dehydrated orange as a garnish.

*Shared by Franz Karl Lagajino at The Pineapple Room in Singapore*

## Irish Cawfee-ish

1 oz. Seedlip Spice 94
1 cup Coffee
1–2 tbsp. Demerara Sugar
¼ cup Whipped Cream
Garnish with Grated Nutmeg

Brew coffee the way you like. Pour into mug and stir in the Demerara until dissolved completely. Add Seedlip. Whip heavy cream until it forms soft peaks. Float whipped cream on top and sprinkle a light dusting of nutmeg.

*Shared by Aidan Bowie, Beverage Director at The Irish Exit in New York City, NY*

## Ivory Jungle

1 oz. Soursop Juice
½ oz. Sweetened Condensed Coconut Milk
1¾ oz. Grapefruit Juice
¾ oz. Lemon Juice
4½ oz. Soda Water
Mint Leaf
Charred Cinnamon Stick

Fill glass with pebble or crushed ice. Stir in juices and coconut milk, and top with soda water. Top off the glass with fresh pebble ice, mint, and charred cinnamon stick.

*Shared by Maxwell Berlin Bartender at Quartz Bar in Phoenix, AZ*

## Jasmine Cooler

1½ oz. Jasmine Syrup
¾ oz. Verjus
¾ oz. Lemon Juice
4–5 Mint Leaves
Club Soda
Lemon Wheel
Mint Sprig

Combine syrup, Verjus, lemon, and mint leaves into a shaker with ice and shake. Strain over ice into Collins glass. Top with club soda and garnish with the lemon wheel and mint sprig.

*Shared by Meaghan Dorman, Bar Director and Partner of Dear Irving on Broadway in New York City, NY*

## Kopi Siew Dai

1.5 oz. of Lyre's American Malt
1 oz. of Dandelion Tea *Kopi* (a traditional Southeast Asian coffee)*
20 mL Cereal-Infused Milk**
Served with Chocolate on the side

Add the Lyre's American Malt and *kopi* into a rocks glass that contains a big ice cube. Pour cereal-infused milk into a small carafe and pour it into the cocktail when serving.

*Shared by Charlie Kim at MO BAR, Mandarin Oriental Singapore in Singapore*
***Kopi Brewed with Dandelion Tea***
8 bags Kopi
8 bags Dandelion Tea
Strain together kopi with dandelion tea.
****Cereal-Infused Milk***
4 oz. Frosted Flakes Cereal
1 quart Whole Milk
Pinch of salt
Combine all ingredients and soak for 1 hour. Strain and remove the frosted flake cereal.

## Love Buzz

4 oz. Hibiscus Rose Mixer
½ oz. Lemon Juice
Splash of Soda
Lemon Peel

Add all ingredients (except lemon peel) into a wine glass with ice and stir. Garnish with the lemon peel and serve.

*Shared by Rollin Colmenares, Head Bartender at RT60 Rooftop Bar and Lounge at Hard Rock Hotel in New York City, NY*

## Lush and Locks

1 oz. Seedlip Grove 42
¾ oz. Phony Negroni
¾ oz. Passion Fruit Syrup
½ oz. Lemon Juice
½ oz. Cinnamon Demerara Syrup
2 dashes All the Bitter New Orleans NA Bitters
Lemon Peel Twist

Add all ingredients (except lemon peel twist) into a shaker. Fill the shaker with ice and shake well. Double strain the mixture into a coupe glass. Garnish with the lemon peel twist.

*Shared by Oscar Simoza Bar manager at The Wigshop in Boston, MA*

## Mama's Garden

1.5 cups Mott's Apple Juice
1 cup Zucchini-Mint Juice*
⅓ cup Giffard NA Ginger
1 cup Seedlip Garden
1 tsp. Sesame Oil

Add all ingredients into the zucchini-mint juice Superbag and stir to mix together. Once combined, pour into a champagne flute.

*Shared by Paul Sauter at The Aviary in Chicago, IL*

CHAPTER 12  **Non-Alcoholic Drinks from Top Bartenders**

**Zucchini-Mint Juice\***
Zucchini
4 Mint Sprigs
Cut off the ends of the zucchini, and peel and cut those ends in half. For each zucchini stump, add one sprig of mint without its stem. Place zucchini and mint in juicer and juice them. Place juice in a Superbag and store.

## Matcha Fizz

1 oz. Fresh Lemon Juice
¾ oz. Simple Syrup
3½ oz. Soda Water
1½ oz. Drinking Water
½ tsp. Matcha Powder
1 tsp. Lemon Zest

In a mixing bowl, whisk matcha powder and drinking water in a number-8 motion until no clumps remain. Set aside. Fill glass with ice, add the lemon juice and simple syrup, and stir to mix well. Top with soda water and stir gently. Quickly whisk the matcha mix to incorporate air into the liquid. Pour onto the surface of the lemonade in the glass. Garnish with the lemon zest.

*Shared by Pae Ketumarn at F\*nkytown in Bangkok, Thailand*

## Mid-Summer

1⅓ oz. Seedlip Grove 42
1.5 oz. Peach Tea Cordial\*
Maison Perrier France Forever Strawberry
Fresh Peach Slice
Sprig of Rosemary

Pour Seedlip Grove 42 and Peach Tea Cordial into a highball glass. Top with Maison Perrier Strawberry and stir gently to combine. Garnish with the peach slice and sprig of rosemary

*Shared by Ron Aransay at Las Palmas in Singapore.*
**\*Peach Tea Cordial**
11 packets of Peach Tea
4.25 cups Hot Water
2.5 cups Sugar
1 tbsp. Citric Acid
Add the packets to the water and steep for 5 minutes. Add in the sugar and stir until fully dissolved. Mix in citric acid until combined.

## Mo' Bettah

10 Thai Basil Leaves
1 oz. Lime Juice
¾ oz. Boiron Passion Fruit Puree
1 oz. Cinnamon Syrup
1½ oz. Pellegrino Sparkling Water
1 Dehydrated Lime wheel
Viola Flower

Gently muddle the basil leaves with lime juice in a cocktail shaker. Add in passion fruit puree and cinnamon syrup with ice and shake. Add in Pellegrino and strain into a coupe glass. Garnish with the dehydrated lime wheel and viola flower.

*Shared by Brian Miller, Bar Manager at Stockton Inn in Stockton, NJ*

# Mockingbird

2 oz. Martini & Rossi Vibrante
2 oz. Pineapple Juice
1 oz. Fresh Lime Juice
½ oz. Blackstrap Molasses Syrup*
2 Pineapple Leaves
1 Dehydrated Pineapple slice

Combine all ingredients (except leaves and dehydrated pineapple) into a shaker with ice and shake. Strain into a rocks glass with ice and garnish with pineapple and leaves.

*Shared by Daniel Maysonet Rivera from Jungle Bird in Puerto Rico*
***Blackstrap Molasses Syrup***
½ cup Sugar
½ cup Water
¼ cup Blackstrap Molasses
Add all ingredients into a pot and bring to a simmer until the sugar is dissolved and combined.

# Naur-Garita

2 oz. Bare 0 Proof Reposado Tequila
¾ oz. Chamomile Syrup*
¾ oz. Fresh Lime Juice
2 Orange Peels
2 tsp. Salt for rimming
Lime Wheel

Combine all ingredients (except salt and lime wheel) in a shaker tin and add ice. Shake for about 10 seconds (or until the tins are cold on the outside). Rim half the glass with salt. Strain the drink into the rocks glass, add fresh ice, and garnish with the lime wheel.

*Shared by Sophie Burton from Junebug in New Orleans, LA*
***Chamomile Syrup***
2 Chamomile Tea Bags
8 oz. Water
8 oz. White Sugar
2 drops Fee Brothers Orange Flower Water
Bring the water to a boil and steep the tea for 5 minutes. Combine tea and white sugar. Gently heat until sugar dissolves. Add in drops of Fee Brothers orange flower water.

# New World

1 oz. Fruitations Cranberry
1 oz. Star Anise Infused Fruitations Tangerine
½ oz. Ginger Syrup
½ oz. Lemon Juice
3 oz. Soda Water
Pinch of Fresh Grated Nutmeg
Lemon Twist

Combine all ingredients (besides soda water, nutmeg, and lemon twist) into a shaker with pebble ice. Quickly shake 5 times to aerate ingredients. Pour ingredients into highball glass without straining. Top off glass with pebble ice and top with soda water. Garnish with nutmeg and lemon twist.

*Shared by Ray Tremblay, Director of Beverage at COJE Management Group in Boston, MA*

## Not a Guava

1½ oz. Alamave NA Reposado Tequila
1 oz. Guava Puree
½ oz. Lime Juice
1 1½ oz. Honey Ginger Syrup
Blood Orange Peel

Add all ingredients (besides blood orange peel) into a cocktail shaker with ice and shake. Dump into a chilled rocks glass and garnish with blood orange peel.

*Shared by Anthony DeSerio*

## Orchard Spritz

4 oz. Martinelli Sparkling Cider
¾ oz. Monin Blackberry Syrup
1 oz. Club Soda
Dash of Rhubarb Bitters
3 Blackberries

Combine all ingredients (except blackberries), along with ice, into a wine glass and stir gently. Garnish with blackberries.

*Shared by Charles Hardwick, Portfolio Mixologist for Moet Hennessy*

## Otra Cosa

1½ oz. Lyre's Agave
½ oz. Brewed Lapsang Souchong Tea
1 oz. M&R Rosso Vibrante
1 oz. Lyre's Aperifit Rosso
Blood Orange Peel

Combine all ingredients in rocks glass. Stir briefly to incorporate. Add in a single large cube of ice and stir cube 5-6 times to chill down the drink. Garnish with the blood orange peel.

You can also batch this drink and pour it chilled from the fridge over the ice cube.

*Shared by Nick Crutchfield*

## Pandan Hi

1.75 oz. Lyre's White Cane with Pandan*
½ oz. Lemongrass Syrup
½ oz. Lemon Juice
Soda Water
Pandan Leaf

Pour all the ingredients into a shaker (except soda and leaf). Add ice to the shaker and shake well for 10 seconds. Double strain into a highball glass and top with soda water. Garnish with the pandan leaf.

*Shared by KT Lam at Sora Bar, Rosewood Phnom Penh in Phnom Penh, Cambodia*

**Lyre's White Cane with Pandan*
1 cup of Pandan Leaves
3.75 cups of Lyre's White Cane
Finely chop pandan leaves into small pieces and sous vide them in a bag with Lyre's White Cane for 30 minutes at 60 degrees. Rest in an ice bucket to cool before fine straining through a coffee filter.

## Papaya Colada

1 oz. Three Spirit Nightcap
1 oz. Papaya-Chamoy Syrup*
1 oz. Lime Juice
¾ oz. Pineapple Juice
¼ oz. Coco Lopez Cream of Coconut
Mint Bouquet

Add all ingredients (besides mint bouquet) into a cocktail shaker with ice and shake. Dump into a highball glass and garnish with the mint bouquet. Serve with a long straw.

*Shared by Abby Durnell and Stuart Weave from Lady Jane in Denver, CO*
**Papaya-Chamoy Syrup:*
1 cup Papaya, peeled and diced
½ cup Sugar
¼ cup Water
2 tbsp. Chamoy Sauce
Place the diced papaya in a blender or food processor and blend until smooth. In a small saucepan, combine the blended papaya, sugar, and water. Heat over medium heat, stirring occasionally, until the sugar is dissolved and the mixture thickens slightly, usually around 5 to 7 minutes. Once the syrup has thickened, stir in the chamoy sauce and allow to cool. Strain the syrup through a fine mesh sieve to remove any pulp. Transfer the syrup to a clean bottle or jar and refrigerate. It will keep for 1 to 2 weeks.

## PB & J

2 oz. Seedlip Garden
½ oz. Caramel Sauce
½ oz. Peanut Butter
1 oz. Grape Juice
1 oz. Lime Juice
1 dash Scrappy's Bitters Firewater Habanero Tincture
Garnish with Parline powder

Cover Collins glass rim with praline powder. Shake all remaining ingredients together, double strain into the Collins glass, and fill with ice.

*Shared by Mohammed Zagha*

CHAPTER 12  Non-Alcoholic Drinks from Top Bartenders

## Pear-Maple Sour

1 oz. Martini & Rossi Floreale
½ oz. Seedlip Spice 94
1½ oz. Pear-Miso-Maple Syrup
1 oz. Lemon Juice
¼ oz. Maple Syrup
Skewered Candied Ginger
Dehydrated Lemon Wheel

Add all ingredients (except for ginger, lemon wheel, and ice) into a cocktail shaker and shake. Fine strain over ice into a rocks. Garnish with ginger and lemon wheel.

*Shared by Nora Hubbell from Lady Jane in Denver, CO*

## Petit Llama

2 oz. Chicha Morada*
1 oz. Purple Corn Syrup**
1 oz. Fresh Lime Juice
1 Fresno Chili, thinly sliced
3 Mint Leaves
Club Soda

Combine chicha morada, purple corn syrup, lime juice, Fresno chili, and mint in a shaker with ice. Shake vigorously until well-chilled. Double-strain into a rocks glass over fresh ice. Top with a splash of club soda. Garnish with a mint sprig or thin slice of Fresno chili, if desired.

*Shared by Chef Ethel J. Salazar from Little Bar in Hoboken, NJ*
**\*Chicha Morada (Purple Corn Punch)**
3 lbs Dried Peruvian Purple Corn
3 quarts Cold Water
3 Large Cinnamon Sticks
1 Medium Pineapple (flesh diced; peel included)
2 Apples, diced
6 Whole Cloves
In a large pot, combine purple corn, water, pineapple flesh and peel, apples, cinnamon sticks, and cloves. Bring to a boil over medium heat. Reduce to medium-low and simmer, partially covered, for 45–60 minutes. Remove from heat, strain out solids, and let the liquid cool completely. Refrigerate until ready to use.
**\*\*Purple Corn Syrup**
1 cup Chicha Morada
1 cup Sugar
In a small saucepan over medium heat, combine chicha morada and sugar. Stir until sugar dissolves and mixture reduces into a syrup, about 5–10 minutes. Remove from heat, let cool, and refrigerate.

## Persimmon Soda

1 oz. Three Spirit Livener
6 oz. Persimmon-Maple Soda
Lemon Wheel

Add Livener and soda into a goblet over Hoshizaki ice and stir. Garnish with lemon wheel and add in straw.

*Shared by Kinsey Whitehill from Lady Jane in Denver, CO*

# Petit Poids

1½ oz. Rhubarb Cordial*
1 oz. Light Snap Peas Syrup**
2 oz. NA Sparkling Wine

Build drink in wine glass over large ice cube. Top with sparkling wine.

Shared by Nathalie Durrieu, Head Bartender at Experimental Cocktail Club in New York City, NY
***Rhubarb Cordial***
4 Cups of Rhubarb Puree
4.25 Cups Water
1⅓ tbsp. 3% Pectinex Ultra SP-L
3 tbsp. Syrup
1 tbsp. Malic Acid
1 tsp. Tartaric Acid
2 tsp. Salt
Combine rhubarb puree and water, then add in Pectinex, to a 100 micron Superbag. Add syrup, malic acid, tartaric acid, and salt.
****Light Snap Peas Syrup***
4.25 Cups Water
2.5 Cups Sugar
3 Cups Snap Peas
Open snap peas up to just use the peas. Combine all ingredients in a saucepan on medium heat. When the mixture starts to simmer, remove from heat. Infuse overnight in the refrigerator. Strain through cheesecloth.

# Pineapple-Banana Frappé

1½ oz. Orange Juice
1 oz. Pineapple Juice
1 oz. Lemon Juice
1 oz. Banana Gum Syrup (infuse banana slices with gum syrup for 24 hours)
½ oz. Egg Whites

Add all ingredients into a cocktail shaker and dry shake. Add ice and shake again. Fine strain into an etched coupe and serve.

Shared by Stuart Weaver from Lady Jane in Denver, CO

# Pineapple No-Groni

1 oz. AMASS Riverine
1 oz. Giffard Aperitif Sirop
¾ oz. Martini & Rossi Vibrante L'Aperitivo
¼ oz. Pineapple Gum Syrup (infuse pineapples slices with gum syrup for 24 hours)
Orange Peel

Add all ingredients into a mixing glass with ice. Stir and strain over a large cube in a rocks glass.

Shared by Stuart Weaver from Lady Jane in Denver, CO

## The Pinery

2 oz. Pineapple Juice
1 oz. Lime Juice
0.75 oz. Agave Syrup
2 tbsp. Chili Salt*
Lime Wedge

Take a lime wedge and move it along half of the rim of a coupe glass then apply it into the chili salt. Measure all the remaining ingredients with a jigger and add to a cocktail shaker. Fill the cocktail shaker with ice cubes and shake for about 20 seconds or until the outside of the shaker is frosty. Strain the cocktail into the rimmed glass and serve.

*Shared by Franz Karl Lagajino at The Pineapple Room in Singapore*
**\*Chili Salt**
*½ cup of Coarse Salt*
*½ cup of Chili Powder*
In a small bowl, combine coarse salt and chili powder. You can adjust the ratio based on your spice preference; for a milder flavor, use more salt than chili powder.

## Rose Marie

1 Muddled Rosemary spring
1 oz. Lemon Juice
¾ oz. Cinnamon Simple Syrup
¼ oz. N/A Giffard Aperitif
Tonic Water
Smoked Rosemary Sprig

Shake and strain all ingredients (except tonic water and rosemary sprig) into a Prosecco glass with ice. Top with tonic water and garnish with the rosemary sprig.

*Shared by Michael Hopper, Bar Manager at Atria in Flagstaff, AZ*

## Scarlet Americano

1.7 oz. Martini Vibrante
1 oz. NA Amaro*
2.4 oz. Cherry Soda
Orange Slice

Pour Martini Vibrante and the amaro into a Collins glass. Add ice and top with cherry soda. Garnish with the orange slice.

*Shared by Nora Koufou, Head Bartender at Line Athens in Athens, Greece*
**\*NA Amaro**
*3.75 cups Vanilla, Caramel, Pomegranate, and Berries Tea\*\**
*2 Cups Monin Bitter*
*1 tsp. Citric Acid*
*¼ tsp. Salt*
*Blend all ingredients and give them a good stir until the solids dissolve.*

**PART 3 Sip & Savor: Non-Alcoholic Drink Recipes**

**\*\*Vanilla, Caramel, Pomegranate & Berries Tea**
4.25 cups Boiling Water
8 bags of Lipton Vanilla & Caramel Tea Mix
8 bags of Lipton Pomegranate & Berries Tea Mix
Heat water until 203 degrees F and pour into a container with the tea. Brew for 10 minutes. Strain tea through a coffee filter. Tip: Changing the tea flavors can give your drink a whole new personality. Have fun with it!

## Shaken and Stoned

1½ oz. Ish Gin
½ oz. Stone Fruit Shrub
½ oz. Orange Juice
½ oz. Lyre's Orange Sec
¾ oz. Mediterranean Tonic
Orange Twist

Shake all ingredients (except the tonic and orange twist), strain into a coupe glass, and top with tonic. Garnish with the orange twist.

*Shared by Conrad C. Helms IV, Beverage Director of Lazy Betty in Atlanta, GA*

## Shanghai Buck

3 oz. Dragon Eye Oolong Tea (brewed)
2 oz. Pomegranate Juice
1 oz. Ginger Beer
3 Cranberries
Rosemary Sprig

Add tea, juice, and ginger beer in a mule mug and stir. Garnish with cranberries and rosemary sprig.

*Shared by Charles Hardwick, Portfolio Mixologist at Moet Hennessy*

## Shrimp Michelada

½ oz. Hot Sauce
¾ oz. Lime Juice
2 oz. Shrimp Consommé\*
12 oz. Atlética N/A Mexican Style Beer
3 cooked shrimp

Add the hot sauce, lime juice, and consommé into the beer glass and stir. Add beer. Garnish with the shrimp on top.

*Shared by Alex Valencia, Co-Owner and Bartender at Vallarta Tropical in New York City, NY*
**\*Shrimp Consommé**
2 cups Clamato
1 pinch Salt
1 pinch Black Pepper
1 pinch Celery Salt
1 oz. Dried Shrimp
1 oz. Dusted Dried Shrimp
Combine the Clamato, salt, black pepper, and celery salt into a medium pot and mix. Add the dried shrimp and dusted dried shrimp. Reduce over medium heat and gently simmer for 15–20 minutes allowing the flavors to combine. Then, let it cool to get ready to serve,

## Snap Pea Sour

1½ oz. Seedlip Garden 108
1 oz. Snap Pea Syrup (snap pea infused simple syrup)
1 oz. Lime Juice
¼ oz. Simple Syrup
1 tsp. Ginger Syrup
8–10 Mint Leaves
Lemon Peel

Add all ingredients (except lemon peel) into a cocktail shaker with ice and shake. Fine strain into a coupe glass and garnish with the lemon peel.

*Shared by Stuart Weaver from Lady Jane in Denver, CO*

## Snow Globe Spritz

1½ oz. Bittersweet Aperitivo
½ oz. Lime Juice
¾ oz. Orange Juice
¾ oz. Simple Syrup
2½ oz. Ginger Beer
Fresh Mint
1 tsp. Powdered Sugar

Add all ingredients to a shaking tin (except for ginger beer, mint bouquet, and powdered sugar). Add ice and shake for 10 seconds. Open the tin and add ginger beer directly to the tin. Strain into a glass over crushed ice. Finish with more ice to fill the glass and create a nice mound. Garnish with the fresh mint bouquet and powdered sugar.

*Shared by Nora Furst of West Bev Consulting*

## Sowing Seeds

1 oz. Seedlip Garden 108
1 oz. Cucumber Juice
1 oz. Ginger Syrup
¼ oz. Lemon Juice
Edible Viola Flower

Add all ingredients (except for edible viola) into a shaker and fill ¾ full with ice. Shake for 10 seconds. Using a Hawthorne strainer and mesh strainer, double strain into a coupe glass. Garnish with flower and serve.

*Shared by Alexa Delgado, Director of Bars at The Miami Beach EDITION in Miami Beach, Florida*

## Spicy Spritz

1 oz. Seedlip Grove 46
½ oz. Lyre's Italian Spritz
1 oz. Spicy Agave
Club Soda
2 slices Jalapeno
Orange Wheel

Add Seedlip, Lyre's, and agave into a shaker with ice and shake. Double strain into a white wine glass with ice. Top with club soda and garnish with the orange wheel. Serve.

*Shared by Gio Olivera of Sirenetta in Hoboken, NJ*

## Squeeze the Day

1½ oz. Seedlip Grove
1 oz. Orange Juice
¾ oz. Yuzu Puree
½ oz. Ginger Syrup
Club Soda
1 Dehydrated Blood Orange wheel
Mint Sprig

Combine all ingredients (except for club soda, blood orange, and mint) into a mixing shaker tin. Add ice, cap tin, and shake well. Uncap tin and pour mocktail into a highball glass. Top with club soda to fill and garnish with the dehydrated blood orange and mint sprig.

*Shared by Inga Tantisalidchai*

## Summer Spritz

1 oz. Martini & Rossi Floreale NA Aperitivo
½ oz. 1883 Peach Syrup
¾ oz. Verjus Blanc
1½ oz. Soda Water
1½ oz. TÖST Rosé Sparkling Tea
Half-moon of Grapefruit
Bundle of Mint

Combine Floreale, peach syrup, and Verjus blanc in a large wine glass or goblet. Add ice until full. Add TÖST Rosé and soda water over ice, stirring to settle and combine ingredients. Garnish with the grapefruit half-moon and bundle of mint.

*Shared by Tom Martinez*

## Sweet Heat

2 oz. Three Spirit Livener
½ oz. Strawberry Syrup
½ oz. Lime Juice
½ oz. Ginger Juice
Soda Water
Pinch Candied Ginger
Pinch Dried Strawberry

Add all ingredients into a cocktail shaker with ice and shake. Strain into a highball glass with ice and top with soda water. Garnish with candied ginger and dried strawberry.

*Shared by Kristine Abrams-Petersman from The Nixer NA Pop-Up Bar in Phoenix, AZ*

CHAPTER 12 **Non-Alcoholic Drinks from Top Bartenders** 173

## Talk to Her

2 oz. Red Verjus
1½ oz. Seedlip Spice 94
¾ oz. Pineapple Juice
½ oz. Cinnamon Syrup
Pineapple Leaf
2 Red Grapes

Add all the ingredients (besides pineapple leaf and grapes) to a rocks glass filled with ice. Give it a quick stir, garnish with the grapes and pineapple leaf, and serve.

Shared by Lynnette Marrero, Co-Founder of the Speed-Rack competition and Co-Author of A Quick Drink: The Speed Rack Guide to Winning Cocktails for Any Mood (Harry N. Abrams)

## Tangerine 75

1½ oz. Lyre's London Spirit
¾ oz. Lemon Juice
¾ oz. Tangerine Syrup*
1½ oz. Prima Pave Blanc de Blanc
Lemon Twist

Add sparkling wine to champagne flute. Add all other ingredients (except for lemon twist) to shaker tin and add ice. Shake hard and fine-strain into the champagne flute. Garnish with the lemon twist.

Shared by Chris Cardone, Founder of Continuous Beverage Solutions in New York City, NY
***Tangerine Syrup**
1 cup Fresh Tangerine Juice
1 cup White Sugar
Add tangerine juice and sugar to a pot and heat over medium heat until all sugar dissolves. Allow to cool for 15 minutes and store in the refrigerator for up to 2 weeks.

## Tea & Crumpets

½ oz. Pumpkin Spice Demerara
1 oz. Cereal Milk (milk infused with cereal)
2 oz. Coconut Black Tea (brewed)
Banana Foam

Add all ingredients (except banana foam) into a mixing glass with ice and stir. Strain into a rocks glass with ice and top with the banana foam.

Shared by Wilson Oliver of Ava's Kitchen & Bar in Kenilworth, NJ

## The Tide Is High

1½ oz. Grapefruit Juice
¾ oz. Lemon Juice
½ oz. Cinnamon Syrup
¼ oz. Giffard Aperitivo
1½ oz. Ginger Beer
Mint Bouquet
1 Dehydrated Lemon wheel

Pour ginger beer into a snifter glass. Combine remaining ingredients (except mint bouquet and dehydrated lemon) into a shaker with ice. Shake and strain over the ginger beer. Garnish with the mint bouquet and dehydrated lemon.

Shared by Neal Bodenheimer at Cure in New Orleans, LA

**PART 3 Sip & Savor: Non-Alcoholic Drink Recipes**

## TLC

1 oz. Almave Reposado NA
½ oz. Spiced Honey Syrup
1½ oz. Carrot and Blood
Orange Shrub
Fever-Tree Tonic Water
Orange Slice

Build in a highball glass and garnish with the slice of orange.

*Shared by Aidan Bowie, Beverage Director at The Dead Rabbit in New York City, NY*

## Tropic Thunder

2 oz. Seedlip Garden
¾ oz. Passion Fruit Juice
¾ oz. Blackberry Syrup
½ oz. Lemon Juice
1 oz. Club Soda
3 Mint Leaves
Mint Sprig

Clap the mint leaves in between your hands, and then add them into a cocktail shaker. Then, add all ingredients except club soda and mint sprig into the shaker tin with ice. Pour the club soda directly in the tin and double strain the mixture into a slim Collins glass. Garnish with the mint sprig.

*Shared by Marcio Ramos, Partner at The Honey Well and Bartender at Sip&Guzzle in New York City, NY*

## Winter Spritz

1½ oz. Citrus Aperitivo
¾ oz. 100% Cranberry Juice
¼ oz. Meyer Lemon Syrup (or ¼ oz. Simple Syrup and ¼ oz. Lemon Juice)
3 oz. NA Sparkling Wine
2-3 Kumquats
Rosemary Sprig

Add all ingredients to the flute (except wine, kumquats, and rosemary) with 1–2 ice cubes. Stir three times to integrate. Top with sparkling wine. Garnish with rosemary sprig and kumquats on a toothpick.

*Shared by Nora Furst of West Bev Consulting*

## Winter White Cosmo

2 oz. Seedlip Grove
½ oz. Lime Juice
¾ oz. White Cranberry Juice
¼ oz. NA Orange Liqueur
Lime Coin

Pour all ingredients (except lime coin) into a cocktail shaker filled with ice. Shake until thoroughly chilled. Strain into a pre-chilled martini glass. Finish by garnishing with the lime coin.

*Shared by Adrienne Smith*

CHAPTER 12  **Non-Alcoholic Drinks from Top Bartenders**   175

## Wuyi

2 oz. Martini and Rossi Vibrante
1 oz. Pineapple Juice
1 oz. Lapsang Souchong Syrup
2 dashes Fee Foam Bitters
1 dash Angostura Bitters
2 Crushed Lapsang Souchong Tea Leaves

Combine all ingredients (except crushed leaves) into a shaker with ice and hard shake until chilled and diluted. Fine strain into a coupe glass and garnish with the crushed tea leaves in the middle of the cocktail.

*Shared by Ray Tremblay, Director of Beverage at COJE Management Group in Boston, MA*

## Zero Paloma

2 oz. Ritual Zero Proof Tequila
1 oz. Fresh Lime Juice
¾ oz. Fresh Grapefruit Juice
Grapefruit Soda
Lime Wheel or Grapefruit Wheel

Combine all ingredients (besides fruit wheel) into your shaker and shake. Strain into a rocks glass with ice and top with grapefruit soda. Garnish with the lime or grapefruit wheel.

*Shared by Alex Valencia, Co-Owner and Bartender at Vallarta Tropical in New York City, NY*

IN THIS CHAPTER

» Making a bucket list of drinks to try

» Finding inspiration for your own NA creations

Chapter **13**

# Non-Alcoholic Drinks from Bars around the World

Creating a menu doesn't come easy, and you have so many things to consider when coming up with the perfect options. Some of the drink recipes in this chapter have gone through multiple rounds of judging and tweaking before even coming close to the bar/restaurant's official menu. Therefore, cocktails that make the menus always count as a big win for the drink creators. This chapter includes some incredibly special non-alcoholic cocktails featured at some of the best bars and restaurants around the globe.

In addition to making these drinks yourself, consider referring to this chapter if you travel so that you can go check these drinks out at the source.

Stay up to date with more recipes featured in *BARTENDER Magazine* at www.bartender.com.

## Almos Healthy

1½ oz. Almave Blanco
½ oz. Hibiscus Syrup
4 oz. Ginger Beer
Rosemary Sprig
Edible Flower

In a highball glass without ice, add the Almave Blanco and hibiscus syrup. Add ice to the glass and stir with a spoon. Top with ginger beer and garnish with a sprig of rosemary and an edible flower.

*Shared by Chef Richard Sandoval of Richard Sandoval Hospitality*

## Butterfly Kisses

1 oz. Passion Fruit Syrup
¾ oz. Lime Juice
½ oz. Simple Syrup
Dash of Black Pepper
1 tsp. Tajin
Lime Wedge

Combine passion fruit syrup, lime juice, simple syrup and black pepper in shaker over ice and shake. Pour into Collins glass and top with club soda. Sprinkle Tajin over the ice. Garnish with lime wedge.

*Shared by Paul Kermizian from Barcade*

## Cardi C

3 oz. Red Grapes & Cardamom Shrub*
3 oz. Ginger Beer
¾ oz. Lemon Juice
2 Blueberries

Add all ingredients (except ice and blueberries) in a shaker and give a small shake. Fine strain into a highball glass with ice. Garnish with the blueberries.

*Shared by Hero Bar in Nairobi, Kenya*
**\*Red Grapes & Cardamom Shrub:**
2.2 pounds Red Grapes
3 ounces Brown Sugar
1.75 oz. Apple Cider Vinegar
Smash grapes in a large container and add in brown sugar and apple cider vinegar. Stir and cover for 7 days leaving it in a dry area. Strain using a fine mesh strainer into bottles and use as needed.

## Chica & Tonic

1 oz. Chicha Morada
1 oz. Elderflower Tonic
½ oz. Agave
1 Edible Flower

Pour chicha morada, elderflower tonic, and agave into a shaker with ice. Shake well and pour over fresh ice into a tall glass. Garnish with an edible flower.

*Shared by Toro Toro in Miami, FL*

## Chichamorada

70 oz. Water
1¼ cup of Dried Purple Corn
2 Cinnamon Sticks
3 Whole Cloves
1 Whole Pineapple
¾ cup Sugar
2 oz. Lime Juice
Green Apple

To make the chicha, peel the pineapple and apple. Add the peels to a large pot with the water, corn, cinnamon, cloves, and sugar. Bring to a boil, then reduce the heat to low and simmer for 45 minutes. Strain and allow to cool completely.

Cut a wedge from the pineapple and set aside for garnish. Juice the pineapple and apple, then refrigerate the juice. Combine the pineapple, apple, and lime juices with the chicha. Garnish with the pineapple wedge.

*Shared by Abricot Bar in Paris, France*

## Chismosa

1 oz. Guava Purée
½ oz. Lime Juice
½ oz. Agave Syrup
2 dashes Peychaud's Bitters
1 oz. Ginger Ale

In a shaker, combine all ingredients (except ginger ale). Shake well and pour over fresh ice. Top with Ginger Ale.

*Shared by Toro Toro in Miami, FL*

## Citron Crush

1½ oz. Ghia Aperitif
1½ oz. Lemon Juice
1 oz. Raspberry Syrup
Orange Wheel
Lemon Wheel
Mint Bouquet

Add aperitif, lemon juice, and raspberry syrup to a shaker. Shake, and strain into a rocks glass with crushed ice. Garnish with mint bouquet, and lemon and orange wheels.

*Shared by Patrick Jobst, Beverage Director at Le Suprême in Michigan, Detroit*

CHAPTER 13  **Non-Alcoholic Drinks from Bars around the World**   179

## Cold Brew Martini

1½ oz. Pathfinder Hemp & Root
1 oz. Cold Brew Coffee
½ oz. Kokuto Syrup*
Garnisha light dusting of
Matcha Powder

Combine all ingredients (except matcha powder) in shaker and shake. Strain into a coupe glass and top with the matcha powder as a garnish.

*Featured at Sip & Guzzle in New York City, NY*
**\*Kokuto Syrup:**
1 cup Kokuto Sugar
1 cup Water
Combine sugar and water in a pan and bring to a boil. Reduce heat and simmer until all the sugar is dissolved.

## Cucumber Basil Bliss

1½ oz. Seedlip Grove 46 NA Spirit
1 oz. Lemon Juice
½ oz. Pineapple Juice
1 oz. Simple Syrup
2 Cucumber Slices
2 Basil Leaves
Top with Ginger Beer
Cucumber Ribbon

Combine all ingredients (except ice, ginger beer, and cucumber ribbon) in a shaker and shake. Double strain over crushed ice in a Collins glass. Top with ginger beer and garnish with a cucumber ribbon.

*Featured at Backstage in Hoboken, NJ*

## Cucumber Cooler

3 oz. Fresh Cucumber Juice
1½ oz. Lemon or Lime Juice (depending on your preference)
1 oz. Simple Syrup
2 oz. Soda Water
Cucumber Slice

In a shaker, add all ingredients (except soda water). Shake until ingredients are mixed. Pour into a Collins glass over ice. Top with soda water and garnish with cucumber slice

*Shared by Aaron Mattis-Robinson, Bartender at Sunken Harbor Club Bermuda in Cambridge Beaches, Bermuda*

## Cucumber Mule

½ oz. Cucumber Shrub
¾ oz. Lime Juice
¾ oz. Simple Syrup
Top with Ginger Beer
Cucumber Wheel

Combine cucumber shrub soda, lime juice, and simple syrup in a shaker with ice and shake. Strain into a Collins glass and fill with ice. Top with ginger beer and garnish with a cucumber wheel.

*Shared by Costera in New Orleans, LA*

## Dear Prudence

¾ oz. Mint Simple Syrup
¾ oz. Lime Juice
½ oz. Roland's Cherry Juice
Top with Tonic Water
Mint Leaf
Amarena Cherry

In a shaker, combine cherry juice, simple syrup, and lime juice over ice. Shake and strain into a Collins glass. Add tonic water and ice; garnish with mint leaf and Amarena cherry.

*Shared by Paul Kermizian from Barcade*

## Disco Dust

1½ oz. Seedlip Garden 108 NA Spirit
2½ oz. Disco Mix*
¾ oz. Lemon Juice
1 Glittered Dehydrated Dragon Fruit

Add all ingredients into a shaker with ice and shake. Add crushed ice into a highball or zombie style glass and strain in mixture. Garnish with dragon fruit and serve.

*Shared by Nickel City in Austin, TX*
***Disco Mix:***
1 cup of Freeze-Dried Strawberry
8 oz. Coconut Milk
2 oz. Mango Juice
2 oz. Guava Juice
9 oz. Passion Tea Extract
12 oz. Sugar
1 tsp. Purple Shimmer (edible glitter)
*Immersion blend all ingredients until smooth. Pour into a food safe bucket and store in the fridge for up to 30 days*

## Don't Be Suspicious

1 oz. Pineapple Juice
½ oz. Lemon Juice
1 oz. Orange Juice
½ oz. Grenadine
2 oz. Ginger Ale
Pineapple Wedge

Add all ingredients (except pineapple wedge) into a highball glass and stir. Garnish with the pineapple wedge and serve.

*Shared by Corsair Kitchen & Bar in Miami, FL*

## Electric Bicycle

1½ oz. Seedlip Garden 108 NA Spirit
1 oz. Grapefruit juice
1 oz. Pomegranate juice
½ oz. Giffard Orgeat Syrup
2-3 oz. Seltzer Water
Mint Leaf

Combine all ingredients (except seltzer and mint leaf), in a shaker tin. Shake hard for 10-15 seconds or until cold. Strain the cocktail into a Collins glass and top with seltzer. Fill the glass with ice and garnish with the mint leaf.

*Shared by Zac Snyder, Creative Lead of Beverage Services at MOLLIE Aspen in Aspen, CO*

## Eliza's Hymns

2 oz. Makrut Lime Infused NA London Dry Gin
¼ oz. NA Aperol Syrup
¼ oz. NA Heirloom Alchermes Syrup
⅓ oz. Spiced Pineapple Cordial
½ oz. Ginger Syrup
¾ oz. Watermelon Real Puree
2 oz. Red Mango Tea Concentrate
½ oz. Yuzu juice
1½ oz. Lemon Juice
0.13 oz. Red Beet Syrup
Guava Yuzu Daisy Dogger
Piece of Lavender-Scented Shortbread

Combine ingredients together and clarify with whole milk. Force carbonate and serve in a Collins glass over a custom cut ice sphere. Garnish with Guava Yuzu Daisy Dogger and shortbread.

*Shared by Century Grand — Platform 18 "Queens of New York" Menu in Phoenix, AZ*

# First Aid

3 oz. Turmeric Rosemary Oleo*
⅔ oz. Lime Juice
3 oz. Soda Water
Fresh Mint Sprig

Add Tumeric Rosemary Oleo and lime over ice in a highball glass and stir. Top with soda water and garnish with mint sprig.

*Shared by Hero Bar in Nairobi, Kenya*
**\*Turmeric Rosemary Oleo:**
2 cups Lemon Peels
¾ cup White Sugar
2 tbsp. Fresh Rosemary (about 3-4 sprigs)
1 tbsp. Fresh Turmeric
Peel the lemons using a peeler, avoiding the white pith. Combine the lemon peels and sugar in a mixing bowl. Use your hands to massage the sugar into the peels. This helps draw out the oils. Add the rosemary and turmeric. Stir to coat everything in sugar. Cover and let sit at room temperature for at least 6-12 hours, or overnight. Stir occasionally to help the sugar dissolve. Once a syrupy consistency has formed, strain out the solids, pressing gently to extract as much liquid as possible. Store in a clean bottle or jar in the fridge for up to two weeks.

# Fizzy Bubblech

4 oz. Strawberry Vanilla Tea
⅔ oz. Blueberry Syrup
1 oz. White Vinegar
3 oz. Soda Water
Cinnamon Stick
Raspberry
Blueberry

Add all ingredients (except ice, raspberry, and blueberry) into a shaker and shake. Fine strain in a highball glass with ice and top with soda water. Garnish with the berries.

*Shared by Hero Bar in Nairobi, Kenya*

# Garden of Eden

1 oz. Seedlip Garden 108 NA Spirit
¾ oz. Lemon Juice
½ oz. Real Lychee Syrup
¼ oz. Simple Syrup
¾ oz. Water
2 oz. Ginger Beer
Cucumber Ribbon
Lemon Wheel
Thyme Sprig
2 Edible Flowers

Place cucumber ribbon and lemon wheel along the sides of the glass, and fill with pebble ice to hold it in place. Combine Seedlip Garden 108, lemon juice, Real lychee syrup, simple syrup, and water in a shaker. Shake and strain into highball glass over pebble ice. Top with ginger beer; add thyme sprig and edible flowers to garnish.

*Shared by Heather Blanchard of The Pool Club at Virgin Hotel in New Orleans, LA*

## Garden Party

2 oz. Seedlip Grove 42 NA Spirit
½ oz. Lemon Juice
½ oz. Simple Syrup
2 oz. Club Soda
Basil Sprig
2 Mint Sprigs

In a mixing glass, combine the Seedlip Grove 42, lemon juice, simple syrup, basil sprig, and 1 mint sprig; muddle together. Strain the mixture into a Collins glass filled with ice. Top with club soda and garnish with remaining sprig of mint.

*Shared by The Americano in Atlanta, GA*

## Ghia Flora

1½ oz. Ghia Aperitif
¾ oz. Giffard NA Elderflower Liqueur
½ oz. Lime Juice
Top with Club Soda
Lemon Wheel
Lime Wheel

Pour all ingredients (except lemon and lime wheels in a wine glass and stir. Garnish with lemon and lime wheels.

*Shared by Gordon Kelley, Beverage Director at Il Premio in Atlanta, GA*

## Giiirl Dinner

1½ oz. Pathfinder Amaro Liqueur
1¼ oz. Hot Girl Cordial*
¾ oz. Lemon Juice
2 Castelvetrano Olives

Add all ingredients (except olives) into a cocktail shaker with ice and shake. Strain into a Collins glass and top with pebble ice. Skewer olives on a toothpick and use as garnish.

*Shared by Kayla LeRoy and Alex Chien from Cobra Bar in Columbus, OH*
**\*Hot Girl Cordial**
**Coconut Watermelon Cordial:**
1 cup of Sugar
1 cup of Coconut Milk
1.5 cups of Cubed Watermelon
Blend all ingredients on high in blender for 3 minutes, and then strain into a food safe container to use for your cocktail.
**Watermelon Shrub:**
1.5 cups of Cubed Watermelon
⅓ cup of White Verjus
⅓ cup of Champagne Vinegar
½ cup Sugar
Macerate the watermelon in the verjus and vinegar for 48 hours. Blend with sugar in a blender and strain into a food safe container to use for your cocktail

## Golden Child

1½ oz. Lyre's Italian Orange NA Spirit
1 oz. Honey Golden Blend*
½ oz. Lemon Juice
1 tsp. Sugar
1 tsp. Black Pepper

Shake the spirit, blend, and lemon juice in a shaker with 1 cup of ice. Rim a rocks glass with sugar and black pepper. Strain drink into the rocks glass and serve.

*Shared by Kimberly Patton-Bragg of Palm & Pine in New Orleans, LA*
**\*Honey Golden Blend:**
⅔ cup Honey
⅓ cup Water
2 tbsp. Golden Milk Mix
Blend all ingredients in a heat-safe blender or with an immersion blender until fully combined and smooth.

## Green Tea Sensation

2 oz. Seedlip Garden 108 NA Spirit
1 oz. Shiso Green Tea Syrup
½ oz. Lime Juice
1 oz. Cucumber Juice
3 dashes NA Chili Bitters
2 oz. Ginger Beer
Shiso Leaf

Add all ingredients (except shiso leaf and ginger beer) in a shaker and shake for 10 seconds. Pour into a teapot. Pour from the teapot into a rocks glass when serving and top with ginger beer and shiso leaf.

*Shared by Dusk at the Ritz-Carlton in Naples, FL*

## Joker Juice

1⅔ oz. Strawberry Juice
1⅔ oz. Raspberry Juice
⅔ oz. Lime Juice
5 oz. Orange Juice
1 oz. Rosemary Syrup
4 Mint Leaves
1 Mint Sprig
1 Dehydrated Orange

Add all ingredients (except ice, mint sprig, and dehydrated orange) in a shaker and shake. Fine strain into a pint glass with ice and garnish with the mint sprig and dehydrated orange.

*Shared by Hero Bar in Nairobi, Kenya*

CHAPTER 13  Non-Alcoholic Drinks from Bars around the World

## Lost in the Fog

1 dash Orange Blossom Water
¼ oz. Orange Juice
¾ oz. Vanilla Spice Syrup*
2½ oz. Earl Grey Tea
Orange Peel

In a chilled stirring vessel, add all ingredients and stir for 20–25 seconds. Strain into a rocks glass filled with ice. Take the orange peel and gentley twist to express the oils over the top of the cocktail, rub the peel around the rim of the glass, and then drop it into the drink along the side of the glass.

*Shared by Courtney Coffee at Good Word Brewing & Public House in Duluth, GA*
***Vanilla Spice Syrup:***
*2 cups of Water*
*2 cups of Sugar*
*2 Vanilla Bean Pods*
*1 tbsp. Black Cardamom*
*½ tsp. Ground Cloves*
*1 tsp. Allspice*
*Combine the water and sugar in a saucepan over medium heat. Stir until the sugar is fully dissolved. Add the vanilla bean pods, black cardamom, cloves, and allspice. Bring to a gentle simmer and let it infuse for 15–20 minutes, stirring occasionally. Avoid boiling. Remove from heat and let cool slightly. Strain out the solids using a fine mesh strainer or cheesecloth. Transfer the syrup to a clean bottle or jar. Store in the refrigerator for up to 2 weeks.*

## The Mad Hatter

1⅓ oz. Rooibos Banana Spiced Tea
2 oz. Raspberry Puree
1 oz. Passion Fruit Pulp
3 oz. Lemon-Lime Soda
1 oz. Honey
5 Mint leaves
Strip of Rooibos Tea (form tea into a strip as a garnish)

Add all ingredients (besides ice and tea strip) in a shaker and shake. Fine strain into a rocks glass with ice and garnish with the strip of tea.

*Shared by Hero Bar in Nairobi, Kenya*

# Nemesis

1 oz. Palette Roots NA Spirit
1 oz. Lime Juice
1 oz. Passion Fruit & Ginger Cordial*
Top with Peach Jasmine Soda
Pineapple Sage Leaf (*a fragrant herb with pineapple-mint aroma*)

Add all ingredients (except soda and pineapple sage leaf) into a mixing glass and stir for 10 seconds. Strain into an old fashioned glass with a large ice cube. Top with peach jasmine soda and garnish with the pineapple sage leaf.

*Shared by Le Bar Aristide in Paris, France*
***Passion Fruit & Ginger Cordial:***
½ cup Passion Fruit Pulp
½ cup Sugar
½ cup Water
1 inch Fresh Ginger, sliced
Simmer all ingredients together for 10 minutes, let cool, strain, and store in the fridge for up to 1 week.

# No-Maro Swizzle

2 oz. Lucano NA Amaro
1 oz. Fresh Lime Juice
¾ oz. Fresh Pineapple Juice
¼ oz. Turbinado Syrup*
½ oz. Lime Oleo**
Pinch of Mint Leaves
Mint Sprig

Add mint leaves to a pint glass, then add all other ingredients (except ice and mint sprig) on top. Fill glass with crushed ice and swizzle until very cold. Top with some more crushed ice, add a straw, and garnish with the mint sprig.

*Shared by Harry Wright, General Manager at Service Bar in Washington, D.C.*
***Turbinado Syrup:***
3.75 cups of Turbinado or Demerara Sugar
2 cups Water
Bring water to a boil. Add in sugar and stir until sugar is well dissolved.
****Lime Oleo:***
Lime
1 qt. Simple Syrup
Use a microplane to zest a lime. Combine about 2 tbsp. of lime zest with ½ cup simple syrup in a sealed jar or container. Store in the fridge for 1–2 days to infuse. Remove from the fridge and strain into a clean bottle or small jar for storage or immediate use.

CHAPTER 13  Non-Alcoholic Drinks from Bars around the World

## The Outfit

15 oz. Verjus
1¾ cups Sugar
5 cups of Water
2 tsp. Crushed Coriander
1 tbsp. Lime Peel
2 tbsp. Orange Peel
½ cup Rose Petals
Drop of Orange Blossom

Add all ingredients into a vacuum-sealed or sous-vide-safe bag. Sous vide at 140 degrees F for 2 hours. Strain into a PET bottle, carbonate, and chill. This recipe makes around 2 quarts.

*Shared by The Savile Row Team from Fortitude Valley, QLD, Australia*

## The Passion

Passion Fruit Half
⅗ oz. Fresh Lime Juice
⅓ oz. Monin Passion Fruit Syrup
3⅓ oz. Fever-Tree Ginger Beer
½ tbsp. of Black Pepper

Add the passion fruit half, fresh passion fruit juice, and lime into a shaker, and shake until combined. Pour into a chilled mule mug filled with ice. Top with ginger beer and a few shakes of freshly ground pepper; stir. Top with another shake of pepper and serve.

*Shared by Zaccaria Medda, Bartender at THE PLACE Firenze in Florence, Italy*

## The Phoenix Fizz

1 oz. NONA NA Gin
1 oz. NONA NA Bitters
½ oz. NONA NA Amaro
⅓ oz. Orange and Olive Syrup*
⅓ oz. Faux Citrus
Egg White
Top with Soda Water
½ Brûléed Orange Wheel (add sugar on top of the orange wheel and use a torch to brûlée)

Add all ingredients (except ice, soda water, and orange wheel) into a shaker and dry shake. Add ice and shake again. Double strain into a highball glass and top with soda water. Garnish with the brûléed orange wheel and serve.

*Shared by Raven Room in Whistler, BC, Canada*
***Orange and Olive Syrup:***
*1 cup fresh orange juice*
*½ cup sugar*
*Zest of 1 orange*
*6–8 pitted green olives*
*Combine the orange juice, sugar, and orange zest in a small saucepan over medium heat. Stir until the sugar dissolves completely. Add the olives then reduce the heat and simmer gently for 10–15 minutes.*

# Pomeriggio Té

2½ oz. Lemongrass Bergamot Tea*
½ oz. Lime Juice
1 oz. Clove Simple Syrup**
¼ oz. Agave Nectar
Clove Rimmer***

Dip a pastry brush in a plate of agave nectar and brush a stripe on the side of your coupe starting at the lip and brushing down. Rim the agave strip with the clove rimmer. Combine lemongrass bergamot tea, lime juice, and clove simple syrup into a cocktail shaker filled with ice. Shake 5–7 times. Double strain into the prepared coupe glass.

*Shared by Serena Pastificio in Atlanta, GA and Boco Raton, FL*
***Lemongrass Bergamot Tea:***
7 oz. Water
Lemongrass Bergamot Tea Bag
Boil water in a kettle on the stove. When water begins to boil, remove from heat and pour into a mug or measuring cup over lemongrass bergamot tea bag. Let steep for 2 minutes, then remove tea bag. Allow to cool.
****Clove Simple Syrup:***
3 tbsp. Whole Cloves
4 cups Water
4 cups Sugar
Using a mortar and pestle, slightly muddle cloves. Add cloves and water to a sauce pan and bring to boil. Remove from heat and cover, letting steep for 20 minutes. Strain with a mesh strainer into mixing bowl or large container, then add sugar and whisk to dissolve.
*****Clove Rimmer:***
1 cup Ground Cloves
½ cup Granulated Suga
¼ cup Ground Cinnamon
Add all ingredients to a bowl and mix to combine.

# Pornstar Mojito

1½ oz. A Cut Above Agave Blanco NA Tequila
¾ oz. Passion Fruit Puree
¾ oz. Lime Juice
¾ oz. Vanilla Syrup
1 pint Mint Leaves
Top with Pima Pavé NA Sparkling Wine

Add all ingredients (except sparkling wine) in a Collins glass. Swizzle briefly and top off with sparkling wine.

*Featured at Sip & Guzzle in New York City, NY*

## Posion De Amor

2 oz. Coconut Cream
1 oz. Mango Purée
1 oz. Simple Syrup
Top with Sparkling Water
3 Pineapple Leaves
3 Blueberries

Add all ingredients (except pineapple leaves and blueberries) in a shaker. Shake and serve in a highball glass with the same ice. Garnish with pineapple leaves and blueberries.

*Shared by Chef Richard Sandoval of Richard Sandoval Hospitality*

## Puppy Pose

7 oz. Lemon Juice
5 oz. Wheatgrass Syrup*
7 oz. Seedlip Garden NA Spirit
3.5 oz. Wilderton Lustre NA Spirit
7 oz. Vanilla Probiotic Yogurt
Large Ice Cube
Grapefruit Peel

Mix all ingredients (except for yogurt, ice, and grapefruit peel) in a food safe bucket until fully incorporated. Pour into yogurt into the mix and let stand for 1 hour. Strain through a coffee filter and restrain the first initial drops that come through for full clarity. Pour into a mixing glass and fill the glass with ice. Stir for about 20 seconds and strain the cocktail into a rocks glass over a large ice cube. Express a grapefruit peel by twisting the peel releasing its oils.

*Featured at Trick Dog in San Francisco, CA*
***Wheatgrass Syrup:***
1 cup Wheatgrass
4½ cups Filtered Water
3.5–4 Cups White Sugar
*Blend wheatgrass in water for 30 seconds. Strain out the wheatgrass through a fine-mesh strainer into a food-safe bucket. Add in sugar and mix until fully incorporated.*

## S&S

2 oz. Pineapple Juice
1½ oz. Lime Juice
2–3 Muddled Jalapeño Slices
½ oz. Mango juice
¼ oz. Grenadine
1 tbsp. Tajín

Rim a Collins glass with Tajín by running a lime wedge around the rim, then dipping the glass into a shallow dish of Tajín to coat. Place jalapeño slices in a shaker and muddle. Add pineapple, lime, and mango juices. Add in ice and shake. Pour over ice into the Collins glass. Top with grenadine.

*Shared by Favorites Bistro Bar in New London, CT*

190   PART 3   Sip & Savor: Non-Alcoholic Drink Recipes

## Sauna Room

1½ oz. Lyre's NA Agave Blanco Spirit
½ oz. Galangal Syrup*
1 oz. Orange and Lime Cordial**
2 tbsp. Malic Acid Powder
2.5 tbsp. Citric Acid Powder
Chocolate Ball

Combine all ingredients (except chocolate ball) to highball glass and stir to dissolve. Garnish with the chocolate ball.

*Shared by Emre Bilgin, Bartender at Maybe Sammy in Sydney, NSW, Australia*
***Galangal Syrup:***
1 cup Water
1 cup Sugar
½ cup Fresh Galangal, thinly sliced
Combine the water and sugar in a saucepan over medium heat. Stir until the sugar fully dissolves. Add the sliced galangal and bring the mixture to a gentle simmer. Simmer for 15–20 minutes, stirring occasionally. Remove from heat and let it steep for 15 more minutes to intensify the flavor. Strain out the galangal slices and let the syrup cool. Store in a clean bottle or jar in the fridge for up to two weeks.
****Orange and Lime Cordial:***
2 cups + 2 tbsp. fresh orange juice
⅔ cup lime juice
3¼ cups caster sugar
Add the orange juice to the lime juice in a large mixing bowl. Add the caster sugar and stir continuously until fully dissolved. (Do not boil.) Once fully combined, transfer to a clean bottle or jar and refrigerate.

## See Saw

1 oz. Verjus
¾ oz. Grenadine
Top with Elderflower Tonic Water
3 Lemon Wheels

Combine verjus, grenadine, and tonic water in a mixing glass and stir. Pour into a wine glass with ice and garnish with the lemon wheels.

*Shared by Natasha David, Creative Beverage Director at Simmer Down in Wilmington, DE*

## Sereno

1 oz. Runneght Hydrosol NA Spirit
2 oz. Coconut Water
1 oz. Fresh Pear Juice
½ oz. Lavender Syrup
½ oz. Fresh Lemon Juice
Top with Tonic Water (Optional)
Mint Leaf
Edible Flower Petal

In a shaker, combine all ingredients (except ice, tonic, mint leaf, and flower petal). Gently shake. Strain the mixture into a rocks glass over fresh ice. Top with a splash of tonic water (optional). Garnish with the mint leaf and an edible flower petal.

*Shared by La Botica Speakeasy in Cabo San Lucas, Mexico*

## Sergeant Pepper Field

2 oz. Strawberry Puree
1 oz. Maple Syrup
2 pinches Black Pepper
⅓ oz. Ginger syrup
½ oz. Lime Juice
⅓ oz. Rosemary Syrup
Rosemary Twig

Add all ingredients (except a pinch of black pepper and the rosemary twig) in a shaker and shake. Fine strain into a rocks glass with ice. Add remaining black pepper and flamed rosemary twig as garnish.

*Shared by Hero Bar in Nairobi, Kenya*

## Snowbird

1½ oz. Three Spirit Nightcap NA Botanical Elixir
¾ oz. Honey Syrup
½ oz. Fresh Lime Juice
2 scoops of Pebble or Crushed Ice
Top with Club Soda
5 Mint Leaves
Mint Sprig
Lime Wedge
½ tsp. Grated Cinnamon

Add elixir, honey syrup, lime juice, and mint leaves into a cocktail shaker with ice and hard shake. Loose strain into a Collins glass. Top with club soda till the glass is ¾ full, and then fill completely with pebble or crushed ice. Garnish with mint sprig, lime wedge, and fresh grated cinnamon.

*Featured at Harry's Bar and Restaurant in New York City, NY*

## Son of a Beecher

2 oz. NA Gin
¼ NA Yuzu Liqueur
¼ oz. NA Cynar
¼ oz. Ginger Syrup
¼ oz. Strawberry Syrup
½ oz. Lemon Juice
½ oz. Pineapple Juice
½ oz. Bamboo Leaf
1 oz. San Pellegrino Prickly Pear Sparkling Fruit Beverage
1 Ice Spear
Bamboo Leaf
Strawberry Half

Mix all ingredients (except ice spear, bamboo leaf, and strawberry half) together in tin shaker and hard shake. Add prickly pear soda to tin. Strain over ice spear and garnish with bamboo leaf and strawberry half.

*Shared by Century Grand — Platform 18 "Queens of New York" Menu in Phoenix, AZ*

## Sparkling Honey Yuzu Lemonade

12 oz. Honey Syrup*
4 oz. Lemon Juice
4 oz. Yuzu Juice
32-48 oz. Soda Water
6-8 bundles of Fresh Herbs
6-8 Lemon Wheels

Combine honey syrup, lemon juice, and yuzu juice in a large pitcher. Stir to combine. Top the pitcher with soda water and gently stir to combine. Add in ice. Garnish with fresh herbs (such as mint, Thai basil, and dill) and lemon wheels. Makes 6-8 drinks

*Shared by Hailey Berkey, Mixologist at Redfish Poke Bar in Honolulu, HI*
***Honey Syrup:***
4 oz. Honey
4 oz. White or Cane Sugar
6 oz. Water
Heat the water to just below a simmer in a small saucepan. Add the honey and sugar and stir until fully dissolved and the mixture is smooth. Let cool, then store in a clean bottle or jar in the refrigerator for up to 2 weeks.

## Spiced Blackberry Fizz

1 oz. Ginger Syrup
1 oz. Spiced Blackberry Shrub Soda
1 oz. Egg Whites
1½ oz. Real Lime Juice
1½ oz. Ginger Beer
1 oz. Soda Water
Blackberry

Pour ginger beer and soda water in chilled highball or collins glass. In a shaker, dry shake the egg whites for about 1 minute. Add ginger syrup, blackberry shrub soda, and lime juice. Fill shaker with ice and shake vigorously for another minute. Strain into the glass that contains the soda water and ginger beer slowly (so it can fizz up). Garnish with blackberry.

*Shared by Commons Club at Virgin Hotels in New Orleans, LA*

## Spiced Sipper

1 oz. Seedlip Spice NA Spirit
½ oz. Honey Syrup
½ oz. Lemon Juice
Top with NA Prosecco or Sparkling Wine
Lemon Twist

In a champagne flute, add Seedlip Spice, honey syrup, and lemon juice. Gently stir and top with Prosecco or other sparkling wine. Garnish with a lemon twist and serve.

*Shared by Laura Royer from The Champagne Bar in New York City, NY*

## Steady Pete's Ginger Brew

1½ oz. Rich Ginger Syrup (2:1 sugar to water)
1½ oz. Lemon Juice
1 oz. Seedlip Spice NA Spirit
3 oz. Athletic Brewing Run Wild
3 Ice Cubes

Add all ingredients (except beer) to a blender and blend. Add beer to your beer glass and top with the blended mixture.

*Featured at Hawksmoor in New York City, NY*

## Strawberry Fizz

½ oz. Fresh Lemon Juice
½ oz. Fresh Lime Juice
4 oz. Strawberry Puree
Splash of Soda Water

Add all ingredients (except soda water) to a shaker tin with ice and shake. Pour into highball glass and top with soda water.

*Shared by Blue Mojito in Key West, FL*

## Sunshine Fun Club

2 oz. Orange Juice
¾ oz. Vanilla Syrup
¼ oz. Ritual Rum Alternative
¼ oz. Seedlip Spice NA Spirit
¼ oz. Seedlip Grove NA Spirit
¾ oz. Heavy Cream
1 dropper of Acid Phosphate
Handful of Pebble Ice
Top with Fever-Tree Soda Water
Orange Slice

Add all ingredients (except soda water and orange slice) to shaker and whip shake. Slowly pour in the soda water. Garnish with an orange slice and serve.

*Shared by Alec Kass, Bartender at Rosevale Cocktail Room in New York City, NY*

## Tembo

3 oz. Apple Juice
⅔ oz. Coconut Vinegar
1½ oz. Ginger Syrup
1 oz. Lemon Juice
1 piece of Dehydrated Coconut
Apple Slice

Add all ingredients (except ice, coconut, and apple slice) in a shaker and shake. Fine strain in a highball glass with ice and garnish with the coconut and apple slice.

*Shared by Hero Bar in Nairobi, Kenya*

## Tick Tock

4 oz. Sweet Chamomile Tea
⅔ oz. Simple Syrup
1 oz. White Vinegar
3 oz. Soda Water
Pickled Pineapple Peel
Thyme Sprig

Add all ingredients (other than ice, pineapple peel, and thyme sprig) in a shaker and shake. Fine strain in a highball glass with ice and top with soda water. Garnish with pineapple peel and thyme sprig.

*Shared by Hero Bar in Nairobi, Kenya*

## Two Worlds

1½ oz. Grapefruit Cordial*
1½ oz. Giffard Grapefruit Alcohol Free
10 drops Orange Blossom Water
½ oz. Egg White
1⁄10 g Maldon Sea Salt
2 oz. Three Cents Soda Water
Zest from ½ grapefruit
Grapefruit Wedge

Add all ingredients (except soda water, grapefruit zest, and grapefruit wedge) into a shaker. Fine strain into a coupe glass and top with the soda water. Garnish with the grapefruit zest and wedge.

*Shared by Christopher McNulty from Candelaria in Paris, France*
**\*Grapefruit Cordial**
*2 cups & 2 tbsp. Grapefruit Juice*
*¾ cup of Cane Sugar*
*1 tbsp. Malic Acid Powder*
*Combine the grapefruit juice, cane sugar, and malic acid powder in a large mixing bowl or pitcher. Stir well until the sugar and acid powder are fully dissolved.*

## Upside-Down Pineapple

¼ oz. Grenadine
1½ oz. Ritual Zero Proof Tequila Alternative
2 oz. Pineapple Juice
½ oz. Lime Juice
1 oz. Vanilla Syrup
1 oz. Lemon-Lime Soda
2 Pineapple Fronds
Lime Wheel

Add ¼ oz. grenadine to a highball glass. Add fresh ice to top of glass. Pour tequila, pineapple and lime juices, and vanilla syrup into a shaker. Add ice all the way to the top. Shake rigorously for 7 seconds. Add lemon-lime soda to shaker. Strain contents over highball glass that contains grenadine. Garnish with pineapple fronds and lime wheel.

*Shared by Ian Welby, Vice President of Beverage and Execution at Bar Louie*

CHAPTER 13  Non-Alcoholic Drinks from Bars around the World

## Watermelon Mint Refresher

6 oz. Club Soda
4 oz. Watermelon Puree
5 Mint Sprigs
Mint Leaf
Lime Wedge

Add all ingredients (except mint leaf and lime wedge) into a highball glass and fill to the top with club soda. Garnish with mint leaf and lime wedge.

*Shared by Four Flamingos in Key West, FL*

## Winter Spritz

2 oz. Chai Concentrate
1 oz. Peach Syrup
½ oz. Fresh Ginger Juice
Splash of Soda Water
Cinnamon Stick

Pour chai, peach syrup, and ginger into a wine glass. Stir until the mixture blends together. Top with a splash of soda water. Add ice and stir. Garnish with cinnamon stick.

*Shared by Birdy's in New Orleans, LA*

## Zero-Proof Negroni

1 oz. ISH NA Gin
1 oz. Lyre's NA Aperitif
1 oz. Wilfred's Bittersweet NA Aperitif
Large Ice Cube
Orange Slice

Add all ingredients (except ice cube and orange slice) to a cocktail mixing glass and stir. Pour into a rocks glass over ice cube and garnish with orange slice.

*Shared by Forza Storico in Atlanta, GA*

# The Part of Tens

### IN THIS PART . . .

Say "Cheers!" and celebrate with anyone around the world.

Talk like a pro by using some of the most common bar slang.

**IN THIS CHAPTER**

» Getting familiar with the jargon

» Talkin' the talk

# Chapter 14
# More Than Ten Tidbits of Bar Slang

Like most businesses, the bar and restaurant industry has its own terminology. This chapter covers some of the most popular sayings. You can sling this slang whether you're serving guests in your home or at a bar. Just don't get 86'd!

## 2 or 3 Deep

The phrase *2 or 3 deep* relates to the number of people waiting for a drink at the bar. In other words, it's busy.

## 86 or 86'd

If you used all of something or you need to remove it from the menu, you *86* it or say it's *86'd*. The restaurant world often uses this term to let the staff know you're out of something, such as a special. For example, you might say, "Vanilla vodka is 86'd" or "86 tonight's drink special."

## Behind

When someone says *"Behind,"* they're alerting you that they're walking behind you so that you don't turn around or back up into them.

## Behind the Stick

Restaurant and bar industry workers call getting behind the bar or working behind the bar as being *behind the stick*.

Here's a little history: It is said that in the early 1900s, bartenders would operate the beer tap handles, which were long wooden sticks. That's how this phrase came into being.

## Call

A *call* drink is when someone says a specific brand in their cocktail. For example, a Tito's & soda or a Jack & Coke.

## Corner

Across the restaurant industry, people say *"Corner"* when they turn a blind corner to make sure that they don't run into someone. This call helps staff avoid spills, breakage, and physical harm.

## Double Shift

Working a *double* or *double shift* means you're working both a morning/afternoon and evening shift on the same day.

# Heard

You use the term *heard* when you understand what someone is asking or telling you, and you want to let them know that you got it. For example, a server at a busy bar calls out, "I need three espresso martinis, please." And the bartender replies with, "Heard!"

# In the Weeds

You use the phrase "in the weeds" to describe being extremely busy or overwhelmed.

The term really took off in the hospitality world during the 1950s and 60s, becoming a common way for bartenders and servers to describe the feeling of moving slowly and struggling through the chaos of a busy bar or restaurant, much like trying to push through thick, tangled weeds.

# Last Call

Bars make a *last call* when patrons have time to order one last drink before the bar closes.

# Neat

Calling a drink *neat* means that it's straight spirit in a rocks glass or champagne flute, poured right from the bottle.

# On the Rocks

A drink served on ice, usually in a rocks glass, is called *on the rocks*.

## Straight Up

You call a shaken or stirred drink that you then strain into a glass (usually martini or coupe) without ice as *straight up*.

## Top-Shelf

*Top-shelf* is a term describing the most expensive liquor and spirits available at the bar.

> **IN THIS CHAPTER**
> » Saying "Cheers!" in 15 languages
> » Celebrating big events

# Chapter 15
# More Than Ten Toasts to Mark Any Occasion

You can make nearly any occasion that involves drinks and a group of friends, relatives, or even strangers special by offering a few words of acknowledgment. The toasts included in this chapter are some of my favorites. But if you ever find yourself at a loss for words, you can always just say, "Cheers!"

## Saying "Cheers" Around the World

In the United States and the UK, toasts usually end with "Cheers!" to wish everyone well. Other countries have similar traditions. Here are ten different ways to wish people well (with a drink) from around the world:

- » **Afrikaans:** *Gesondheid* (literally: To your health)
- » **Chinese:** *Gānbēi* (literally: Dry cup)
- » **Danish/Swedish:** *Skål* (literally: Bowl)
- » **Dutch:** *Proost* (literally: Good health)
- » **Greek:** *Yamas* (literally: To our health)

- **Italian:** *Cin cin* (literally: words that mimic the sound of glasses clinking)
- **Korean:** *Geonbae* (literally: Dry cup)
- **Finnish:** *Kippis*
- **French:** *Santé* (literally: Health)
- **German:** *Prost* (literally: May it benefit you)
- **Irish Gaelic:** *Sláinte* (literally: Health)
- **Japanese:** *Kanpai* (literally: Dry the glass)
- **Polish:** *Na zdrowie* (literally: To your health)
- **Portuguese:** *Saúde* (literally: Health)
- **Spanish:** *Salud* (literally: Health)

## Saluting Special Occasions

Birthdays, retirements, weddings, and holidays often call for someone to stand up and say a few words. Whether you're toasting the guest of honor or celebrating a new phase of life, these toasts can make you sound clever and give your guests something to think about:

- "Every baby born into the world is a finer one than the last." — Charles Dickens, *Nicholas Nickleby*
- "Then let us be merry and taste the good cheer,

    And remember old Christmas but comes once a year." — From an old Christmas carol
- "May good fortune follow you all your days . . . and never catch up with you!" — Old Irish toast
- "May you never lie, steal, or drink. But, if you lie, lie with each other at night. If you steal, steal each other's sorrows. And if you must drink . . . drink with us. Cheers to the newlyweds!" — Unknown
- "Here's to the good time I must have had!" — Raymond P. Foley, founder, BARTENDER® Magazine

# Recipe Index

## A
Æcorn Dry NA Aperitif
  Martino, 107
AÉR
  Age of Discovery, 150
agave & agave nectar/syrup
  Beer-Paloma, 80
  Beer-Rita, 80
  Butterfly Tea Lemonade, 153
  Pa-Faux-Ma, 113
  Spicy Cucumber Margarita, 123
  Tranquilita, 128
Agave Amargo, 77
Agave Espresso Martini, 78
Agave Royal Hawaiian, 78
Age of Discovery, 150
Agua de Jamaica, 156
Aline sitoé Diatta, 150
Almave
  FauxMelo, 157
Almave Blanco
  Almos Healthy, 178
Almave NA Resposado Tequila
  Not a Guava, 166
  TLC, 175
almond milk
  Coconut Nog Margarita, 90
Almos Healthy, 178
aloe vera juice
  Cucumber Cooler, 155
Amaro (NA), 170
AMASS Riverine
  Pineapple No-Groni, 169
Ambrosia Punch, 136
Amethyst Lemon
  Celery Gimlet, 153
Amore, 151
Aperitivo (NA)
  Chocolate Almond Negroni, 87
  Notorious F.I.G., 111

Aperol Syrup (NA)
  Eliza's Hymns, 182
Apple Cider, 136
  Apple Cider Whiskey Smash, 78
  Apple & Ginger, 78
  Beer at the Orchard, 79
  EYE See You Punch, 144
  Hot Apple & Ginger, 101
  Isaac's Apple, 101
Apple Cider Whiskey Smash, 78
Apple & Ginger, 78
Apple-Rol Spritz, 151
apples & apple juice/syrup
  Apple & Ginger, 78
  Berry Punch, 136
  Chicha Morada (Purple Corn Punch), 168
  Chichamorada, 179
  Crisp Valley Spritz, 93
  Cucumber Apple Smoothie, 93
  Fall Apples, 148
  Kona Coast, 103
  Tembo, 194
apricot nectar
  Ambrosia Punch, 136
aquafaba
  Clover Club, 70, 89
  Jack of Clubs, 102
  Whiskey Sour, 76
arbol chilies
  Spiced Ginger Syrup, 152
Arnold Palmer, 68
Athletic Brewing Run Wild
  Steady Pete's Ginger Brew, 194
Atlética N/A Mexican Style Beer
  Shrimp Michelada, 171
Aviation, 78
Avocado Margarita, 79
avocados
  Avocado Margarita, 79
  Chocolate Avocado Smoothie, 87

# B

Banana Oleo, 151
baNANana, 151
bananas
- Blueberry-Banana Slushie, 82
- Chocolate Avocado Smoothie, 87
- Chocolate Banana Colada Shake, 87
- Citrus Serenade, 137
- Grapefruit Banana Shake, 139
- Tropical Fruit Smoothie, 141

Bare 0 Proof Reposado Tequila
- Naur-Garita, 165

basil
- Cantaloupe Crush, 86
- Caprese Spritz, 153
- Citrus Seltzer, 88
- Cucumber Basil Bliss, 180
- Golden Bloom, 160
- Mo' Bettah, 164
- Pineapple Seltzer, 116
- Tea & T, 126
- Watermelon-Basil Sweet Tea, 142

beer (NA)
- Beer at the Orchard, 79
- Beer-Mojito, 79
- Beer-Mojito Mule, 79
- Beer-Mosa, 79
- Beer-Paloma, 80
- Beer-Rita, 80
- Beer-Sour, 80
- Berry Lemonade & Beer, 81
- Michelada, 109
- Shandy, 122

Beer at the Orchard, 79
Beer-Mojito, 79
Beer-Mojito Mule, 79
Beer-Mosa, 79
Beer-Paloma, 80
Beer-Rita, 80
Beer-Sour, 80
Bee's Kiss, 80
Bee's Knees, 69, 81
Bellini, 81

berries. *See also specific berries*
- Berry Lemonade & Beer, 81
- Berry Smash, 68
- Mint Berry Smash, 110

Berry Lemonade & Beer, 81
Berry Punch, 136
Berry Smash, 68
Bitter Spritz, 152
Bitter Sweet Moment, 81
black tea
- Zing Zang Iced Tea-Rita, 133

blackberries & blackberry syrup
- Blackberry Lemonade, 82
- Blackberry Mojito, 82
- Blackberry Scramble, 81
- Jack of Clubs, 102
- Spiced Blackberry Fizz, 193

Blackberry Lemonade, 82
Blackberry Mojito, 82
Blackberry Scramble, 81
Blackstrap Molasses Syrup, 165
Blanco tequila (NA)
- Paloma, 75, 113
- Spicy Pineapple Non-Alcoholic Margarita, 144
- Tommy's Margarita, 128

Blood Orange Daiquiri, 82
blood oranges & blood orange juice
- Blood Orange Daiquiri, 82
- Stillman, 124

Bloody Maria, 82
Bloody Mary, 70
blueberries & blueberry juice/puree/syrup
- Berry Punch, 136
- Blueberry Cream Dirty Soda, 83
- Blueberry Daiquiri, 83
- Blueberry Mojito, 83
- Blueberry Smash, 83
- Blueberry-Banana Slushie, 82
- Blueberry-Lemon Slushie, 83
- Mint Berry Smash, 110
- Watermelon NA Tequila Punch, 142

Blueberry Cream Dirty Soda, 83
Blueberry Daiquiri, 83
Blueberry Mojito, 83

Blueberry Simple Syrup, 144
Blueberry Smash, 83
Blueberry-Banana Slushie, 82
Blueberry-Lemon Slushie, 83
Bodega Daiquiri, 152
Bourbon (NA)
   Eggnog, 95
   Falling For You, 95
   Green Tea Highball, 99
   Holiday Bourbon Punch, 139
   John Collins, 102
   Maple Old Fashioned, 106
   Matcha Highball, 107
   Mint Julep, 74
   The Moonraker, 110
   Pumpkin Old Fashioned, 117
   Red, White, and Blueberry Blast, 144
   Revolver, 75, 119
   Takeaway, 126
   Very Peachy, 129
brandy (NA)
   Scorpion Bowl, 141
Brave Bull, 84
Breakfast in Oaxaca, 84
Brooke Bravely, 84
Brown and Stormy, 152
Brown Derby, 84
Brown Derby #2, 84
Bruce the Hairdresser, 85
Brunch Punch, 136
Butterfly Kisses, 178
Butterfly Tea Lemonade, 153

## C

Café con Rhum, 85
Calamansi Curd, 158
Calpico
   Ginger Blossom, 159
Candy Cane Crush, 85
Cantaloupe Crush, 86
Caprese Spritz, 153
Cardi C, 178
carrot juice
   Garden Jynn, 97
   Spring Sunrise, 124, 146

Catching Smoke, 85
Ceder's Crisp NA spirit
   Crisp Stinger, 93
   Crisp Valley Spritz, 93
Ceder's Pink rose NA spirit
   Pink Rose Garden, 117
Ceder's Wild NA spirit
   Spiced Wild, 122
Celery Gimlet, 153
Celestial, 154
Cereal-Infused Milk, 163
   Kopi Siew Dai, 163
   Tea & Crumpets, 174
chai
   Falling For You, 95
   Winter Spritz, 196
chamomile tea
   Golden Bloom, 160
   Tick Tock, 195
Champagne (NA)
   Fall Symphony Punch, 138
   Hugo Spritz, 101
   Midnight Kiss, 143
   Mimosa, 73, 109
   Raspberry Champagne, 118
Cham-Painless, 154
Chemin de Pamplemousse, 86
cherries & cherry cola/puree/soda/syrup
   Cherry Blossom, 146
   Cherry Daiquiri, 86
   Cherry Dark 'N' Stormy, 86
   Scarlet Americano, 170
Cherry Blossom, 146
Cherry Daiquiri, 86
Cherry Dark 'N' Stormy, 86
Cherry Vanilla Dirty Soda, 86
Chica & Tonic, 178
Chicha Morada (Purple Corn Punch)
   Chica & Tonic, 178
   Petit Llama, 168
   Purple Corn Syrup, 168
Chichamorada, 179
Chili-Lime Pineapple Soda, 88
Chinese 5 Spice Dark 'N' Stormy, 87
Chismosa, 179

**Recipe Index**    **207**

chocolate
  Cracked Coffee, 92
  Gelt Hot Chocolate, 145
Chocolate Almond Negroni, 87
Chocolate Avocado Smoothie, 87
Chocolate Banana Colada Shake, 87
Chocolate Colada Shake, 88
chocolate ice cream. *See* ice cream
chocolate milk
  Chocolate Avocado Smoothie, 87
chocolate syrup
  Chocolate Banana Colada Shake, 87
  Chocolate Colada Shake, 88
cinnamon & cinnamon syrup/sticks
  Chicha Morada (Purple Corn Punch), 168
  Mo' Bettah, 164
  Party Punch, 140
Citron Crush, 179
Citrus Aperitivo
  Dirty Spritz, 157
  Winter Spritz, 175
Citrus Beer Spritz, 88
Citrus Seltzer, 88
Citrus Serenade, 137
Clamato Cocktail, 88
Clamato juice
  Clamato Cocktail, 88
Clearer Twist Premium French Pink Mixer
  Bitter Sweet Moment, 81
Clearer Twist Premium Tonic Water
  Tea & T, 126
Clove Rimmer, 189
Clove Simple Syrup, 189
Clover Club, 70, 89
cloves
  Chicha Morada (Purple Corn Punch), 168
Coco Lopez Cream of Coconut
  Ambrosia Punch, 136
  Chocolate Banana Colada Shake, 87
  Chocolate Colada Shake, 88
  Coco Lopez Shake, 89
  Double Berry Coco Punch, 138
  New Orleans Day, 111
  Orange Coconut Frost, 140
  Orange Smoothie, 112

Painkiller, 113
Peaches & Cream, 114
Pina Colada, 69, 75
Piña Colada, 115
Piña Colada Shake, 115
Secret Admirer, 143
Tropical Fruit Smoothie, 141
Coco Lopez Shake, 89
Coconut Bay Breeze, 89
coconut black tea
  Tea & Crumpets, 174
coconut & coconut syrup
  lemon-lime soda, 94
  Pineapple Coconut Dirty Soda, 116
coconut cream/milk/water. *See also* Coco Lopez Cream of Coconut
  Candy Cane Crush, 85
  Coconut Dirty Soda, 89
  Coconut Limeade, 90
  Coconut Nog Margarita, 90
  Coquito Lemonade, 154
  Disco Mix, 181
  PEEPstini, 115
  Pineapple Coconut Dirty Soda, 116
  Posion De Amor, 190
  Raspberry Dirty Soda, 118
  Ruhm With a View, 120
  Sereno, 191
  Spring Sunrise, 146
  That's-a-CoCo, 127
  Tropical Dirty Soda, 128
Coconut Dirty Soda, 89
Coconut Limeade, 90
Coconut Mango Sunrise, 90
Coconut Margarita, 89
Coconut Mojito, 90
Coconut Nog Margarita, 90
Coconut Watermelon Cooler, 91
coffee ice cream. *See* ice cream
coffee liqueur (NA)
  Cool Coffee Club, 91
  Revolver, 75
coffee/coffee beans/cold brew coffee. *See also* Cold Brew Concentrate
  Brave Bull, 84
  Breakfast in Oaxaca, 84

Café con Rhum, 85
Cold Brew Martini, 180
Irish Cawfee-ish, 162
Irish Coffee, 72
The Moonraker, 110
Peppermint Irish Coffee, 146
Takeaway, 126
cola
   Blueberry Cream Dirty Soda, 83
   Coconut Dirty Soda, 89
   Dirty Soda, 94
   Grape Dirty Soda, 98
   Peach Dirty Soda, 114
   Pineapple Coconut Dirty Soda, 116
   Raspberry Dirty Soda, 118
   Roy Rogers, 69, 120
   Vanilla Pop, 129
Cold Brew Concentrate
   Agave Espresso Martini, 78
   Cold-Brew Old Fashioned, 91
   Espresso Martini, 71, 95
   Mezcal Mole Martini, 108
Cold Brew Martini, 180
Cold-Brew Negroni, 91
Cold-Brew Old Fashioned, 91
Confetti Punch, 137
Cool Coffee Club, 91
Coquito Lemonade, 154
Coral Paradise, 137
Cosmopolitan, 70
CosNOpolitan, 92
Cracked Coffee, 92
cranberries & cranberry juice
   Berry Punch, 136
   Coconut Bay Breeze, 89
   Cosmopolitan, 70
   CosNOpolitan, 92
   Cranberry Collins, 92
   Cranberry Punch, 137
   Cranberry Smash, 92
   Cranberry Spritz, 93
   Cran-Rosemary Soda, 146
   Double Berry Coco Punch, 138
   Fruit Punch, 68
   Ginger Blossom, 159
   Party Punch, 140

   Pink Lemonade, 116
   Poinsettia Punch, 140
   Red Racket, 119
   Ruby Cooler, 120
   Rum Madras, 121
   Shanghai Buck, 171
Cranberry Collins, 92
Cranberry Punch, 137
Cranberry Smash, 92
Cranberry Spritz, 93
Cran-Rosemary Soda, 146
Crimson and Clover, 155
Crisp Stinger, 93
Crisp Valley Spritz, 93
Cucumber Apple Smoothie, 93
Cucumber Basil Bliss, 180
Cucumber Cooler, 93, 155, 180
Cucumber Mule, 155, 181
Cucumber Shrub
   Cucumber Mule, 181
cucumbers & cucumber puree/juice
   Crisp Valley Spritz, 93
   Cucumber Apple Smoothie, 93
   Cucumber Basil Bliss, 180
   Cucumber Cooler, 93, 155, 180
   Cucumber Mule, 155, 181
   East Side, 71
   Going Green, 160
   Green Tea Sensation, 185
   Kiwi Cooler, 103
   Sowing Seeds, 172
   Spicy Cucumber Margarita, 123
   Tranquilita, 128
Cut Above Agave Blanco NA Tequila
   Agave Royal Hawaiian, 78
   Fall Symphony Punch, 138
   Pornstar Mojito, 189
   Tranquilita, 128
   Watermelon NA Tequila Punch, 142
Cut Above Bourbon
   Apple Cider Whiskey Smash, 78
Cut Above Gin
   Chocolate Almond Negroni, 87
   Honey & Fig G&T, 100
   Rosemary Gin Fizz, 120
   Strawberry Gin Collins, 126

Cut Above Mezcal
  Brave Bull, 84
  Cantaloupe Crush, 86
  Mezcal Bramble, 108
  Mezcal Mole Martini, 108
  Tiger Lily, 127
Cut Above Whiskey
  Blackberry Scramble, 81
  Cold-Brew Old Fashioned, 91
  Fool's Gold, 96
  Notorious F.I.G., 111
  Whiskey Collins, 132
  Whiskey Peach Lemonade, 132
cynar (NA)
  Son of a Beecher, 192

# D

Daiquiri, 70, 94
dandelion tea
  Kopi Brewed with Dandelion Tea, 163
  Kopi Siew Dai, 163
Dark 'N' Stormy, 71, 94
dark rum (NA)
  Bee's Kiss, 80
  Brown and Stormy, 152
  Coconut Bay Breeze, 89
  Kath's Clockin In, 103
  Mai Tai, 73, 105
  NA Eggnog, 138
  NA Planter's Punch, 139
  Rum Flip, 121
  Rum Madras, 121
  Rum Old Fashioned, 121
  Water Rush, 130
Dear Prudence, 181
Desert Bloom, 156
Desert Rose, 94, 156
Dill-Infused Simple Syrup, 154
Dirty Soda, 94
Dirty Spritz, 157
Disco Dust, 181
Disco Mix, 181
Don't Be Suspicious, 182

Double Berry Coco Punch, 138
Dragon Eye Oolong tea
  Shanghai Buck, 171
Dragon Fruit Cordiale, 157
dragon fruit & dragon fruit juice
  Dragon Fruit Margarita, 94
  Dragon Fruit Highball, 157
  Dragon Fruit Margarita, 94
dry vermouth (NA)
  Gibson, 71
Dust Cutter, 94

# E

Earl Grey tea
  High Tea, 100
  Lost in the Fog, 186
East Side, 71
Egg Hunt, 143
Eggnog, 95
eggs & egg whites
  Clover Club, 70, 89
  Eggnog, 95
  Granata, 161
  Hibiscus Sour, 100
  Illegal Backflip, 161
  Jack of Clubs, 102
  NONA Ginger & Pink Grapefruit, 111
  The Phoenix Fizz, 188
  Pineapple-Banana Frappé, 169
  Rum Flip, 121
  Spiced Blackberry Fizz, 193
  Two Worlds, 195
  Violette Lady, 129
  Whiskey Sour, 76
elderflower tonic water
  Chica & Tonic, 178
Electric Bicycle, 182
Eliza's Hymns, 182
espresso
  Cracked Coffee, 92
Espresso Martini, 71, 95
Euphoric Spritz, 95
EYE See You Punch, 144

## F

Fall Apples, 148
Fall Symphony Punch, 138
Falling For You, 95
Fancy Sorbet, 96
FauxMelo, 157
Featherweight Smash, 158
Fee Brothers Orange Flower Water
   Chamomile Syrup, 165
Fever-Tree Ginger Beer
   The Passion, 188
Fever-Tree Sicilian Lemon Soda
   Caprese Spritz, 153
Fever-Tree tonic water
   TLC, 175
Filipino Flip, 158
First Aid, 183
Fizzy Bubblech, 183
Fool's Gold, 96
Freddy Bartholomew, 96
French 05, 96
French 71, 96
Fresca Tonic, 159
Frosé, 96
Frozen Daiquiri, 97
Frozen Margarita, 97
Frozen Negroni, 97
fruit. *See also specific fruit*
Fruit Bowl, 97
fruit cocktail
   Confetti Punch, 137
Fruit Punch, 68, 139
Fruitations Cranberry
   New World, 165
Fun in the Sun, 159

## G

Garden Jynn, 97
Garden of Eden, 183
Garden Party, 184
The Garnet, 98
Gelt Hot Chocolate, 145
Ghia Aperitif
   Citron Crush, 179
   Ghia Flora, 184

Ghia Flora, 184
Gibson, 71
Giffard Aperitif Sirop
   Bitter Spritz, 152
   Pineapple No-Groni, 169
Giffard Aperitivo
   Rose Marie, 170
Giffard NA
   FauxMelo, 157
Giffard NA Elderflower Liqueur
   Ghia Flora, 184
Giffard NA Ginger
   Mama's Garden, 163
Giffard NA Grapefruit
   Two Worlds, 195
Giffard Orgeat syrup
   Scorpion Bowl, 141
Giiirl Dinner, 184
gin (NA)
   Bee's Knees, 69, 81
   Clover Club, 70, 89
   Cosmopolitan, 70
   French 71, 96
   Gibson, 71
   Gin Fizz, 72
   Gin Rickey, 72
   Gin & Tonic, 72, 98
   Gold Minded, 98
   Jack of Clubs, 102
   Ruby Cooler, 120
   Son of a Beecher, 192
   Southside, 124
   Tom Collins, 76, 128
Gin Fizz, 72
Gin Rickey, 72
Gin & Tonic, 72, 98
ginger ale/soda
   Chismosa, 179
   Don't Be Suspicious, 182
   Freddy Bartholomew, 96
   Fruit Punch, 68, 139
   Gunner, 99
   Hole-in-One, 100
   Kona Coast, 103
   Pomegranate Punch, 140
   Ruby Cooler, 120

**Recipe Index    211**

ginger beer
  Almos Healthy, 178
  Cardi C, 178
  Catching Smoke, 85
  Chinese 5 Spice Dark 'N' Stormy, 87
  Cucumber Mule, 155
  Dark 'N' Stormy, 71, 94
  Desert Rose, 156
  Fall Apples, 148
  Garden of Eden, 183
  Green Tea Sensation, 185
  Gunner, 99
  Mango Mule, 106
  Mezcal Mule, 108
  Mezcal Passion Mule, 109
  Mule, 74, 110
  Party Punch, 140
  Perfect Storm (Rum Mule), 115
  Shanghai Buck, 171
  Snow Globe Spritz, 172
  Spiced Blackberry Fizz, 193
  Spring Sunrise, 124
  Strawberry Mule, 125
  The Tide Is High, 174
  Tiger Lily, 127
Ginger Blossom, 159
ginger & ginger juice/syrup
  Apple & Ginger, 78
  Beer at the Orchard, 79
  Hot Apple & Ginger, 101
  Passion Fruit & Ginger Cordial, 187
  Snap Pea Sour, 172
  Sowing Seeds, 172
  Spiced Blackberry Fizz, 193
  Spiced Ginger Syrup, 152
  Spring Sunrise, 146
  Steady Pete's Ginger Brew, 194
  Tembo, 194
Gingerbread Martini, 145
Going Green, 160
Gold Minded, 98
Gold Mosey, 160
Golden Bloom, 160
Golden Child, 185
Granata, 161
Grape Dirty Soda, 98
Grapefruit Banana Shake, 139

Grapefruit Cooler, 98
Grapefruit Cordial, 195
grapefruit & grapefruit juice/soda
  Beer-Paloma, 80
  Brown Derby, 84
  Brown Derby #2, 84
  Chemin de Pamplemousse, 86
  Citrus Seltzer, 88
  Confetti Punch, 137
  Electric Bicycle, 182
  Fruit Bowl, 97
  Grapefruit Cooler, 98
  Grapefruit Cordial, 195
  Ivory Jungle, 162
  Lady Nora, 103
  Paloma, 75, 113
  Red Racket, 119
  Shower Punch, 141
  Spicy Paloma, 123
  The Tide Is High, 174
  Two Worlds, 195
grapes & grape juice/syrup
  Fruit Bowl, 97
  Grape Dirty Soda, 98
  Hole-in-One, 100
  Maverick's Caddy, 107
  PB & J, 167
  Perrier Mimosa, 115
  Red Grapes & Cardamom Shrub, 178
Green Curry Syrup
  Filipino Flip, 158
green tea
  Green Tea Highball, 99
  Tea & T, 126
  Zing Zang Iced Tea-Rita, 133
Green Tea Highball, 99
Green Tea Sensation, 185
Green With Envy, 161
grenadine
  Roy Rogers, 69
  Shirley Temple, 69
Grilled Lemonade, 99
guava juice/purée
  Chismosa, 179
  Not a Guava, 166
Gunner, 99

## H

half-and-half
  Cherry Vanilla Dirty Soda, 86
  Coco Lopez Cream of Coconut, 111
  Dirty Soda, 94
  Grape Dirty Soda, 98
  Hazelnut Italian Soda, 99
  Lime Dirty Soda, 104
  NA Eggnog, 138
  Peach Dirty Soda, 114
  Root Beer Dirty Soda, 120
Hazelnut Italian Soda, 99
heavy cream
  Bee's Kiss, 80
  Blueberry Cream Dirty Soda, 83
  Eggnog, 95
  Gelt Hot Chocolate, 145
  Gingerbread Martini, 145
Heirloom Alchermes Syrup (NA)
  Eliza's Hymns, 182
Hibiscus Cooler, 99
hibiscus rose mixer
  Love Buzz, 163
Hibiscus Sour, 100
hibiscus tea
  Hibiscus Sour, 100
  Zing Zang Iced Tea-Rita, 133
High Tea, 100
Hole-in-One, 100
Holiday Bourbon Punch, 139
honey
  Blueberry Smash, 83
  Brown Derby, 84
  Honey Syrup, 193
  The Mad Hatter, 186
Honey & Fig G&T, 100
Honey Golden Blend, 185
Honey Limeade, 101
Honey Syrup, 193
  Bee's Knees, 69
  Cran-Rosemary Soda, 146
  Pink Rose Garden, 117
  Sparkling Honey Yuzu Lemonade, 193

Hot Apple & Ginger, 101
Hot Girl Cordial, 184
Hot Toddy, 72, 101
Hugo Spritz, 101

## I

ice cream
  Chocolate Banana Colada Shake, 87
  Chocolate Colada Shake, 88
  Coco Lopez Shake, 89
  Cool Coffee Club, 91
  Egg Hunt, 143
  Kath's Clockin In, 103
  NA Eggnog, 138
  Orange Smoothie, 112
  Piña Colada Shake, 115
  Shake Those Shamrocks!, 143
iced coffee
  The Moonraker, 110
Iced Tea, 68
  Arnold Palmer, 68
  P.G.'s Tea, 113
  Whiskey Tea, 132
Iki, 161
Illegal Backflip, 161
Indian Summer, 162
Irish Cawfee-ish, 162
Irish Coffee, 72
Isaac's Apple, 101
Ish NA Gin
  Apple-Rol Spritz, 151
  Shaken and Stoned, 171
  Zero-Proof Negroni, 196
Island Oasis Wildberry Mix
  Mezcal Bramble, 108
Italian orange liqueur (NA)
  Josh Cellars Sparkling Italian Spritz, 102
Ivory Jungle, 162

## J

J & T, 102
Jack of Clubs, 102

**Recipe Index**    213

jalapeño peppers
  Pa-Faux-Ma, 113
  Spicy Cucumber Margarita, 123
  Spicy Margarita, 75, 123
  Spicy Paloma, 123
  Spicy Pineapple Non-Alcoholic Margarita, 144
  Spicy Raspberry Margarita, 123
  Spicy Spritz, 173
  S&S, 190
Jasmine Cooler, 162
jasmine & jasmine syrup
  Cherry Blossom, 146
  Jasmine Cooler, 162
John Collins, 102
Joker Juice, 185
Josh Cellars Sparkling Italian Spritz, 102
Jumping Jack, 102

## K

Kath's Clockin In, 103
Kiwi Cooler, 103
Kiwi Seltzer, 103
kiwis
  Kiwi Cooler, 103
  Kiwi Seltzer, 103
  Strawberry-Kiwi Slushie, 125
Kombucha
  Euphoric Spritz, 95
  French 05, 96
Kona Coast, 103
Kopi Siew Dai, 163

## L

Lady Nora, 103
Lapsang Souchong tea
  Catching Smoke, 85
  Otra Cosa, 166
  Wuyi, 176
lavender & lavender syrup
  Lavender Non-Collins, 104
Lavender Lemonade, 104
Lavender Non-Collins, 104
Lemon Amethyst
  Cucumber Mule, 155

Lemonade, 68, 104
  Arnold Palmer, 68
  Berry Lemonade & Beer, 81
  Blackberry Lemonade, 82
  Honey Limeade, 101
  Shandy, 122
  Strawberry Lemonade, 125
lemonade concentrate
  Confetti Punch, 137
Lemongrass Bergamot Tea, 189
Lemon-Lime Seltzer, 104
lemon-lime soda
  Blueberry Cream Dirty Soda, 83
  Coconut Dirty Soda, 89
  Dirty Soda, 94
  EYE See You Punch, 144
  Grape Dirty Soda, 98
  Lime Dirty Soda, 104
  The Mad Hatter, 186
  Mango Daiquiri, 105
  Maverick's Caddy, 107
  Peach Dirty Soda, 114
  Pineapple Coconut Dirty Soda, 116
  Raspberry Dirty Soda, 118
  Shirley Temple, 69
  Strawberry Daiquiri, 125
  Upside-Down Pineapple, 195
lemons & lemon juice
  Beer-Sour, 80
  Bee's Knees, 69
  Blackberry Scramble, 81
  Blueberry-Lemon Slushie, 83
  Butterfly Tea Lemonade, 153
  Citron Crush, 179
  Citrus Beer Spritz, 88
  Clover Club, 89
  Coquito Lemonade, 154
  Cucumber Basil Bliss, 180
  Cucumber Cooler, 180
  Eliza's Hymns, 182
  Featherweight Smash, 158
  Frosé, 96
  Fruit Punch, 139
  Fun in the Sun, 159
  Gin Fizz, 72
  Grilled Lemonade, 99
  Hibiscus Cooler, 99

**214** Non-Alcoholic Drinks For Dummies

Iki, 161
Jack of Clubs, 102
John Collins, 102
Lavender Non-Collins, 104
Lemonade, 68, 104
Lemon-Lime Seltzer, 104
Matcha Fizz, 164
NONA June Collins, 111
Pear-Maple Sour, 168
Pineapple-Banana Frappé, 169
Pink Lemonade, 116
Puppy Pose, 190
Raspberry Lemonade, 118
Rose Marie, 170
Rosemary Gin Fizz, 120
Scorpion Bowl, 141
Snow Blower, 141
Southside, 124
Sparkling Honey Yuzu Lemonade, 193
Sparkling Raspberry Lemonade, 147
Steady Pete's Ginger Brew, 194
Strawberry Lemonade, 125
Tembo, 194
Tom Collins, 76, 128
Vanilla-Rosemary Lemonade, 142
Whiskey Collins, 132
Whiskey Tea, 132
Light Snap Peas Syrup, 169
Lime Dirty Soda, 104
Lime Oleo, 187
limes & lime juice/syrup
  Beer-Mojito, 79
  Beer-Mojito Mule, 79
  Beer-Paloma, 80
  Beer-Rita, 80
  Blackberry Mojito, 82
  Blood Orange Daiquiri, 82
  Blueberry Daiquiri, 83
  Blueberry Mojito, 83
  Blueberry Smash, 83
  Brown Derby #2, 84
  Cherry Daiquiri, 86
  Chichamorada, 179
  Chili-Lime Pineapple Soda, 88
  Clamato Cocktail, 88
  Coconut Limeade, 90
  Coconut Mojito, 90

Coconut Watermelon Cooler, 91
Cosmopolitan, 70
Cranberry Collins, 92
Cranberry Smash, 92
Cucumber Cooler, 93, 180
Daiquiri, 94
Fall Apples, 148
Frozen Daiquiri, 97
Frozen Margarita, 97
Fruit Punch, 139
Green With Envy, 161
Honey Limeade, 101
Indian Summer, 162
Kona Coast, 103
Lemon-Lime Seltzer, 104
Lime Dirty Soda, 104
Livener XS Picante, 105
Michelada, 109
Mint Berry Smash, 110
Mo' Bettah, 164
Mockingbird, 165
Mojito, 74, 110
Nemesis, 187
No-Maro Swizzle, 187
Papaya Colada, 167
PB & J, 167
Peach Daiquiri, 113
Petit Llama, 168
Pineapple Daquiri, 116
The Pinery, 170
Pomegranate Punch, 140
Prickly Pear, 117
Ranch Water, 119
Raspberry Daiquiri, 118
Raspberry Mojito, 119
Snap Pea Sour, 172
Spiced Blackberry Fizz, 193
Spicy Cucumber Margarita, 123
S&S, 190
Strawberry Mule, 125
Tommy's Margarita, 128
Tranquilita, 128
Watermelon Daiquiri, 130
Watermelon NA Tequila Punch, 142
Yeehaw, Beebaw!, 133
Zero Paloma, 176

**Recipe Index**    **215**

Livener XS NA spirit
   Livener XS Picante, 105
Livener XS Picante, 105
Lost in the Fog, 186
Love Buzz, 163
Lucano NA Amaro
   No-Maro Swizzle, 187
Lush and Locks, 163
Lyre's Agave
   Otra Cosa, 166
Lyre's Amaretti
   Chocolate Almond Negroni, 87
Lyre's American Malt
   Kopi Siew Dai, 163
Lyre's Apéritif Rosso
   Cold-Brew Negroni, 91
   Frozen Negroni, 97
   Negroni, 74
Lyre's Coffee Originale NA coffee liqueur
   Revolver, 119
Lyre's Dry London spirit
   Cold-Brew Negroni, 91
   Frozen Negroni, 97
   Negroni, 74
Lyre's Dry White Cane spirit
   Daiquiri, 70, 94
   Pineapple Daquiri, 116
Lyre's Italian Orange NA spirit
   Apple-Rol Spritz, 151
   Cold-Brew Negroni, 91
   Frozen Negroni, 97
   Golden Child, 185
   Indian Summer, 162
   Negroni, 74
   Valhalla, 129
Lyre's Italian Spritz
   Spicy Spritz, 173
Lyre's London Spirit
   Tangerine 71, 174
Lyre's NA Agave Blanco Spirit
   Sauna Room, 191
Lyre's NA Aperitif
   Zero-Proof Negroni, 196
Lyre's White Cane with Pandan
   Pandan Hi, 166

# M

The Mad Hatter, 186
Mai Tai, 73, 105
Makrut Lime Infused NA London Dry Gin
   Eliza's Hymns, 182
Mama's Garden, 163
Mango Daiquiri, 105
Mango Margarita, 105
Mango Mule, 106
Mango-Pineapple Slushie, 106
mangos & mango nectar/juice/purée/syrup
   Coconut Mango Sunrise, 90
   Mango Daiquiri, 105
   Mango Margarita, 105
   Mango Mule, 106
   Mango-Pineapple Slushie, 106
   Nora's Tiger Lilly, 111
   Posion De Amor, 190
Manhattan, 73, 106
Maple Old Fashioned, 106, 147
maple syrup
   Maple Old Fashioned, 106
   Pear-Maple Sour, 168
   Sergeant Pepper Field, 192
Margarita, 73, 107
Martinelli Sparkling Cider
   Orchard Spritz, 166
Martini & Rossi Floreale NA Aperitivo
   Agave Amargo, 77
   Pear-Maple Sour, 168
   Summer Spritz, 173
Martini & Rossi Vibrante L'Aperitivo
   Bitter Spritz, 152
   Mockingbird, 165
   Otra Cosa, 166
   Pineapple No-Groni, 169
   Scarlet Americano, 170
   Wuyi, 176
Martino, 107
Matcha Fizz, 164
Matcha Highball, 107
matcha powder
   Matcha Fizz, 164
   Matcha Highball, 107
   Matcha Tonic, 107

Matcha Tonic, 107
Maverick's Caddy, 107
Mexican Hot Tea, 108
Mezcal (NA)
   Breakfast in Oaxaca, 84
   Catching Smoke, 85
   Mezcal Mule, 108
   Mezcal Passion Mule, 109
Mezcal Bramble, 108
Mezcal Gilda, 108
Mezcal Mole Martini, 108
Mezcal Mule, 108
Mezcal Passion Mule, 109
Mezkahl Chiller, 109
Miami Vice, 109
Michelada, 109
Midnight Kiss, 143
Mid-Summer, 164
milk
   Chocolate Banana Colada Shake, 87
   Chocolate Colada Shake, 88
   Cool Coffee Club, 91
   Cracked Coffee, 92
   Egg Hunt, 143
   Eggnog, 95
   Gelt Hot Chocolate, 145
   NA Eggnog, 138
   Shake Those Shamrocks!, 143
Mimosa, 73, 109
mint
   Beer-Mojito, 79
   Beer-Mojito Mule, 79
   Blackberry Mojito, 82
   Blueberry Mojito, 83
   Coconut Mojito, 90
   Crisp Stinger, 93
   Cucumber Apple Smoothie, 93
   East Side, 71
   Featherweight Smash, 158
   Fun in the Sun, 159
   The Garnet, 98
   Jasmine Cooler, 162
   Mint Berry Smash, 110
   Mint Julep, 74
   Mojito, 74, 110

Old Cuban, 112
Petit Llama, 168
Pornstar Mojito, 189
Raspberry Mojito, 119
Snap Pea Sour, 172
Southside, 124
Tea & T, 126
Tequila Julep, 127
Watermelon Mint Refresher, 196
Watermelon NA Tequila Punch, 142
Watermelon Seltzer, 131
Zucchini-Mint Juice, 164
Mint Berry Smash, 110
mint chocolate ice cream. *See* ice cream
mint iced tea
   Mezkahl Chiller, 109
Mint Julep, 74
mint simple syrup
   Dear Prudence, 181
Mionetto Spritz, 110
Mo' Bettah, 164
Mockingbird, 165
Mojito, 74, 110
Monday Zero Alcohol Gin
   Green With Envy, 161
Monin Desert Pear Syrup
   Egg Hunt, 143
The Moonraker, 110
Mott's apple juice
   Mama's Garden, 163
mozzarella ball
   Caprese Spritz, 153
Mule, 74, 110

# N

NA Eggnog, 138
NA Planter's Punch, 139
Naur-Garita, 165
Negroni, 74
Nemesis, 187
New Orleans Day, 111
New World, 165
No-Maro Swizzle, 187
NONA Ginger & Pink Grapefruit, 111

**Recipe Index**    **217**

NONA June Collins, 111
NONA June NA spirit
   NONA June Collins, 111
NONA NA Amaro
   The Phoenix Fizz, 188
NONA NA Bitters
   The Phoenix Fizz, 188
NONA NA Gin
   The Phoenix Fizz, 188
Nora's Tiger Lily, 111
Not a Guava, 166
Notorious F.I.G., 111

# O

Oaxacan Old Fashioned, 112
Ocean Spray Cranberry Juice Cocktail
   Citrus Serenade, 137
Ocean Spray Ruby Mango Grapefruit Juice Cocktail
   Coral Paradise, 137
Ocean Spray White Grapefruit Juice
   Grapefruit Banana Shake, 139
Ocho Verde Spirit
   Tranquilita, 128
Old Cuban, 112
Old Fashioned, 75
olives & olive brine
   Martino, 107
Orange and Lime Cordial, 191
Orange and Olive Syrup, 188
orange blossom & orange blossom water
   Two Worlds, 195
Orange Coconut Frost, 140
orange liqueur (NA)
   Fall Symphony Punch, 138
   P.G.'s Tea, 113
Orange Margarita, 112
Orange Smoothie, 112
oranges & orange juice
   Ambrosia Punch, 136
   Beer-Mosa, 79
   Beer-Rita, 80
   Brooke Bravely, 84
   Citrus Beer Spritz, 88
   Coral Paradise, 137

Cranberry Punch, 137
Crimson and Clover, 155
Don't Be Suspicious, 182
Fruit Bowl, 97
Fruit Punch, 68, 139
The Garnet, 98
Holiday Bourbon Punch, 139
Joker Juice, 185
Lost in the Fog, 186
Mimosa, 73, 109
Nora's Tiger Lily, 111
Orange Coconut Frost, 140
Orange Margarita, 112
Orange Smoothie, 112
Painkiller, 113
Party Punch, 140
Perrier Mimosa, 115
Pineapple-Banana Frappé, 169
Poinsettia Punch, 140
Pumpkin Patch, 118
Rum Madras, 121
Scorpion Bowl, 141
Shower Punch, 141
Squeeze the Day, 173
Sunshine Fun Club, 194
Tennessee Punch, 141
Tequila Sunrise, 76, 127
Tropical Fruit Smoothie, 141
Orchard Sour, 112
Orchard Spritz, 166
Otra Cosa, 166
The Outfit, 188

# P

Pa-Faux-Ma, 113
Painkiller, 113
Palette Roots NA spirit
   Nemesis, 187
Paloma, 75, 113
Pandan Hi, 166
Papaya Colada, 167
Papaya-Chamoy Syrup, 167
Party Punch, 140
Passion Fruit & Ginger Cordial, 187

passion fruit & passion fruit pulp/juice/puree/syrup
 Butterfly Kisses, 178
 The Mad Hatter, 186
 Mezcal Passion Mule, 109
 The Passion, 188
 Softcore Martini, 122
Passion Fruit Vanilla Syrup, 150
The Passion, 188
Pathfinder Amaro Liqueur
 Giiirl Dinner, 184
Pathfinder Hemp & Root
 Cold Brew Martini, 180
The Pathfinder NA spirit
 Chemin de Pamplemousse, 86
 Featherweight Smash, 158
PB & J, 167
Peach Daiquiri, 113
Peach Dirty Soda, 114
Peach Fizz, 114
peach jam
 Very Peachy, 129
peach jasmine soda
 Nemesis, 187
peach lemonade
 Whiskey Peach Lemonade, 132
Peach Tea Cordial, 164
Peaches & Cream, 114
peaches & peach nectar/puree/syrup
 Bellini, 81
 Peach Daiquiri, 113
 Peach Dirty Soda, 114
 Sobrii Peach Bellini, 124
 Sweet Peach Tea, 126
 Whiskey Peach Lemonade, 132
 Winter Spritz, 196
peach-infused NA Bourbon
 Peach Fizz, 114
pear jam
 Orchard Sour, 112
Pear Vanilla, 114
Pear-Maple Sour, 168
pears and pear juice
 Pear Vanilla, 114
 Sereno, 191
PEEPstini, 115

Pellegrino sparkling water
 Mo' Bettah, 164
Peppermint Irish Coffee, 146
Perfect Storm (Rum Mule), 115
Peroni 0.0
 Desert Bloom, 156
Perrier
 The Garnet, 98
 Perrier Mimosa, 115
Perrier Mimosa, 115
Persimmon Soda, 168
Petit Llama, 168
Petit Poids, 169
P.G.'s Tea, 113
Philters Jynn
 Aviation, 78
 Garden Jynn, 97
 J & T, 102
 Lavender Non-Collins, 104
 Ruby Slippers, 120
 Violette Lady, 129
 Winter Bee, 132
Philters Mezkahl
 Desert Rose, 94
 Mezcal Gilda, 108
 Mezkahl Chiller, 109
 Oaxacan Old Fashioned, 112
 Pa-Faux-Ma, 113
 See No Evil, 121
 Spicy Cucumber Margarita, 123
Philters Ruhm
 Café con Rhum, 85
 Cherry Dark 'N' Stormy, 86
 Chinese 5 Spice Dark 'N' Stormy, 87
 Dark 'N' Stormy, 71, 94
 Isaac's Apple, 101
 Playful Punch, 117
 Pumpkin Patch, 118
 Root Beer Dark 'N' Stormy, 119
 Ruhm With a View, 120
 Vanilla Dark 'N' Stormy, 129
Philters Wiski
 Brown Derby, 84
 Brown Derby #2, 84
 High Tea, 100

Recipe Index  219

The Phoenix Fizz, 188
Piña Colada, 69, 75, 115
  Miami Vice, 109
Piña Colada Shake, 115
Pineapple Coconut Dirty Soda, 116
Pineapple Daquiri, 116
Pineapple No-Groni, 169
Pineapple Princess, 116
Pineapple Seltzer, 116
Pineapple-Banana Frappé, 169
pineapples & pineapple juice/puree/soda/syrup
  Ambrosia Punch, 136
  baNAnana, 151
  Brooke Bravely, 84
  Chicha Morada (Purple Corn Punch), 168
  Chichamorada, 179
  Chili-Lime Pineapple Soda, 88
  Coconut Bay Breeze, 89
  Coral Paradise, 137
  Cranberry Punch, 137
  Desert Bloom, 156
  Don't Be Suspicious, 182
  Fruit Bowl, 97
  Fruit Punch, 68, 139
  Fun in the Sun, 159
  Grapefruit Banana Shake, 139
  Green With Envy, 161
  Jumping Jack, 102
  Mango-Pineapple Slushie, 106
  Mockingbird, 165
  Painkiller, 113
  Party Punch, 140
  Peaches & Cream, 114
  Pina Colada, 69, 75
  Piña Colada, 115
  Piña Colada Shake, 115
  Pineapple Coconut Dirty Soda, 116
  Pineapple Daquiri, 116
  Pineapple Princess, 116
  Pineapple Seltzer, 116
  Pineapple-Banana Frappé, 169
  The Pinery, 170
  Playful Punch, 117
  Pumpkin Patch, 118
  Secret Admirer, 143

Spiced Wild, 122
Spicy Pineapple Non-Alcoholic Margarita, 144
S&S, 190
Tiger Lily, 127
Tropical Dirty Soda, 128
Tropical Fruit Smoothie, 141
Upside-Down Pineapple, 195
VIP Welcome, 130
Walter, 130
Wuyi, 176
The Pinery, 170
pink grapefruit juice
  NONA Ginger & Pink Grapefruit, 111
  Pink Rose Garden, 117
Pink Lemonade, 116
Pink Rose Garden, 117
Playful Punch, 117
Poinsettia Punch, 140
Pomegranate Punch, 140
pomegranates & pomegranate juice
  Electric Bicycle, 182
  EYE See You Punch, 144
  Fresca Tonic, 159
  The Garnet, 98
  Granata, 161
  Holiday Bourbon Punch, 139
  Pomegranate Punch, 140
  Ruby Slippers, 120
  Shanghai Buck, 171
Pomeriggio Té, 189
Pop-in-Prosecco, 117
Pornstar Mojito, 189
Posion De Amor, 190
Prickly Pear, 117
Prima Pave Blanc de Blanc
  Tangerine 71, 174
Prosecco (NA)
  Bellini, 81
  French 71
  Pop-in-Prosecco, 117
Pumpkin Old Fashioned, 117
Pumpkin Patch, 118
Puppy Pose, 190
Purple Corn Syrup
  Chichamorada, 179
  Petit Llama, 168

# R

Ranch Water, 119
raspberries & raspberry juice/puree/syrup
    Berry Punch, 136
    Citron Crush, 179
    Clover Club, 70, 89
    Joker Juice, 185
    The Mad Hatter, 186
    Mint Berry Smash, 110
    Perrier Mimosa, 115
    Raspberry Champagne, 118
    Raspberry Daiquiri, 118
    Raspberry Dirty Soda, 118
    Raspberry Lemonade, 118
    Raspberry Mojito, 119
    Rum Raspberry Lemonade, 121
    Secret Admirer, 143
    Sparkling Raspberry Lemonade, 147
    Spicy Raspberry Margarita, 123
Raspberry Champagne, 118
Raspberry Daiquiri, 118
Raspberry Dirty Soda, 118
raspberry iced tea
    Bruce the Hairdresser, 85
Raspberry Lemonade, 118
    Rum Raspberry Lemonade, 121
Raspberry Mojito, 119
Raspberry-Black Pepper Syrup, 155
Raspberry-Infused Lyre's Italian Spritz, 150
Red, White, and Blueberry Blast, 144
Red Grapes & Cardamom Shrub, 178
Red Racket, 119
Red Verjus
    Talk to Her, 174
red wine (NA)
    EYE See You Punch, 144
Reposado tequila (NA)
    Hibiscus Cooler, 99
Revolver, 75, 119
Rhubarb Cordial, 169
rhubarb simple syrup
    Brunch Punch, 136
Ritual rum alternative
    Sunshine Fun Club, 194
Ritual tequila alternative

Avocado Margarita, 79
Coconut Margarita, 89
Mango Margarita, 105
Margarita, 73, 107
Spicy Margarita, 75, 123
Spicy Raspberry Margarita, 123
Ritual whiskey alternative
    Old Fashioned, 75
    VIP Welcome, 130
Ritual Zero Proof Non-Alcoholic Whiskey, 160
Ritual Zero Proof Tequila
    Upside-Down Pineapple, 195
    Zero Paloma, 176
Rooibos Banana Spiced Tea
    The Mad Hatter, 186
root beer
    Root Beer Dark 'N' Stormy, 119
    Root Beer Dirty Soda, 120
Root Beer Dark 'N' Stormy, 119
Root Beer Dirty Soda, 120
Rose Marie, 170
rose water & rose water syrup
    Desert Rose, 94
Rosé wine (NA)
    Frosé, 96
    Lady Nora, 103
Rosemary Gin Fizz, 120
rosemary & rosemary syrup
    Cran-Rosemary Soda, 146
    Joker Juice, 185
    Rose Marie, 170
    Turmeric Rosemary Oleo, 183
    Vanilla-Rosemary Lemonade, 142
Roy Rogers, 69, 120
Ruby Cooler, 120
Ruby Slippers, 120
Ruhm With a View, 120
rum (NA). *See also* dark rum (NA); white rum (NA)
    Ambrosia Punch, 136
    Blood Orange Daiquiri, 82
    Blueberry Daiquiri, 83
    Cherry Daiquiri, 86
    Double Berry Coco Punch, 138
    Frozen Daiquiri, 97
    Fruit Punch, 139

Recipe Index    **221**

rum (NA). *See also* dark rum (NA); white rum (NA) *(continued)*
   Green Tea Highball, 99
   Hot Toddy, 101
   Jumping Jack, 102
   Mango Mule, 106
   Mojito, 110
   Old Cuban, 112
   Painkiller, 113
   Peach Daiquiri, 113
   Peaches & Cream, 114
   Perfect Storm (Rum Mule), 115
   P.G.'s Tea, 113
   Piña Colada, 75, 115
   Raspberry Daiquiri, 118
   Rum Raspberry Lemonade, 121
   Scorpion Bowl, 141
   Secret Admirer, 143
   Shower Punch, 141
   Snow Blower, 141
   Watermelon Daiquiri, 130
   Zing Zang Piñita Colada, 133
Rum Flip, 121
Rum Madras, 121
Rum Old Fashioned, 121
Rum Raspberry Lemonade, 121
Runneght Hydrosol NA spirit
   Sereno, 191

# S

San Pellegrino Prickly Pear Sparkling Fruit Beverage
   Son of a Beecher, 192
Sauna Room, 191
Scarlet Americano, 170
Scorpion Bowl, 141
Secret Admirer, 143
See No Evil, 121
See Saw, 191
Seedlip 90
   Age of Discovery, 150
Seedlip Garden
   Celestial, 154
   Mama's Garden, 163
   PB & J, 167
   Tropic Thunder, 175

Seedlip Garden 108 NA spirit
   Disco Dust, 181
   East Side, 71
   Electric Bicycle, 182
   Garden of Eden, 183
   Green Tea Sensation, 185
   Martino, 107
   Orchard Sour, 112
   Puppy Pose, 190
   Snap Pea Sour, 172
   Sowing Seeds, 172
   Symbole d'Espoir, 126
   Valhalla, 129
Seedlip Grove
   Amore, 151
   Granata, 161
   Squeeze the Day, 173
   Sunshine Fun Club, 194
   Winter White Cosmo, 175
Seedlip Grove 42 NA spirit
   CosNOpolitan, 92
   French 05, 96
   Garden Party, 184
   Lush and Locks, 163
   Mid-Summer, 164
   Turkey Trot, 145
Seedlip Grove 46 NA spirit
   Cucumber Basil Bliss, 180
   Fun in the Sun, 159
   Spicy Spritz, 173
Seedlip Notas de Agave NA spirit
   Agave Espresso Martini, 78
   Desert Bloom, 156
   Desert Rose, 156
Seedlip Spice 94 NA spirit
   Cherry Blossom, 146
   Espresso Martini, 71, 95
   Irish Cawfee-ish, 162
   Pear-Maple Sour, 168
   Spiced Sipper, 193
   Steady Pete's Ginger Brew, 194
   Sunshine Fun Club, 194
   Talk to Her, 174
Sereno, 191
Sergeant Pepper Field, 192
Shake Those Shamrocks!, 143

Shaken and Stoned, 171
Shandy, 122
Shanghai Buck, 171
Shirley Temple, 69
Shiso Green Tea Syrup
   Green Tea Sensation, 185
Shower Punch, 141
Shrimp Consommé
   Shrimp Michelada, 171
Shrimp Michelada, 171
simple syrup. *See also specific types*
Snap Pea Sour, 172
Snow Blower, 141
Snow Globe Spritz, 172
Snowbird, 192
Sobrii 0-gin
   Candy Cane Crush, 85
   Sobrii Peach Bellini, 124
Sobrii 0-tequila
   Coconut Nog Margarita, 90
   Dragon Fruit Margarita, 94
   Watermelon Paloma, 131
Sobrii Peach Bellini, 124
Softcore Martini, 122
Son of a Beecher, 192
sorbet
   Fancy Sorbet, 96
Southside, 124
Sowing Seeds, 172
Spa Water, 122
sparkling apple cider
   Party Punch, 140
Sparkling Honey Yuzu Lemonade, 193
sparkling lemonade
   Euphoric Spritz, 95
Sparkling Raspberry Lemonade, 147
sparkling wine (NA)
   Bitter Sweet Moment, 81
   Brooke Bravely, 84
   Cranberry Spritz, 93
   Fancy Sorbet, 96
   French 71, 96
   Holiday Bourbon Punch, 139
   Hugo Spritz, 101
   Josh Cellars Sparkling Italian Spritz, 102

Nora's Tiger Lilly, 111
Old Cuban, 112
Peach Fizz, 114
Petit Poids, 169
Poinsettia Punch, 140
Softcore Martini, 122
Winter Spritz, 175
Spiced Blackberry Fizz, 193
Spiced Ginger Syrup, 152
Spiced Sipper, 193
Spiced Wild, 122
spicy agave
   Spicy Spritz, 173
Spicy Cucumber Margarita, 123
Spicy Margarita, 75, 123
Spicy Paloma, 123
Spicy Pineapple Non-Alcoholic Margarita, 144
Spicy Raspberry Margarita, 123
Spicy Spritz, 173
spirit (NA)
   Mule, 74, 110
Spring Sunrise, 124, 146
Spritzer, 124
Squeeze the Day, 173
S&S, 190
Steady Pete's Ginger Brew, 194
Stillman, 124
Strange-Water Sparkling Coconut Water
   Cucumber Cooler, 155
strawberries & strawberry juice/puree/syrup
   Berry Punch, 136
   Double Berry Coco Punch, 138
   Frosé, 96
   Joker Juice, 185
   Midnight Kiss, 143
   Sergeant Pepper Field, 192
   Strawberry Daiquiri, 125
   Strawberry Fizz, 194
   Strawberry Lemonade, 125
   Strawberry Margarita, 147
   Strawberry Mule, 125
   Strawberry-Kiwi Slushie, 125
   Strawberry-Watermelon Slushie, 125
Strawberry Daiquiri, 125
   Miami Vice, 109

**Recipe Index**

Strawberry Fizz, 194
Strawberry Gin Collins, 126
Strawberry Lemonade, 125
  Brunch Punch, 136
Strawberry Margarita, 147
Strawberry Mule, 125
Strawberry Vanilla Tea
  Fizzy Bubblech, 183
Strawberry-Kiwi Slushie, 125
Strawberry-Watermelon Slushie, 125
Summer Spritz, 173
Sunshine Fun Club, 194
Sweet Heat, 173
Sweet Peach Tea, 126
sweet vermouth (NA)
  Chocolate Almond Negroni, 87
  Manhattan, 73, 106
Symbole d'Espoir, 126

# T

tajin
  Chili-Lime Pineapple Soda, 88
Takeaway, 126
Talk to Her, 174
Tangerine 71, 174
tea
  Eliza's Hymns, 182
  Fizzy Bubblech, 183
  Golden Bloom, 160
  Iced Tea, 68
  Kopi Siew Dai, 163
  Lemongrass Bergamot Tea, 189
  Lost in the Fog, 186
  The Mad Hatter, 186
  Otra Cosa, 166
  Peach Tea Cordial, 164
  Shanghai Buck, 171
  Sweet Peach Tea, 126
  Tea & Crumpets, 174
  Tennessee Punch, 141
  Tick Tock, 195
  Watermelon Iced Tea, 131
  Watermelon-Basil Sweet Tea, 142
  Wuyi, 176
  Zing Zang Iced Tea-Rita, 133

Tea & Crumpets, 174
Tea & T, 126
Tembo, 194
Tennessee Punch, 141
tequila (NA)
  Agave Amargo, 77
  Bloody Maria, 82
  Frozen Margarita, 97
  Kiwi Cooler, 103
  Lady Nora, 103
  Mexican Hot Tea, 108
  Orange Margarita, 112
  Pineapple Princess, 116
  Prickly Pear, 117
  Ranch Water, 119
  Spicy Paloma, 123
  Strawberry Margarita, 147
  Tequila Julep, 127
  Tequila & Soda, 127
  Tequila Sunrise, 76, 127
  That's-a-CoCo, 127
  Yeehaw, Beebawl, 133
Tequila Julep, 127
Tequila & Soda, 127
Tequila Sunrise, 76, 127
That's-a-CoCo, 127
Three Cents soda water
  Two Worlds, 195
Three Spirit Livener
  Bitter Spritz, 152
  Euphoric Spritz, 95
  Persimmon Soda, 168
  Sweet Heat, 173
Three Spirit Nightcap NA Botanical Elixir
  Papaya Colada, 167
  Snowbird, 192
Three Spirit Social
  Illegal Backflip, 161
Three Spirit Spark
  Bitter Spritz, 152
Tick Tock, 195
The Tide Is High, 174
Tiger Lily, 127
TLC, 175
Tom Collins, 76, 128

tomatoes & tomato juice
  Bloody Maria, 82
  Bloody Mary, 70
  Caprese Spritz, 153
Tommy's Margarita, 128
Topo Chico sparkling water
  Cantaloupe Crush, 86
  Ranch Water, 119
  Symbole d'Espoir, 126
TÖST Rosé sparkling tea
  Summer Spritz, 173
Tranquilita, 128
Triple Sec (NA)
  Orange Margarita, 112
Tropic Thunder, 175
Tropical Dirty Soda, 128
Tropical Fruit Smoothie, 141
Turkey Trot, 145
Turmeric Rosemary Oleo, 183
Two Worlds, 195

## U

Upside-Down Pineapple, 195

## V

Valhalla, 129
vanilla chai
  baNAnana, 151
vanilla cola
  Vanilla Dark 'N' Stormy, 129
  Water Rush, 130
Vanilla Dark 'N' Stormy, 129
vanilla ice cream. *See* ice cream
Vanilla Infused Ritual Whiskey Alternative, 147
Vanilla Pop, 129
Vanilla Rosemary Syrup, 142
Vanilla Spice Syrup, 186
vanilla & vanilla syrup
  Cherry Vanilla Dirty Soda, 86
  Upside-Down Pineapple, 195
  Vanilla Pop, 129

vanilla yogurt
  Puppy Pose, 190
vanilla-infused NA Bourbon
  Pear Vanilla, 114
Vanilla-Rosemary Lemonade, 142
Verjus
  baNAnana, 151
  The Outfit, 188
  See Saw, 191
Very Peachy, 129
Violette Lady, 129
VIP Welcome, 130
Vita Coco Original coconut water
  Coconut Mango Sunrise, 90
  Coconut Mojito, 90
  Coconut Watermelon Cooler, 91

## W

Walter, 130
Water Rush, 130
Watermelon Daiquiri, 130
Watermelon Iced Tea, 131
Watermelon Mint Refresher, 196
Watermelon NA Tequila Punch, 142
Watermelon Paloma, 131
Watermelon Seltzer, 131
Watermelon Shrub, 184
Watermelon Slushie, 131
watermelon & watermelon juice/puree/syrup
  Celestial, 154
  Coconut Watermelon Cooler, 91
  Strawberry-Watermelon Slushie, 125
  Watermelon Daiquiri, 130
  Watermelon Mint Refresher, 196
  Watermelon NA Tequila Punch, 142
  Watermelon Paloma, 131
  Watermelon Seltzer, 131
  Watermelon Slushie, 131
  Watermelon-Basil Sweet Tea, 142
Watermelon-Basil Sweet Tea, 142
wheat beer (NA)
  Citrus Beer Spritz, 88

Wheatgrass Syrup, 190
    Puppy Pose, 190
whiskey (NA)
    Bruce the Hairdresser, 85
    Fruit Punch, 139
    Hot Toddy, 72, 101
    Irish Coffee, 72
    Manhattan, 73, 106
    NA Eggnog, 138
    Peppermint Irish Coffee, 146
    Whiskey Sour, 76
    Whiskey Tea, 132
Whiskey Collins, 132
Whiskey Peach Lemonade, 132
Whiskey Sour, 76
Whiskey Tea, 132
white rum (NA)
    Mai Tai, 73, 105
white wine (NA)
    Spritzer, 124
wild berry tea
    PEEPstini, 115
Wilderton Bittersweet Aperitivo
    Agave Amargo, 77
Wilderton Lustre NA spirit
    Puppy Pose, 190
Wilfred's Bittersweet NA Aperitif
    Zero-Proof Negroni, 196

Winter Bee, 132
Winter Spritz, 175, 196
Winter White Cosmo, 175
Worcestershire sauce
    Bloody Mary, 70
Wuyi, 176

# Y

Yeehaw, Beebaw!, 133
yuzu juice/puree
    Golden Bloom, 160
    Sparkling Honey Yuzu Lemonade, 193
yuzu liqueur (NA)
    Son of a Beecher, 192

# Z

Zero Paloma, 176
Zero-Proof Negroni, 196
Zing Zang Iced Tea-Rita, 133
Zing Zang Lemon Fizz, 134
Zing Zang Mango Fizz, 133
Zing Zang Piñita Colada, 133
Zing Zang Strawberry Fizz, 133
Zucchini-Mint Juice, 164

# Topics Index

## A

ABV (alcohol by volume), 10, 45
Afrikaans, saying Cheers in, 203
age, as a consideration for purchases, 39
alcohol by volume (ABV), 10, 45
alcohol-free bars, stores, and events, 64
alcohol-free drinks. *See* non-alcoholic (NA) drinks
Almave, 64
amber ale, 47
Anheuser Busch, 9
Ariel, 54
arrack, 135
Atopia, 57

## B

bar napkins, 14
bar spoon, 13
bar tools, 37–38
bar towels, 13
BARE Zero Proof, 57
bars
   alcohol-free, 64
   serving at, 60–62
*BARTENDER Magazine*, 149, 177
basic bar setup, 34
*Beer For Dummies* (Nachel and Ettlinger), 46
Behind, 200
behind the stick, 200
Betty Buzz, 64
blender, 14
Bordeaux, 52
Boston shaker
   about, 12–13
   shaking cocktails in, 19–20
botanicals, for flavor profiles, 56
bottle opener, 14
bowls, 15
brands
   celebrity-backed, 64
   non-alcoholic, 49–50
   of non-alcoholic spirits, 56–57
   of non-alcoholic wine, 54
brandy snifter, 18
breathe, 16
Budweiser, 47
Bull in China PDX, 38
Burgundy, 52

## C

Cabernet Sauvignon, 52
calculating supply needs, 38–42
call, 200
Carl Jung, 54
Ceder's, 57
celebrity-backed brands, 64
Champagne
   about, 54
   opening bottles of, 30
Champagne flute, 16, 18
Chardonnay, 53
Cheat Sheet (website), 2–3
Cheers!, 203–204
Chenin Blanc, 53
cherries, maraschino, 29
Chinese, saying Cheers in, 203
Christmas, 145
church key, 14
cider, 47, 49
Cinco De Mayo, 144
classic cocktails, recipes for, 67–76
Clausthaler, 47
coasters, 14

Cobbler shaker, 12–13
cocktail glass, 18
cocktail shaker, 12–13
cocktails
   adding flavor with infusions, 21
   muddling, 20–21
   naming, 61
   shaking, 19–20
   stirring, 20
Collins, John (waiter), 128
Collins glass, 16, 18
complete bar setup, 35
condiment caddy, 15
Corner, 200
costs
   for basic bar setup, 34
   for complete bar setup, 35
   considerations for, 61–62
   for ultimate bar setup, 36
coupe, 16
coupe glass, 18
crushed ice, 22
cucumber ribbons, 27–28
cups, 15
Cut Above, 57
cutting
   cucumber ribbons, 27–28
   lemon slices, 25–26
   lemon twists, 23–24
   lemon wheels, 25–26
   orange slices, 25–26
   orange wheels, 25–26
   pineapple wedges, 26–27
   wedges, 23
cutting board, 15

# D

Danish, saying Cheers in, 203
De Soi, 64
dirty pour, 121
Dom Pérignon, 54
double shift, 200

drinks
   adding flavor with infusions, 21
   muddling, 20–21
   naming, 61
   shaking, 19–20
   stirring, 20
Dutch, saying Cheers in, 203

# E

Easter, 143
86/86'd, 199
essences, creating flavors using, 56
Ettlinger, Steve (author)
   *Beer For Dummies*, 46
events, alcohol-free, 64
Everleaf, 57
Ewing-Mulligan, Mary (author)
   *Wine For Dummies*, 51
extracts, creating flavors using, 56

# F

fall cocktails, 147–148
fermentation, 46
fermentation cessation, 51–52
Finnish, saying Cheers in, 204
flavors
   adding with infusions, 21
   creating using essences and extracts, 56
   for simple syrups, 22
Fluère Drinks, 57
food pairings, 64
FRE, 54
French, saying Cheers in, 204
future, of non-alcoholic (NA) drinks, 62–64

# G

garnishes
   about, 22–23
   lemon and lime wedges, 23
geographical location, as a consideration for purchases, 40

German, saying Cheers in, 204
Ghia, 57
glassware
  about, 16–17
  rimming, 24, 28–29
golden ale, 49
grater, 14
Greek, saying Cheers in, 203
Grenache, 52

# H

Halloween, 144
Hamilton, Lewis, 64
Hanukkah, 145
Hawthorn strainer, 13, 14
head, 19
heard, 201
Heineken, 47
highball glass, 16, 18
history
  of non-alcoholic beer, 47
  of non-alcoholic (NA) drinks, 9
holiday cocktails, 143–145
home bars
  about, 31
  location for, 32
  preparing, 31–33
  serving at, 32–33, 59–60
  stocking, 33–38
*Homebrewing For Dummies* (Nachel), 46

# I

ice, 22
ice bucket, 14
ice scoop, 14
ice tongs, 14
icons, explained, 2
In Good Spirits, 64
in the weeds, 201
Independence Day, 144
India pale ale (IPA), 47, 49–50
infusions, adding flavor with, 21

Irish Gaelic, saying Cheers in, 204
Italian, saying Cheers in, 204

# J

Japanese, saying Cheers in, 204
Jefferson, Thomas, 47
jigger, 15
juicer, 15
Julep strainer, 13, 14

# K

knife, 15
Korean, saying Cheers in, 204

# L

lager, 48, 49, 50
last call, 201
lemons
  slices, 25–26
  twists, 23–24
  wedges, 23
  wheels, 25–26
Lewis ice bag, 15
light beer, 49
limes
  slicing, 24–25
  wedges, 23
liquor, calculating needs for, 38–40
Lively, Blake, 64
location, for home bar, 32
low ABV, 10
Lumette, 57
Lussory, 54
Lyre's, 57

# M

making simple syrup, 21–22
Malbec, 52
maraschino cherries, 29
margarita glass, 18

Topics Index    **229**

Martini, 57
martini glass, 16, 18
mason jar, 16
*Mayflower*, 47
McCarthy, Ed (author)
   *Wine For Dummies*, 51
measuring glass, 15
Merlot, 52
miscellaneous tools, 13–16
mixers
   about, 36–38
   calculating needs for, 40–42
   future of, 63
mixing glass, 15
mocktails, 8
muddler, 16
muddling drinks, 20–21
mule mug, 18

# N

NA (non-alcoholic) beer
   about, 45
   brands of, 49–50
   future of, 63
   history of, 47
   how it's made, 46
   serving, 48
   storing, 48
   types of, 47–48
NA (non-alcoholic) drinks
   about, 7–8
   future of, 62–64
   history of, 9
   new wave of drinkers, 9
   options for at bars, 10
   rise of, 7–10
   shift towards, 8–9
NA (non-alcoholic) seltzers, future of, 63
NA (non-alcoholic) spirits
   about, 55
   brands of, 56–57
   future of, 63
   how they're made, 56
   serving, 57–58
   storing, 57–58
NA (non-alcoholic) wine
   about, 51
   brands of, 54
   future of, 63
   how it's made, 51–52
   styles of, 52–54
Nachel, Marty (author)
   *Beer For Dummies*, 46
   *Homebrewing For Dummies*, 46
naming cocktails, 61
NCSolutions, 9
near beer, 9, 47
neat, 201
New Year's Eve, 143
no ABV, 10
non-alcoholic (NA) beer
   about, 45
   brands of, 49–50
   future of, 63
   history of, 47
   how it's made, 46
   serving, 48
   storing, 48
   types of, 47–48
non-alcoholic (NA) drinks
   about, 7–8
   future of, 62–64
   history of, 9
   new wave of drinkers, 9
   options for at bars, 10
   rise of, 7–10
   shift towards, 8–9
non-alcoholic (NA) seltzers, future of, 63
non-alcoholic (NA) spirits
   about, 55
   brands of, 56–57
   future of, 63
   how they're made, 56
   serving, 57–58
   storing, 57–58

non-alcoholic (NA) wine
  about, 51
  brands of, 54
  future of, 63
  how it's made, 51–52
  styles of, 52–54
Noughty, 54

# O

Oddbird, 54
old-fashioned glass, 17
on the rocks, 201
opening
  Champagne bottles, 30
  sparkling wine bottles, 30
  wine bottles, 29–30
orange slices, 25–26
orange wheels, 25–26

# P

pale ale, 48
parties, estimating liquor for, 38–39
peeler, 16
Penn, William, 47
Perry, Katy, 64
Philters, 57
pilsners, 48, 49, 50
pineapple wedges, 26–27
Pinot Grigio, 53
pint glass, 18
Polish, saying Cheers in, 204
Portuguese, saying Cheers in, 204
pourer, 16
preparing home bars, 31–33
Prosecco, 54
Proxies, 54
punch, 135
Putnam, Israel (General), 47

# R

ready-to-drink (RTD) non-alcoholic drinks, future of, 63
red ale, 47
red wine glass, 16, 18
red wines, 52
Remember icon, 2
reverse osmosis, 46
ribbons, cucumber, 27–28
Riesling, 53
rimming glasses, 24, 28–29
Ritual, 57
rocks glass, 17, 18
rocks ice, 22
rosé wines, 53
RTD (ready-to-drink) non-alcoholic drinks, future of, 63

# S

Sauvignon Blanc, 53
season, as a consideration for purchases, 40
seasonal cocktails, 145–148
Seedlip, 55, 57
serving
  about, 59
  at bars, 60–62
  at home, 59–60
  at home bars, 32–33
  non-alcoholic beer, 48
  non-alcoholic spirits, 57–58
sessionable, 10
shaking drinks, 19–20
Shiraz (Syrah), 52
shot glass, 17, 18
simple syrup, making, 21–22
skunked beer, 48
slang, 199–202
slicing
  lemon, 25–26
  limes, 24–25
  orange, 25–26

Society De La Rassi, 54
sour, 48
Spanish, saying Cheers in, 204
sparkling wine
  about, 53–54
  opening bottles of, 30
special occasions
  drinks for, 135–148
  toasts for, 204
spinning cone process, 52
St. Patrick's Day, 143
standard ice, 22
stemless glass, 17, 18
stirrers, 16
stirring drinks, 20
stocking home bars, 33–38
stores, alcohol-free, 63
storing
  non-alcoholic beer, 48
  non-alcoholic spirits, 57–58
stout, 48, 49
straight up, 202
strainer, 13
straws, 16
styles, of non-alcoholic wine, 52–54
summer cocktails, 147
supplies, calculating needs for, 38–42
Swedish, saying Cheers in, 203

# T

Thanksgiving, 145
Tip icon, 2
toasts, 203–204
tongs, 14
tools
  about, 11
  checklist for, 37–38
  cocktail shaker, 12–13
  glassware, 16–17
  miscellaneous, 13–16
  strainer, 13
  wine opener, 12

top-shelf, 202
twists, lemon, 23–24
2 or 3 deep, 199

# U

ultimate bar setup, 35–36

# V

vacuum distillation, 46, 47
Valentine's Day, 143

# W

Warning icon, 2
Washington, George, 47
websites
  *BARTENDER Magazine*, 177
  Bull in China PDX, 38
  Cheat Sheet, 2–3
  In Good Spirits, 63
  Seedlip, 55
wedges
  lemon, 23
  lime, 23
  pineapple, 26–27
wheat beer, 48, 49, 50
wheels, lemon and orange, 25–26
white wine glass, 17, 18
white wines, 53
Wilfred's, 57
wine bottles, opening, 29–30
*Wine For Dummies* (McCarthy and Ewing-Mulligan), 51
wine opener, 12
winter cocktails, 146
worm, 12

# Z

Zinfandel, 52, 53

# About the Author

Ryan Foley is a proud father to his daughter, Nora, husband to his beautiful wife, Caitlin, and son to Ray and Jackie Foley. Ryan has spent his whole life in the hospitality industry and loves spending time with his family and friends in various bars and restaurants across the world.

His parents, Ray and Jackie Foley, are the founders of BARTENDER Magazine and The BARTENDER Hall of Fame, which honors the best bartenders all over the globe, not only for their abilities as bartenders, but also for their involvement in their communities. Ray Foley wrote Bartending For Dummies (Wiley) in 1996, and it's now in its 6th edition.

Ryan is also the co-author of Bartending For Dummies (Wiley) and Running a Bar For Dummies (Wiley).

For more information about BARTENDER Magazine, please contact us at info@bartender.com and visit our website at www.bartender.com.

# Dedication

This book is dedicated to my dad, Ray Foley, who loved me the best. And to the women in my life who keep my heart and glass full: Nora Foley, Caitlin Fallon Foley, Jackie Foley, Martha Michels, and Kathleen Fallon.

# Author's Acknowledgments

I'd like to pour out my gratitude to Alicia Sparrow and the overflowing enthusiasm at John Wiley & Sons.

For mixing together all the ingredients properly for this project, I'd like to thank Tim Gallan and Laura K. Miller.

I humbly acknowledge those at BARTENDER® Magazine for serving this up at record speed, especially Jackie Foley and Caitlin Fallon Foley.

A big thank you to John Henderson, who helped and supported me throughout this book. A true friend!

A very special thank you to all the great folks who bartend, and who make, market, and sell all the amazing non-alcoholic wine, beer, and spirits around the globe.

To some of my personal favorite bar guests: Hymie Lipshitz, Colin and Molly Mackey, John Victor Muskett III, Phoebe Getzow, Sean T. Gregory Fallon, Conor Fallon, Lydia Stinson, John and Kathleen Fallon, Kevin Brix, Ted Cocuzza, Steve and Destiny Troullos, William Bard, John and Brenna D'Alessandro, Curly P. Foley, Kevin and Brooke Marren, Zach Baine, Vince and Taylor Voiro, Mike and Cat Zuppe, Drew and Katie Saine, Alex and Chris Farrell, Kelly Landrigan, Jayme Laurash and the Laurash girls; and the Fallon, Brix, and O'Neill families.

And finally, toasting a special glass to those who are no longer with us: Ray Foley, Anne Loffredo, Emma Foley, Howard and Delia Wilson, Danny Brix, and LeRoy Neiman.

## Publisher's Acknowledgments

**Acquisitions Editor:** Alicia Sparrow
**Development Editor:** Tim Gallan
**Copy Editor:** Laura Miller
**Senior Managing Editor:** Kristie Pyles

**Production Editor:** Magesh Elangovan
**Cover Image:** © Maryna Voronova/stock.adobe.com